THIS

Workbook BELONGS TO:

_____

Published by Best Seller Publishing®, St. Augustine, FL
Best Seller Publishing® is a registered trademark.
Printed in the United States of America.
ISBN: 978-1-959840-97-8

This workbook is designed to provide assistance with the subject matter covered. The author does not provide financial, legal, health, psychological, or any other professional services or advice. If specific advice is needed while organizing your essential life details or while completing this workbook or digital version, please contact a competent professional in the appropriate area of expertise.

For more information, please write:
Best Seller Publishing®
1775 US-1 #1070
St. Augustine, FL 32084
or call 1 (626) 765-9750
Visit us online at: www.BestSellerPublishing.org

Author's Dedication

To those whose lives are, or will be, deeply affected by a Just In Case scenario of an accident, illness, or the passing of a loved one. I dedicate this workbook to all of you and your loved ones, hoping it makes a difficult time a little easier.

I dedicate Just In Case Solutions to those who struggle with organization or need help with capturing all aspects of their life that go beyond the professional planning process. My intention in creating the 10 easy Steps was to assist people in gathering their unique and essential details from the comfort of their own homes. This way, everyone can benefit from the convenience and simplicity of the process privately.

Experiencing an accident, illness, or the loss of a loved one can be a very difficult and overwhelming time for family and friends. I hope this workbook will help ease the stresses and sorrows of that period and provide help during those trying times for the ones most loved.

My dedication extends to the family and friends of those who have completed this workbook.
Concentrating can be challenging when dealing with sadness or anxiety, making it difficult to focus. Someone who cares about you has made these preparations to help you when they cannot do so themselves. As the author, I hope this workbook will support you with where to begin and help you navigate your responsibilities through those hard times.

To my family, with a special message for my cherished daughter. If I become unable to speak for myself, need your assistance handling my daily tasks, or when my death eventually comes, this workbook prepares you with everything you should need. Feeling heartache or anxiety might be inevitable; however, feel how much I love you. I committed to reviewing and updating all my essential life details annually to show my appreciation for your help when it comes time to manage my life and to provide my support when I cannot physically help you. I will forever love you more! *Mom* xoxo

Wendy Michelle

TABLE OF CONTENTS

- Step Completion Dates
- Annual Review
- Assign a Person to be Responsible for this Workbook
- Storage Location

- Responsibility Checklist (Helpful Guide for Loved Ones)

- User Name(s)
- Purse, Wallet, Handbag
- Designated Personal Representative or Entity
- Birth Information, Birth Certificate, Citizenship, Adoption
- Social Security Number (SSN)/Individual Taxpayer Identification Number (ITIN), Other
- Marital Status
  - Marriage Certificate, Nuptial Agreement, Death Certificate, Divorce Decree, Partnerships, Family Certificates
- Telephone Number(s)
  - Answering Machine, Cell Phone(s)
- Email Address(es)
- Residential Address (Main and Secondary)
  - Mailing Address, Keys, Combination Lock, PO Box, Previous Address
- Vote/Politics
- Passport(s), Global Entry/Trusted Traveler
- Local Town, City, or Government Offices
- Emergency Contacts
- License(s) and/or Identification
  - Driver's, Commercial, Fishing, Hunting, Notary Public
  - Other Identification or Specialty License
- Firearms: License, Ownership, Storage, Inventory
- Computers: PC, Laptop, Tablet, Devices
  - Passwords/Login Credentials, Wi-Fi, Router, Modem
  - Computer Details
  - Cloud Storage, Technology Backup, Digital Photographs, Important Folders, Files

INTRODUCTION

Welcome to the Just In Case Solutions workbook designed for you and your loved ones.

What is a Just In Case **Scenario**?

These are unfortunate scenarios that may occur, such as an accident, illness, or loss of life. We all need to prepare for these Just In Case scenarios, especially for the inevitable scenario of death. Luckily, we have the ability and the power within ourselves to plan ahead for these types of events.

What is **Just In Case Solutions**?

Just In Case Solutions is a comprehensive workbook that provides individuals or couples an easy way to organize, record, and deliver all their essential life details to their loved ones (or responsible person) in a consolidated manner. In the case of an unexpected event, such as an accident, illness, or death, all important information will be readily available.

This workbook is an all-inclusive and well-organized resource that contains all your important information. When overwhelming life situations are difficult to handle, having completed Just In Case Solutions will help bring life-changing assistance to those who care about you, alleviating any pondering thoughts of confusion or uncertainty, such as, "Where would Mom keep that?" or "Does my uncle have a safe-deposit box someplace?" or "Does Dad have more than one retirement account?" Your loved ones can use this workbook as a reference guide to simplify tasks listed on the responsibility checklist.

Before you start, Ask Yourself: Is your loved one (or responsible person) prepared to handle your entire life should you be in an unexpected accident, or suddenly stricken with an illness and unable to speak for yourself, or when your death inevitably comes?

Maybe one of the following situations pertains to you:
- You are a business traveler with a spouse and minor children at home.
  - You would want to ensure that your spouse is well-informed about essential details, especially those they may not know or are not currently responsible for.
- You are a mature couple needing to organize your life, your papers and finalize your end-of-life affairs.
  - Together, you would want to compile a comprehensive inventory to guarantee that your beloved is well-prepared to face the tough times ahead when one of you passes on.
- You are dealing with a chronic medical condition, and living with this long-term illness makes caring for yourself and your household difficult.
  - You would want to provide a thorough reference and guide for someone to step in and assist you.
- You have a single adult child living alone far away, and you're not familiar with their current situation.
  - Your adult child can complete this workbook to provide you with their information in case of an emergency.
- You are a retired person without a spouse or children and live alone with your beloved dog.
  - You would want an all-inclusive way to deliver all your necessary information to your designated personal representative to ensure no crucial details are overlooked, including instructions for the person who will be taking care of your dog.

Ask Yourself, In the scenario of an accident, illness, or death:

- Does your loved one know what medications you are taking and your medical history? Do they know what kind of health insurance you have and how you pay the premium?
- Are they familiar with what vital legal documents you have and where the originals are stored?
- Does your loved one know what bills you have? Do they know if your vehicle is paid off and where you keep the title? Are all your expenses organized in one place for them to step in to handle your situation smoothly and efficiently?
- Do they know the location, registration and beneficiary status of your financial accounts and insurance policies, including whether those accounts and policies will close or continue?
- Does your loved one or designated personal representative know how to care for your children or pets? Do they know at least one of your good friends or neighbors who could lend a helping hand?
  - If you have a child with a health condition or disability, do they have the essential information on how to care for that child?
- Does your loved one know the name and contact information of the house of worship you attend, as well as the phone numbers of your closest friends?
- Do your loved ones know if you belong to a club or have a volunteer job that may require them to notify others in case of an emergency?
- Does your loved one know if you have a preferred funeral home or cemetery? Do they know if you already made prepaid arrangements and where those documents are located? Do they know your preference for cremation or burial, open or closed casket, and visiting hours?
- Can they distinguish between your cherished sentimental possessions and those with a financial value? Are they aware if any of the valuable items have been appraised, and if yes, where do you keep the appraisals?

We cannot dictate or control what happens after we pass away. But, whether it's your spouse, child, distant relative, friend, or designated personal representative, they will appreciate following your directions and fulfilling your wishes. The intense grief following the loss of a loved one is unavoidable. However, being proactive in making all the heavy decisions for them before our passing WILL help ease some anxiety and leave them with a grateful memory during those hard times.

How does **Just In Case Solutions** work?

Just In Case Solutions has 10 simple Steps that enable the User (you) to enter information easily. As the User, you will see a short message at the beginning of each Step, followed by a NOTE directed to your loved ones. It's designed to assist both you and your loved ones.

Dividing up this process into 10 easy Steps allows you to tackle one Step at a time. This approach makes it less overwhelming and helps it not be such a daunting task because, let's be honest, no one wants to do this, but it's something we all should!

You can complete this workbook at your own pace, in the comfort of your home, and in any order that works best for you, although it helps to start with the basics in Step 1.

This workbook partners well with the retirement, caregiving, estate, and funeral planning process by bridging the gap and consolidating all the details outside of the professional planning process. The 10 Steps will gather every aspect related to your daily and monthly routines, critical legal documents, financial accounts, insurance policies, health and medical information, end-of-life plans, and so much more!

When it comes to our own lives, we are the experts!

We have access to all sorts of professionals who share their expertise with us. Financial advisors and banks can help us manage our money and plan for retirement, accountants help with tax-related matters, doctors support our physical and emotional well-being, and attorneys assist with legal issues, including estate planning.

However, **Ask Yourself**, what professional helps us organize and document our important life information?

If your loved ones need to sell your property, they would seek the assistance of a professional Realtor. However, if they need to know where you keep the spare set of keys to your car, the professional they would need is YOU. People only know what they know. When the time comes for someone to step in and become the expert for your life, you have the ability to prepare them. Given that everyone's situation is unique, this information will vary accordingly. For instance:

- You may have a last will and testament, but the storage location of that legal document can differ depending on the individual.
- You might keep a handwritten list of passwords; someone else might store them electronically.
- You may have a waterproof/fireproof safe hidden on your property; someone else may have a storage facility.

There are numerous essential aspects of your life that only you know. Take charge, be your own professional, and ease the burden on those who care deeply about you. **Be your own expert because no one knows your life better than you!**

What does this workbook _not_ do?

- Just In Case Solutions does not ask who is getting what in your will; it simply asks if you have one and where it is located.
- It does not ask how much money you have; it asks what accounts you have and where they are located.
  - Regardless of your financial status, loved ones will have the same struggle to determine what you have or don't have. Once they know something exists, where it's located, and how to access it, they can act accordingly.
- It does not provide or offer professional services; it asks you thought-provoking questions.
  - However, if you are unsure about answers, please seek guidance from a qualified professional.

HELP YOUR LOVED ONES GO FROM GRIEF TO GRATITUDE!

This workbook allows you to effectively prepare those who love you the most. Locating essential documents or stepping in to pay your bills during a difficult time can be emotional, confusing, and overwhelming. By completing Just In Case Solutions, you can provide your loved ones with guidance so they don't have to deal with disorganization and express statements like, "What do I do now?" or "Where do I even begin?" or "I wish they had been more organized and not such a mess."

You want your family and friends to have good memories of you and not the lasting thoughts of what a gigantic mess you left for them to figure out.

- Without this workbook, your loved ones could wait years for probate to be settled while they try to make sense of the disorderly way you left things.
- Without this workbook, your loved ones could waste time figuring out your bills and how to pay them.

Stop procrastinating and start taking action!

Please take a moment to self-reflect and identify the underlying reasons why it is so difficult to have a conversation as important as this - a conversation that provides details and prepares for scenarios like an accident, illness or death. Some of us repeat things to ensure our loved ones remember, while others will not share anything at all. Sometimes one person wants to discuss this topic, and the other person is unwilling to listen, responding with phrases like "We can talk later," "We have plenty of time," or "I don't want to talk about it." Many of us encounter challenges with this subject due to fear, worry, anxiety, or avoidance, which can be uncomfortable to deal with. However, we must push all these roadblocking feelings aside, do what is best for ourselves, and ultimately help our loved ones.

- <u>Note for Couples</u>: In some relationships, not all tasks are evenly divided, and sometimes one partner may lack the knowledge to perform certain responsibilities. If you are the person who handles a specific responsibility, such as paying the bills or interacting with professionals, take the time to teach your partner how to do it themselves and introduce them to the right contacts.

To make sure you finish completing this workbook, establish a timeframe or create a schedule for yourself and commit to it. This will help with holding yourself accountable. If you are an overachiever, the math is simple: Completing one Step a day will result in finishing in 10 days!

**It's beneficial to take action <u>NOW</u> while you still have the opportunity,
as it will ultimately help those close to you in the future.**

Please note: While you gather information for your 10 Steps, it's worth tidying up any clutter or disarray. Imagine what you would want your loved ones to encounter or walk into if something happened to you.

- Maybe it's time to finish any pending projects you have been putting off.
- Maybe it's time to shred those old documents in the basement or declutter those old boxes in the attic.
- Maybe it's time to tidy up your home office, desk, and file cabinet!

Achieving a completely organized life is nearly impossible. Some of us are prone to be naturally messy, while others tend to maintain a high level of tidiness. <u>We should embrace ourselves for who we are; however, it's important to remember that we don't need to change who we are as a person in order to write down what truly matters</u>.

We all wish for our loved ones to encounter less hardship during challenging times. We want to prepare our responsible person with the necessary reference guide to help alleviate confusion and avoid massive struggles during those difficult moments. This workbook offers an organized solution to share your secure information, essential details, and other crucial aspects of your life. Provide your loved ones or a designated personal representative with a consolidated inventory of all your important information and give yourself peace of mind.

Now it's time for you to take the first step toward organizing and recording your Just In Case Solutions!

FUN MEMORY!

At the end of each Step, there will be a page to write something personal to your loved ones. Adding a little fun at the end of each Step may bring some joy into this tedious process and create lasting memories.

Sharing a memory, a funny story about yourself, a fact about a time in your past, inserting a photograph, or simply writing a loving thought to your loved one will bring a smile during a difficult time.

10 Steps... 10 Fun Memories... 10 Smiles...
that you will be able to deliver when you are unable to do so!

HOW TO USE THIS WORKBOOK
(For the Users)

Review the Table of Contents before getting started to familiarize yourself with each Step.

At the start of each Step, there is a brief message to you as the User, followed by a note directed to your loved ones. Each Step's opening message includes information regarding what's included within that Step. It also has questions to ponder and some valuable tips that may assist you, your loved ones, or a responsible person when an accident, illness, or death occurs.

- Use this workbook to start your planning process, stimulate your thoughts, or initiate hard conversations that people tend to shy away from.
- Be aware that you may need to search for information if it's not readily accessible.
- If you need to take action on something, bookmark the page for future reference. This will serve as a reminder to easily draw your attention back to any outstanding items.

How long does it take to complete Just In Case Solutions? The completion time varies because everyone's situation is different. A Step that takes 20 minutes for one person may take longer for someone else.
- For example, if you only have one vehicle, you will complete the Vehicle and Transportation (Step 8) more quickly than someone with two vehicles, a motorcycle, a camper, a boat, and a trailer.

Create a schedule: To ensure that you complete this workbook, establish a timeframe or schedule for yourself and commit to following it. You've got this!

HOW TO COMPLETE THE 10 EASY STEPS

This 10-Step solution was created to make it simple to follow and easy to complete. Organizing important life details into 10 manageable Steps can greatly assist in completing this valuable resource.

Start with Step 1. After finishing Step 1, you can complete the remaining Steps in any order that best suits you and your situation.
- **Answer the questions by filling in the blanks** that pertain to you.
- You will be asked to **circle "Yes or No,"** and depending on your answer, you will proceed by either answering more questions or skipping to the next section.

- **Note**: If there is a question or section that is not relevant to you, then cross it out. This way, you can show that you have seen it, and your loved one will see that it was not overlooked.
  - For example, if you do not have children, circle "No" children, strike out all the children-related sections, and proceed to the next item.

Consider taking a photo of any significant pages in this workbook. Having it accessible on your mobile device will allow you to easily share it with a loved one or medical professional.

NEXT STEPS

Step Completion Dates: At the end of each Step, there will be a place to record the date when you completed that specific Step.

Annual Review: It's advisable to review this workbook annually to see if any modifications are needed to guarantee that your loved ones will have up-to-date, accurate information. If life changes after completion, simply add new information, cross out anything that is no longer relevant, or make adjustments so your loved ones know about the change. Consider writing a note in the margins if an explanation is needed.

Annual Review Month/Date: _____

> Completing this workbook is a huge achievement.
> Please take time to celebrate your accomplishment and feel a sense of comfort knowing you have taken the initiative to go above and beyond to help the ones you love the most.

Assign a person to be responsible for this workbook: After finishing this workbook, have a discussion with your loved ones or designated personal representative. Inform them that you have completed this workbook and explain it's a valuable resource containing all your essential information they will need to know.

Choose a storage location: Decide on a safe and secure location to store this workbook, and tell your responsible person where it will be located.

Who will be responsible for this workbook? Name: _____

NOTE TO LOVED ONES

The purpose of **Just In Case Solutions** is to simplify a challenging time by breaking down all the necessary information into 10 Steps, to use as a reference guide in the future, making it less overwhelming. It has been created to help the loved ones of the person who is completing this workbook (the Users).

Each Step begins with a message to the Users, followed by a NOTE intended for their loved ones that provides guidance and tips that may assist those using the completed workbook.

HOW LOVED ONES SHOULD USE THIS WORKBOOK

Below is a checklist to help guide you during this difficult time.

TO LOVED ONES, IN THE CASE OF DEATH

Losing someone can be a very stressful experience for those left behind. The feeling of grief can be consuming; however, your loved one took the time to record their vital information to make it easier for you.

To get a better understanding of what's inside:
- Review the Table of Contents; it can help you find whatever you need quickly.
- Review the "NOTE TO LOVED ONES" section at the beginning of each Step. This will provide you with a brief overview and valuable guidance regarding what has been completed within that Step, along with helpful tips or suggestions.

When life gets overwhelming, use the CHECKLIST below. Take one Step at a time or one page at a time.
- Mark items off once you have completed a task. Consider sticky notes to mark pages and write reminders for tracking and follow-ups.
- If this is your first experience handling the affairs of a loved one who has passed away, you may be shocked at all the paperwork and tasks you need to complete. Don't be afraid to ask someone to help you. You don't have to do this alone.
- Remember to always ask a qualified professional for guidance and advice regarding all financial, tax, and legal matters.

RESPONSIBILITY CHECKLIST

☐ Notification of the Death: This workbook should contain all important people to contact.

Family Members: Steps 1 & 2	Non-family, Close Friends/Neighbors: Steps 2 & 9
Funeral Home: Step 10	House of Worship/Religion: Steps 9 & 10
Employer/Military: Step 4	Professionals: Step 5
Doctors: Step 3	Clubs, etc.: Step 9

☐ End of Life Services: Take action on their wishes (Step 10).
- If Military: review military experience (Step 4) and funeral wishes (Step 10) to honor their time served.

☐ Death Certificate: Consider requesting extra death certificates. You could need 10, 15, or perhaps even 20. Obtaining extras will save you the hassle of needing to request more later. The funeral director (Step 10) or the town/city clerk's office (Step 1) will be able to help you.

☐ Social Security: Notify the Social Security Administration of the death (Step 6). The payments and Medicare benefits should be immediately stopped for the deceased. Ask if survivor benefits are applicable.

- ☐ Security During Funeral/Services:
  - Who will watch the residence during the services?
    - If you don't know someone who can keep an eye on the residence during the services, consider contacting local law enforcement to notify them of the death and ask if they would watch or do a frequent drive-by during the services.
- ☐ Local Town, City, or Government Offices: Familiarize yourself with their list of important local offices and their locations (Step 1).
- ☐ Residence(s), Bills, and Debts: This will help you handle the household chores and daily/monthly expenses (Step 7).
  - Who will collect the mail? Do you need to have the mail forwarded?
  - Who will continue to watch and care for the residence?
  - Familiarize yourself with household services, utilities, and bills. They may need to be paid, canceled, or transferred into someone else's name, or the deceased spouse's name may need to be removed.
  - Compile a List of Debts: Review this entire workbook and make notes for all items.
  - Credit Reports: It may be helpful to keep an eye on your loved one's credit reports. See if they mentioned having an account with a reporting agency (Step 7).
- ☐ Legal Documents: Locate legal documents, such as their will and trusts (Step 5). If you are the responsible party (trustee), familiarize yourself with the contents of the legal documents and reach out to their estate planning attorney for assistance.
- ☐ Life Insurance: Locate any life insurance policies (Step 6) and contact the company or a professional for assistance on how to claim the death benefit for the beneficiaries.
- ☐ Technology/Digital Life: Review technology items provided (Step 1).
  - Locate cell phones, answering machines, computers, email accounts, social media, etc., and see how to access them.
  - Login Credentials: Some usernames and passwords are provided throughout this workbook, and some might be referenced in EXTRAS. See the passwords section (Step 1) to learn where and how they store all their login credentials.
  - ☐ Respond to any voicemails, text messages, or emails. Consider creating an Auto-Reply message for digital communication to avoid repeatedly informing people of the passing of your loved one.
    - Auto-Reply Example: "It is with great sadness we share the news of _<name/relationship>_ who passed on _<date>_. If you need to reach a family member, please contact _<name>_ at _<phone/email>_. Thank you for your understanding and support during this difficult time."
  - Eventually you will need to close their email accounts; however, consider triple-checking to ensure that you no longer need that email address before closing it.
  - ☐ If they use social media, refer to the list provided (Step 1).
- ☐ Location of Important Items: Locate their wallet or purse, identification cards, driver's license, passport, keys, combinations, certificates, firearms, etc. (Step 1).
  - ☐ Review the Document Storage and Storage Location section (Step 5). Remember that some items might be stored at a location away from the residence, such as a safe deposit box.
  - ☐ Locate inventory lists for personal possessions and valuable items. Locate these items and match them up with any appraisals. (Step 5 & EXTRAS)
    - Or, consider contacting an appraiser to value certain things for the estate (Step 5). Please contact a professional if you need assistance with an estate sale.
  - ☐ Cancel driver's license and other forms of ID.

- ☐ Real Estate: If real estate is involved, contact a reliable agent/broker and attorney to inform them of your situation. Telling them in advance will enable them to be better prepared to help you when you are ready to proceed (Steps 5 & 7).
    - ☐ If necessary, contact a real estate appraiser. Having a date-of-death valuation (or time-of-death appraisal) helps determine the value of any real estate they own.
    - ☐ If your loved one owns or has a financial interest in a timeshare or vacation club, review the details provided (Step 9) and locate the necessary documents to enable you to act accordingly.
- ☐ Taxes: Locate past years' tax returns and contact their accountant and legal professional to assist you with filing all the necessary final tax returns (Step 5). Make sure to stay informed about any deadlines.
- ☐ Employee and/or Military Benefits:
    - ☐ Employer or Union: Review (Step 4) and learn whom to contact to assist with any benefits their employer provides.
    - ☐ Military: Review the military details provided to you (Step 4). VA health care benefits (Step 3).
- ☐ Medical Coverage and Long-Term Care Insurance: Cancel health, dental, vision, and other supplemental insurance policies (Step 3). Ask if survivor benefits are applicable.
- ☐ Financial Accounts and Other Policies: Familiarize yourself with what they have for accounts and policies (Step 6), and contact any financial professionals, companies, and insurance agents/agencies they listed for assistance (Step 5).
    - ☐ Digital Assets: Do not forget to locate any digital assets that have value and if they carry a balance in a digital wallet (Step 6).
    - ☐ Accounts and Policies: Review (Step 6). This will lay out all their bank accounts, investment accounts (retirement and non-retirement), annuities, insurance policies, CDs, bonds, college funds, and more.
        - ☐ Continued Ownership and Beneficiary Distribution: Look at how the financial accounts are registered/titled/owned and the listed beneficiaries.
        - • Ask Yourself, will you be canceling the account, changing the name/ownership of the account to either have it continue in your name or someone else's name? Will the account need to be transferred, disbursed, or closed?
            - • If the ownership changes, ensure the new account is registered appropriately and beneficiaries are added. Contact a professional if you have questions!
                - • For example, if there is a joint savings account and one owner dies, the deceased's name must be removed. If the account will continue for the other joint owner, consider an individual account with a TOD (transfer on death), which adds a beneficiary to the newly established individual account. This could avoid a future hassle.
            - • If the account is closing, contact the beneficiaries to obtain the necessary information to facilitate the transfer of assets.
    - ☐ Ask companies and professionals to give you detailed instructions on handling their paperwork and what needs to be submitted along with their specific forms. It might be helpful to inquire about the estimated processing time of their process.
- ☐ Vehicles and Transportation: Review (Step 8).
    - ☐ Determine what's necessary to handle vehicle ownership, registrations, and license plates, such as canceling a plate, transferring ownership (locate original title), or selling or gifting a car.
    - ☐ If needed, cancel/return any toll tag accounts; disability parking permits/placards; and bus, ferry, or train passes. Cancel or transfer ownership of any roadside assistance programs and satellite radio accounts.

- ☐ Clubs, Subscriptions, Memberships, and Volunteer Commitments:
    - ☐ Review (Step 9) and learn if they joined a club or have any active memberships or subscriptions (mail or online) requiring cancellation or modification of ownership.
    - ☐ If your loved one volunteered, contact the organization or charity to inform them of their passing.
    - ☐ Find their list of streaming services (Step 1) and cancel or change the name on those accounts.

Notes:

_____
_____
_____
_____
_____
_____
_____
_____
_____
_____
_____
_____
_____
_____
_____
_____
_____
_____
_____

As the author, my heart goes out to you during this difficult time, and please accept my deepest condolences for your loss. If you are reading this, you are very fortunate that someone in your life took the time to organize all this information to help make things easier for you.

Step 1

Personal Details and Technology

(Primary User and Secondary User)

In Step 1, you will list personal details and computer-related items. There is a section to list essential life details for a Primary User – you – and a section for a Secondary User, such as your spouse or partner.

Personal details include many of the facts that quickly come to mind, such as full legal and maiden names, birth and citizenship information, marital status, residential addresses, post office boxes, and telephone numbers. They also include the location of family documents such as birth and death certificates, marriage licenses, and divorce decrees. Includes if you have the originals and/or copies.

Here are more items and actions that will be helpful to your loved ones in case of an accident, illness, or death:

- A list of emergency contacts.
- The location of your driver's license, identification cards, passport, or specialty licenses, such as a commercial or nursing license.
- Make things easier by organizing your wallet or handbag.
- Go the extra mile and provide the contact information for your local town or city offices.
- Share details regarding your computer, tablet, and mobile devices, including any computer maintenance or security subscriptions you may have.
- Describe how to access your wireless network and the location of your modem and/or router.

Ask Yourself, how many email addresses do you have? What is the purpose of each email? Such as, do you use one for correspondence and one just for electronic statements and paying bills? This will be helpful to your loved ones should they need a copy of your last statement or to assist you with bills.

- Provide the username and passwords for any email addresses and websites that you use. Ensure that all your login credentials are written down and stored somewhere private and list where they are kept.
- Specify how you organize your electronic files and photos.

Ask Yourself, are spreadsheets in a particular folder on your computer? Do you save memorable photos to an external hard drive? Do you have electronic copies of legal documents in a special folder?

- List your social media accounts and passwords. Describe what you would like to happen to your account/profile upon your death.
- Compile a list of all streaming services or app subscriptions and how you pay for them. This provides an orderly way for your loved ones to either change the name on the account or cancel the service.
- If you own firearms, appoint someone who can be legally responsible. Your loved ones may need assistance with opening your firearm safe, handling firearms, or transporting or selling them and accessories. Write an inventory of everything related to your firearms and provide the location of all paperwork. Be sure your wishes comply with state law.

Ask Yourself, what else do you own that requires a physical key, combination code, or keycard to access?

Help your loved ones struggle less by recording what is important to your unique situation.

Please take a moment to review what's included in this Step:

STEP 1: PERSONAL DETAILS AND TECHNOLOGY (Primary User and Secondary User)
- User Name(s)
- Purse, Wallet, Handbag
- Designated Personal Representative or Entity
- Birth Information, Birth Certificate, Citizenship, Adoption
- Social Security Number (SSN)/Individual Taxpayer Identification Number (ITIN), Other
- Marital Status
  - Marriage Certificate, Nuptial Agreement, Death Certificate, Divorce Decree, Partnerships, Family Certificates
- Telephone Number(s)
  - Answering Machine, Cell Phone(s)
- Email Address(es)
- Residential Address (Main and Secondary)
  - Mailing Address, Keys, Combination Lock, PO Box, Previous Address
- Vote/Politics
- Passport(s), Global Entry/Trusted Traveler
- Local Town, City, or Government Offices
- Emergency Contacts
- License(s) and/or Identification
  - Driver's, Commercial, Fishing, Hunting, Notary Public
  - Other Identification or Specialty License
- Firearms: License, Ownership, Storage, Inventory
- Computers: PC, Laptop, Tablet, Devices
  - Passwords/Login Credentials, Wi-Fi, Router, Modem
  - Computer Details
  - Cloud Storage, Technology Backup, Digital Photographs, Important Folders, Files
- Streaming Services, App Subscriptions
- Social Networking/Social Media Sites
- Step 1 Completion Date and Fun Memory!

Step 1: NOTE TO LOVED ONES

In Step 1, your loved ones have provided many personal details about themselves to make things easier for you.

This information will assist you with filling out forms and finding important marital status paperwork such as marriage, divorce, or death certificates. You'll learn where your loved ones receive their mail and how to access it.

This Step also covers what they have for technology, including where to find their list of usernames and passwords. Ensure you know any email addresses and how to log in to them.

Here are some additional ways in which Step 1 can help:

- Learn where to locate their wallet or handbag, keys, and combinations to open locks.
- If you need to step in and handle technology for your loved ones, you have been provided with details about the home network, Wi-Fi access, and devices.
- You can obtain access codes for cell phones in order to respond to voicemails or text messages before you proceed with terminating cell phone plans.
- If your loved one has passed away, you will be able to honor their intentions on what to do with their social networking sites.
- You will be able to easily cancel streaming services or change the name on the accounts.

> **READ:** As you complete this workbook, you will write information about the Primary User in the Primary User sections and information for the Secondary User in the Secondary User sections.

What is a Primary User?

The **Primary User** is someone who is entering their essential life details into this workbook.

Primary User

Who is the **Primary User** of this workbook?

Full Name:_____

What is a Secondary User?

The **Secondary User** is someone who shares their life with the Primary User.

Note: If you don't have a Secondary User or don't want to fill out the sections for a Secondary User, you can leave those sections blank.

<u>Single individual</u>, you would not have a secondary user.

<u>Married couples</u>, you can complete this workbook together or individually by filling out a separate workbook.

Question:

Do you want to enter information for a Secondary User?   Yes or No

If yes: What is the Secondary User's relationship to the Primary User?_____

(Spouse, life partner, etc.)

Secondary User

Who is the **Secondary User** for this workbook?

Full Name:_____

Primary User	Secondary User
Name	**Name**
Prefix: _____ (Mr., Mrs., Ms., Miss, Gov., Dr., Capt., etc.)	Prefix: _____ (Mr., Mrs., Ms., Miss, Gov., Dr., Capt., etc.)
First name: _____	First name: _____
Middle name: _____	Middle name: _____
Last name: _____	Last name: _____
Suffix: _____	Suffix: _____
Do you have a nickname? Yes or No	Do you have a nickname? Yes or No
If yes: Nickname: _____	If yes: Nickname: _____
Do you have a maiden name? Yes or No	Do you have a maiden name? Yes or No
If yes: Maiden name: _____	If yes: Nickname: _____
Do you have an alias? Yes or No (Also known as)	Do you have an alias? Yes or No (Also known as)
If yes: Alias: _____	If yes: Alias: _____

Purse, Wallet, Handbag	Purse, Wallet, Handbag

Do you have a purse, wallet, or handbag?
                              Yes or No
Location: *Where do you typically keep it?*
_____
	Do you have a purse, wallet, or handbag?
	                              Yes or No
	Location: *Where do you typically keep it?*
	_____

Note: Take a moment to organize your wallet. Consider adding essential items that may be needed in a crisis, such as emergency contacts.	

Designated Personal Representative or Entity	Designated Personal Representative or Entity

Have you designated a personal representative?
                              Yes or No
If yes, Name: _____
Phone: _____
Email: _____
If Entity: Additional Details:
	Have you designated a personal representative?
	                              Yes or No
	If yes, Name: _____
	Phone: _____
	Email: _____
	If Entity: Additional Details:

Primary User	**Secondary User**

Birth Information	**Birth Information**
Date of birth: _____	Date of birth: _____
Place of birth: _____	Place of birth: _____
Do you have a copy or original birth certificate?	Do you have a copy or original birth certificate?
_____	_____
Where is your birth certificate located?	Where is your birth certificate located?
_____	_____
Are you a U.S. citizen? Yes or No	**Are you a U.S. citizen?** Yes or No
If no, are you a:	If no, are you a:
Resident Alien or Non-Resident Alien	Resident Alien or Non-Resident Alien
What is your citizenship? _____	What is your citizenship? _____
Where is your citizenship paperwork located?	Where is your citizenship paperwork located?
_____	_____
What is your race and ethnicity?	What is your race and ethnicity?
_____	_____
Gender Identity: _____	Gender Identity: _____
Sex Assigned at Birth: _____	Sex Assigned at Birth: _____
Were you adopted? Yes or No	**Were you adopted?** Yes or No
Where is your adoption paperwork located?	Where is your adoption paperwork located?
_____	_____
Details: Agency name/Documentation/Family medical history/Ethnic background/etc. _____	Details: Agency name/Documentation/Family medical history/Ethnic background/etc. _____
_____	_____
_____	_____
_____	_____
_____	_____

Social Security Number (SSN) **Individual Taxpayer Identification Number (ITIN)** **Other (SIN)**	**Social Security Number (SSN)** **Individual Taxpayer Identification Number (ITIN)** **Other (SIN)**
Do you have a Social Security Number? Yes or No	Do you have a Social Security Number? Yes or No
If yes: What is your SSN? _____	If yes: What is your SSN? _____
If no SSN, what do you have? _____	If no SSN, what do you have? _____
ITIN: _____	ITIN: _____
Tax File Number: _____	Tax File Number: _____
National ID: _____	National ID: _____
SIN: _____	SIN: _____
Other: _____	Other: _____
Additional details:	Additional details:
_____	_____

Note: Step 6 has additional details pertaining to Social Security.

Primary User and Secondary User

1

Marital Status

What is your marital status? _____
(Married, divorced, separated, widowed, lifetime partner, never married, etc.)

Full legal name of your spouse/life partner: _____

If Married: Do you have a copy and/or original marriage certificate?   Yes or No
                                                                Original or Copy

Where is the marriage certificate located? _____
(Safe-deposit box, office file cabinet, box in a closet, etc.)

Do you have any nuptial agreements?   Yes or No
    Is there a sunset provision?   Yes or No   If yes: Expiration date: _____
    Are there stipulations Just In Case of an accident or death?

_____

Where is the agreement located? _____

If Widowed: Do you have a copy and/or original death certificate?   Yes or No
                                                                Original or Copy

Name of late spouse: _____

Where is the death certificate located? _____
(Safe-deposit box, office file cabinet, box in a closet, etc.)

If Single: Full legal name of your next of kin: _____

If Divorced: Are you legally divorced?   Yes or No
              Number of divorces?   # _____
              Did you have an annulment of your marriage?   Yes or No

Where is the paperwork and divorce decree located? _____
(Safe-deposit box, office file cabinet, box in a closet, etc.)

Details: _____

If Civil Union/Civil Partnership: Do you have a copy and/or original certificate?   Yes or No   Original or Copy

Where are civil records/certificates located? _____
(Safe-deposit box, office file cabinet, box in a closet, etc.)

Details: _____

Do you have a family certificate?   Yes or No   What country? _____

Where is the certificate located? _____ Original or Copy

Details: _____

Primary User	**Secondary User**
Telephone Number(s)	**Telephone Number(s)**
Home (Landline): _____	Home (Landline): _____
Voicemail password: _____	Voicemail password: _____
Work: _____	Work: _____
Voicemail password: _____	Voicemail password: _____
Other: _____	Other: _____
Other: _____	Other: _____
Do you have a stand-alone **answering machine**?	Do you have a stand-alone **answering machine**?
Yes or No	Yes or No
If yes: Password: _____	If yes: Password: _____

Cell Phone(s)	**Cell Phone(s)**
Do you own a cell phone?　　　　　Yes or No	Do you own a cell phone?　　　　　Yes or No
If yes: How many?　　　# _____	If yes: How many?　　　# _____
Cell # 1. Cell number: _____	**Cell # 1.** Cell number: _____
Type of cell phone: _____ *(Android, iPhone, etc.)*	Type of cell phone: _____ *(Android, iPhone, etc.)*
Device password: _____	Device password: _____
Voicemail password: _____	Voicemail password: _____
Does anyone else besides you know the password?	Does anyone else besides you know the password?
Yes or No	Yes or No
If yes: Who? _____	If yes: Who? _____
Cell # 2. Cell number: _____	**Cell # 2.** Cell number: _____
Type of cell phone: _____ *(Android, iPhone, etc.)*	Type of cell phone: _____ *(Android, iPhone, etc.)*
Device password: _____	Device password: _____
Voicemail password: _____	Voicemail password: _____
Does anyone else besides you know the password?	Does anyone else besides you know the password?
Yes or No	Yes or No
If yes: Who? _____	If yes: Who? _____

Primary User – Email Address

Do you have an email address?   Yes or No

If yes: How many?   # _____

Email Address	Password	Purpose of this email? *(Personal, shopping, bills, work, etc.)*

Secondary User – Email Address

Do you have an email address?   Yes or No

If yes: How many?   # _____

Email Address	Password	Purpose of this email? *(Personal, shopping, bills, work, etc.)*

Additional details: _____

_____

_____

Primary User and Secondary User

Main Residence - Address

#, Street Name_____Apt./Suite/Other _____

City, State, and ZIP _____

County _____ Country _____

Mailing Address
Is your mailing address the same as your main residence address?   Yes or No

   If no: What is your mailing address? _____

Where do you keep your **key(s)** for your main residence? _____
Who else has a key to your main residence? _____
What other keys are kept on your key chain? _____

_____

Do you have a **combination lock** to access your main residence? *(door/garage)*   Yes or No
   If yes: What is the combination? _____
Who else has a combination, and what is their code? _____

_____

Do you have a **PO Box**?   Yes or No
   If yes: What is your PO Box number? _____
          PO Box location: _____
   Do you have a key for this PO Box, or is it a combination lock? _____
      If keys: How many keys and where are they located? _____
      If combination lock: What is the combination? _____

Optional: Previous Address
Would you like to enter a previous address and the date last lived there?   Yes or No
   If yes: What is your last known previous address? _____
          What is the date you moved from the previous address? _____

Second Residence – Address

Do you have a second residence?   Yes or No
   If yes: What is the address of the second residence? _____

   Mailing address: _____

   _____

   Where do you keep your **key(s)** for your second residence? _____
   Who else has a key to your second residence? _____
   Do you have a **combination lock** to access your second residence? *(door/garage)*   Yes or No
      If yes: What is the combination? _____
   Who else has a combination, and what is their code? _____

_____

Primary User	Secondary User

Vote/Politics

Are you registered to vote?　　　Yes or No

If yes: How are you currently registered?

_____
(Democrat, Independent, Libertarian, Republican, etc.)

Where is your voting location?

_____

Absentee ballot details: _____

_____

Vote/Politics

Are you registered to vote?　　　Yes or No

If yes: How are you currently registered?

_____
(Democrat, Independent, Libertarian, Republican, etc.)

Where is your voting location?

_____

Absentee ballot details: _____

_____

Primary User	Secondary User

Passport/Trusted Traveler

Do you have a **passport**?　　　Yes or No
　If yes: Where is your passport located?

_____

　Expiration date of passport: _____

Do you have a **foreign passport**?　　Yes or No
　If yes: Where is your passport located?

_____

　Expiration date of passport: _____

Do you have a **Global Entry, Trusted Traveler number**?　　　Yes or No
　If yes: Where is your card located?

_____

　Number: _____
　Details: _____

Passport/Trusted Traveler

Do you have a **passport**?　　　Yes or No
　If yes: Where is your passport located?

_____

　Expiration date of passport: _____

Do you have a **foreign passport**?　　Yes or No
　If yes: Where is your passport located?

_____

　Expiration date of passport: _____

Do you have a **Global Entry, Trusted Traveler number**?　　　Yes or No
　If yes: Where is your card located?

_____

　Number: _____
　Details: _____

Just In Case of Death:

- Contact the local Homeland Security office and notify them of the death associated with Trusted Traveler Number/Global Entry.
- Passports can be kept as a memento or submitted to be destroyed. If you decide to keep it, consider submitting the passport for cancellation and have it returned to you.

Primary User and Secondary User

Local Town, City, or Government Offices

It's helpful to provide your loved ones with the contact information of your local offices.

Write the address and telephone numbers below:

Town/City Hall and Clerk's Office:
County Offices / Probate Court:
Post Office:
Registry of Motor Vehicles (RMV)/Department of Motor Vehicles (DMV):
Police Department:
Fire Department:
Transfer Station/Dump:
Social Security Office:
Other: _____

_____

_____

_____

Primary User and Secondary User - Emergency Contact(s)

1. Emergency Contact name:

   Telephone number(s):

   Email address:

   Your relationship to this Emergency Contact: *(Spouse, daughter, cousin, friend, etc.)*

2. Emergency Contact name:

   Telephone number(s):

   Email address:

   Your relationship to this Emergency Contact: *(Spouse, daughter, cousin, friend, etc.)*

3. Emergency Contact name:

   Telephone number(s):

   Email address:

   Your relationship to this Emergency Contact: *(Spouse, daughter, cousin, friend, etc.)*

4. Emergency Contact name:

   Telephone number(s):

   Email address:

   Your relationship to this Emergency Contact: *(Spouse, daughter, cousin, friend, etc.)*

Additional details:

_____

_____

_____

_____

Primary User	Secondary User

License(s) and/or Identification

Primary User

Do you have a **driver's license**?   Yes or No

    If yes: What state? _____
    License location: _____

    If no: Do you have another type of photo ID?
    Location/Details: _____
    _____

Do you have a **commercial driver's license**?
                                    Yes or No
    If yes: What state? _____

Do you have a **boating license**?   Yes or No
Do you have a **fishing license**?   Yes or No

    If yes: What state(s)? _____

    Recreational or Commercial

Do you have a **hunting license**?   Yes or No

    If yes: What state(s)? _____

    Recreational or Commercial

All commercial licenses:

Do you have paperwork or documentation as to whom you would like your permit transferred to?
                                    Yes or No

Location and details:

_____
_____

Are you a **notary public**?   Yes or No

    If yes: Where is your notary seal (stamp) kept?

    _____

What are your state's requirements if you are unable to fulfill notary duties? *(Report death to the Secretary of State, destroy or surrender your seal, journals, etc.)*

_____
_____

Do you have any **other identification or specialty licenses**?   Yes or No
(Teacher, nurse, pilot, trade, medical, etc.)

If yes: Details:

_____
_____

Secondary User

Do you have a **driver's license**?   Yes or No

    If yes: What state? _____
    License location: _____

    If no: Do you have another type of photo ID?
    Location/Details: _____
    _____

Do you have a **commercial driver's license**?
                                      Yes or No
    If yes: What state? _____

Do you have a **boating license**?   Yes or No
Do you have a **fishing license**?   Yes or No

    If yes: What state(s)? _____

    Recreational or Commercial

Do you have a **hunting license**?   Yes or No

    If yes: What state(s)? _____

    Recreational or Commercial

All commercial licenses:

Do you have paperwork or documentation as to whom you would like your permit transferred to?
                                    Yes or No

Location and details:

_____
_____

Are you a **notary public**?   Yes or No

    If yes: Where is your notary seal (stamp) kept?

    _____

What are your state's requirements if you are unable to fulfill notary duties? *(Report death to the Secretary of State, destroy or surrender your seal, journals, etc.)*

_____
_____

Do you have any **other identification or specialty licenses**?   Yes or No
(Teacher, nurse, pilot, trade, medical, etc.)

If yes: Details:

_____
_____

Primary User	Secondary User
Firearms License and Firearms Storage	**Firearms License and Firearms Storage**
Do you have a **firearms license**? Yes or No	Do you have a **firearms license**? Yes or No
Is it a concealed-carry license? Yes or No	Is it a concealed-carry license? Yes or No
What state(s)? _____	What state(s)? _____
Ownership:	**Ownership:**
Do you own a firearm? Yes or No	Do you own a firearm? Yes or No
If yes: How many? #_____	If yes: How many? #_____
Paperwork location: _____	Paperwork location: _____
Firearms Storage	**Firearms Storage**
Are the firearms locked? Yes or No	Are the firearms locked? Yes or No
Details:_____	Details:_____
_____	_____
_____	_____
Where are the firearms stored? In a safe?	Where are the firearms stored? In a safe?
Details:_____	Details:_____
_____	_____
_____	_____
How do you access the firearms storage/safe?	How do you access the firearms storage/safe?
Keys,combination lock, thumbprint, and/or keycard, etc.	Keys,combination lock, thumbprint, and/or keycard, etc.
Details:_____	Details:_____
_____	_____
Combination: _____	Combination:_____
If you become unable to use, maintain, or store your firearms properly/safely, what's your plan?	If you become unable to use, maintain, or store your firearms properly/safely, what's your plan?
_____	_____
_____	_____
_____	_____
Upon your death: Name of person in charge of your firearms: _____	**Upon your death**: Name of person in charge of your firearms: _____
Who can assist your loved ones if help is needed with your firearms? Name/Telephone:	Who can assist your loved ones if help is needed with your firearms? Name/Telephone:
_____	_____
Details: _____	Details: _____
_____	_____
Firearms Inventory: _____	**Firearms Inventory:** _____
_____	_____
_____	_____
_____	_____
_____	_____
_____	_____

> Please consult an estate planning attorney with any questions about including your firearms in your will

Primary User and Secondary User

Computers: PC, Laptop, Tablet, Devices

Do you own a **computer, desktop, or laptop**?   Yes or No

    If yes: How many? **Primary User #**_____ **Secondary User #**_____

Do you own an **iPad or other type of tablet**?   Yes or No

    If yes: How many? **Primary User #**_____ **Secondary User #**_____

Primary User: Passwords (login credentials)

Do you have a **written list** of usernames and passwords?   Yes or No

Do you use an **app or software** to store your passwords?   Yes or No

If **written list**   Where is it located or saved? *(Paper, digital, flash drive, etc.)* _____

If **app/software** Name: _____

                Details on how to access app or software: _____

_____

Additional details regarding **where to locate your login credentials**: _____

_____
_____

Secondary User: Passwords (login credentials)

Do you have a **written** list of usernames and passwords?   Yes or No

Do you use an **app or software** to store your passwords?   Yes or No

If **written list**   Where is it located or saved? *(Paper, digital, flash drive, etc.)* _____

If **app/software** Name: _____

                Details on how to access app or software: _____

_____

Additional details regarding **where to locate your login credentials**: _____

_____

Username and Password List with Security Questions:
If you haven't created a list of your login credentials yet, you can find a **Username and Password List with Security Questions** chart in the EXTRAS section, at the end of this workbook, to help you create one.

Wi-Fi, Router, Modem

Do you have a modem and/or router?   Yes or No

   If yes: Where is the modem and/or router located? _____

Do you have a wireless network? Wi-Fi?   Yes or No

   If yes: Network name:_____Password:_____

       Network name:_____Password:_____

Primary User and Secondary User

Computer Details: PC, Laptop, Tablet, Etc.

Bookmarks/Favorites for Websites: In your web browser, you can bookmark all the websites that you frequently use. This will help your loved ones easily navigate to your important sites.

Legacy Contacts: On certain accounts, you can designate a legacy contact and/or a trusted contact. This can provide the ability to access the data saved within that account.

Inactive Account Managers: For accounts that offer inactivity notifications, you can add a contact to be notified when an account remains inactive for a certain period of time.

Primary User	Secondary User
List any accounts that you use across all your devices. *(Google account, Microsoft, Apple ID, Cloud, etc.)* Note: Make sure to add these to your Username and Password List	
1. Details:	1. Details:
2. Details:	2. Details:
3. Details:	3. Details:

Provide details for each of your technological devices.

Include: Cloud Storage / Technology Backup / Digital Photographs / Important Folders / Saved Files
(Keep in mind you may have more than one way of backing up your data depending on your devices.)

1. **Name/Type Computer or Device:** _____

   (Wendy's Microsoft surface laptop, family desktop computer, George's iPad, Samsung Tablet, etc.)

   Purpose: *(Personal, work, fun only, etc.)* _____

   How to access: *(Complete what is necessary to unlock the device)*
   PIN: _____   Username: _____
   Other: _____   Password: _____

   Do you have important software installed? *(Antivirus, Microsoft Office, Outlook, etc.)*   Yes or No
   If yes: Software name/Details: _____
   _____

   Do you pay a recurring fee for any software?   Yes or No
   If yes: Payment details: _____

Computer/Device Backup/Storage Used: _____
Where is it located:_____How do you access it: _____

Important Items, Folders, saved files on computer/device: *(Legal documents, bills, address book, etc.)*
_____
_____

Where are digital photos saved? _____

What web browser do you use? *(Google Chrome, Microsoft Edge, Apple Safari, etc.)* _____

Additional details: *(Recover Key, Google Doc, or OneDrive usage, directions to find a saved document or letter, etc.)* _____
_____

2. **Name/Type Computer or Device:** _____
   (Wendy's Microsoft surface laptop, family desktop computer, George's iPad, Samsung Tablet, etc.)

   Purpose: *(Personal, work, fun only, etc.)* _____

   How to access: *(Complete what is necessary to unlock the device)*
   PIN: _____   Username: _____
   Other: _____   Password: _____

   Do you have important software installed? *(Antivirus, Microsoft Office, Outlook, etc.)*   Yes or No
   If yes: Software name/Details: _____
   _____

      Do you pay a recurring fee for any software?   Yes or No
      If yes: Payment details: _____

Computer/Device Backup/Storage Used: _____
Where is it located:_____How do you access it: _____

Important Items, Folders, saved files on computer/device: *(Legal documents, bills, address book, etc.)*
_____
_____

Where are digital photos saved? _____
What web browser do you use? *(Google Chrome, Microsoft Edge, Apple Safari, etc.)* _____
Additional details: *(Recover Key, Google Doc, or OneDrive usage, directions to find a saved document or letter, etc.)* _____
_____

---

3. **Name/Type Computer or Device:** _____
   (Wendy's Microsoft surface laptop, family desktop computer, George's iPad, Samsung Tablet, etc.)

   Purpose: *(Personal, work, fun only, etc.)* _____

   How to access: *(Complete what is necessary to unlock the device)*
   PIN: _____   Username: _____
   Other: _____   Password: _____

   Do you have important software installed? *(Antivirus, Microsoft Office, Outlook, etc.)*   Yes or No
   If yes: Software name/Details: _____
   _____

      Do you pay a recurring fee for any software?   Yes or No
      If yes: Payment details: _____

Computer/Device Backup/Storage Used: _____
Where is it located:_____How do you access it: _____

Important Items, Folders, saved files on computer/device: *(Legal documents, bills, address book, etc.)*
_____
_____

Where are digital photos saved? _____
What web browser do you use? *(Google Chrome, Microsoft Edge, Apple Safari, etc.)* _____
Additional details: *(Recover Key, Google Doc, or OneDrive usage, directions to find a saved document or letter, etc.)* _____
_____

4. Name/Type Computer or Device: _____
(Wendy's Microsoft surface laptop, family desktop computer, George's iPad, Samsung Tablet, etc.)

Purpose: *(Personal, work, fun only, etc.)* _____

How to access: *(Complete what is necessary to unlock the device)*

PIN: _____   Username: _____

Other: _____   Password: _____

Do you have important software installed? *(Antivirus, Microsoft Office, Outlook, etc.)*   Yes or No

If yes: Software name/Details: _____

_____

Do you pay a recurring fee for any software?   Yes or No

If yes: Payment details: _____

Computer/Device Backup/Storage Used: _____

Where is it located:_____How do you access it: _____

Important Items, Folders, saved files on computer/device: *(Legal documents, bills, address book, etc.)*

_____

_____

Where are digital photos saved? _____

What web browser do you use? *(Google Chrome, Microsoft Edge, Apple Safari, etc.)* _____

Additional details: *(Recover Key, Google Doc, or OneDrive usage, directions to find a saved document or letter, etc.)* _____

_____

---

5. Name/Type Computer or Device: _____
(Wendy's Microsoft surface laptop, family desktop computer, George's iPad, Samsung Tablet, etc.)

Purpose: *(Personal, work, fun only, etc.)* _____

How to access: *(Complete what is necessary to unlock the device)*

PIN: _____   Username: _____

Other: _____   Password: _____

Do you have important software installed? *(Antivirus, Microsoft Office, Outlook, etc.)*   Yes or No

If yes: Software name/Details: _____

_____

Do you pay a recurring fee for any software?   Yes or No

If yes: Payment details: _____

Computer/Device Backup/Storage Used: _____

Where is it located:_____How do you access it: _____

Important Items, Folders, saved files on computer/device: *(Legal documents, bills, address book, etc.)*

_____

_____

Where are digital photos saved? _____

What web browser do you use? *(Google Chrome, Microsoft Edge, Apple Safari, etc.)* _____

Additional details: *(Recover Key, Google Doc, or OneDrive usage, directions to find a saved document or letter, etc.)* _____

_____

Primary User	Secondary User

Streaming Services, App Subscriptions

(Amazon Prime, Netflix, Hulu, Disney+, Spotify, Apple Music, HBO, YouTube, Xbox, PlayStation, Casino Games, Pandora, Sling TV, Roku, News, etc.)

Do you have a subscription/membership to streaming software or any apps?　　Yes or No

If yes: How many **require payment?**　#＿＿＿＿＿

1. App name: ＿＿＿＿＿＿＿＿＿＿＿＿＿＿＿＿
 Name(s) on subscription: ＿＿＿＿＿＿＿＿

＿＿＿＿＿＿＿＿＿＿＿＿＿＿＿＿＿＿＿＿＿

Email used: ＿＿＿＿＿＿＿＿＿＿＿＿＿＿＿
How do you pay? ＿＿＿＿＿＿＿＿＿＿＿＿＿
(Credit card, debit, PayPal, Apple Pay on iPhone, etc.)

Is this on auto-renew?　　Yes or No
Payment method:　　Monthly or Annually
Amount $ ＿＿＿＿＿　Renewal month: ＿＿＿

2. App name: ＿＿＿＿＿＿＿＿＿＿＿＿＿＿＿＿
 Name(s) on subscription: ＿＿＿＿＿＿＿＿

＿＿＿＿＿＿＿＿＿＿＿＿＿＿＿＿＿＿＿＿＿

Email used: ＿＿＿＿＿＿＿＿＿＿＿＿＿＿＿
How do you pay? ＿＿＿＿＿＿＿＿＿＿＿＿＿
(Credit card, debit, PayPal, Apple Pay on iPhone, etc.)

Is this on auto-renew?　　Yes or No
Payment method:　　Monthly or Annually
Amount $ ＿＿＿＿＿　Renewal month: ＿＿＿

3. App name: ＿＿＿＿＿＿＿＿＿＿＿＿＿＿＿＿
 Name(s) on subscription: ＿＿＿＿＿＿＿＿

＿＿＿＿＿＿＿＿＿＿＿＿＿＿＿＿＿＿＿＿＿

Email used: ＿＿＿＿＿＿＿＿＿＿＿＿＿＿＿
How do you pay? ＿＿＿＿＿＿＿＿＿＿＿＿＿
(Credit card, debit, PayPal, Apple Pay on iPhone, etc.)

Is this on auto-renew?　　Yes or No
Payment method:　　Monthly or Annually
Amount $ ＿＿＿＿＿　Renewal month: ＿＿＿

4. App name: ＿＿＿＿＿＿＿＿＿＿＿＿＿＿＿＿
 Name(s) on subscription: ＿＿＿＿＿＿＿＿

＿＿＿＿＿＿＿＿＿＿＿＿＿＿＿＿＿＿＿＿＿

Email used: ＿＿＿＿＿＿＿＿＿＿＿＿＿＿＿
How do you pay? ＿＿＿＿＿＿＿＿＿＿＿＿＿
(Credit card, debit, PayPal, Apple Pay on iPhone, etc.)

Is this on auto-renew?　　Yes or No
Payment method:　　Monthly or Annually
Amount $ ＿＿＿＿＿　Renewal month: ＿＿＿

Streaming Services, App Subscriptions

Do you have a subscription/membership to streaming software or any apps?　　Yes or No

If yes: How many **require payment?**　#＿＿＿＿＿

1. App name: ＿＿＿＿＿＿＿＿＿＿＿＿＿＿＿＿
 Name(s) on subscription: ＿＿＿＿＿＿＿＿

＿＿＿＿＿＿＿＿＿＿＿＿＿＿＿＿＿＿＿＿＿

Email used: ＿＿＿＿＿＿＿＿＿＿＿＿＿＿＿
How do you pay? ＿＿＿＿＿＿＿＿＿＿＿＿＿
(Credit card, debit, PayPal, Apple Pay on iPhone, etc.)

Is this on auto-renew?　　Yes or No
Payment method:　　Monthly or Annually
Amount $ ＿＿＿＿＿　Renewal month: ＿＿＿

2. App name: ＿＿＿＿＿＿＿＿＿＿＿＿＿＿＿＿
 Name(s) on subscription: ＿＿＿＿＿＿＿＿

＿＿＿＿＿＿＿＿＿＿＿＿＿＿＿＿＿＿＿＿＿

Email used: ＿＿＿＿＿＿＿＿＿＿＿＿＿＿＿
How do you pay? ＿＿＿＿＿＿＿＿＿＿＿＿＿
(Credit card, debit, PayPal, Apple Pay on iPhone, etc.)

Is this on auto-renew?　　Yes or No
Payment method:　　Monthly or Annually
Amount $ ＿＿＿＿＿　Renewal month: ＿＿＿

3. App name: ＿＿＿＿＿＿＿＿＿＿＿＿＿＿＿＿
 Name(s) on subscription: ＿＿＿＿＿＿＿＿

＿＿＿＿＿＿＿＿＿＿＿＿＿＿＿＿＿＿＿＿＿

Email used: ＿＿＿＿＿＿＿＿＿＿＿＿＿＿＿
How do you pay? ＿＿＿＿＿＿＿＿＿＿＿＿＿
(Credit card, debit, PayPal, Apple Pay on iPhone, etc.)

Is this on auto-renew?　　Yes or No
Payment method:　　Monthly or Annually
Amount $ ＿＿＿＿＿Renewal month: ＿＿＿

4. App name: ＿＿＿＿＿＿＿＿＿＿＿＿＿＿＿＿
 Name(s) on subscription: ＿＿＿＿＿＿＿＿

＿＿＿＿＿＿＿＿＿＿＿＿＿＿＿＿＿＿＿＿＿

Email used: ＿＿＿＿＿＿＿＿＿＿＿＿＿＿＿
How do you pay? ＿＿＿＿＿＿＿＿＿＿＿＿＿
(Credit card, debit, PayPal, Apple Pay on iPhone, etc.)

Is this on auto-renew?　　Yes or No
Payment method:　　Monthly or Annually
Amount $ ＿＿＿＿＿　Renewal month: ＿＿＿

Primary User	Secondary User
Streaming Services, App Subscriptions	**Streaming Services, App Subscriptions**

5. App name: _____
   Name(s) on subscription: _____
   _____

   Email used: _____
   How do you pay? _____
   (Credit card, debit, PayPal, Apple Pay on iPhone, etc.)

   Is this on auto-renew?   Yes or No
   Payment method: Monthly or Annually
   Amount $ _____ Renewal month: _____

5. App name: _____
   Name(s) on subscription: _____
   _____

   Email used: _____
   How do you pay? _____
   (Credit card, debit, PayPal, Apple Pay on iPhone, etc.)

   Is this on auto-renew?   Yes or No
   Payment method: Monthly or Annually
   Amount $ _____ Renewal month: _____

6. App name: _____
   Name(s) on subscription: _____
   _____

   Email used: _____
   How do you pay? _____
   (Credit card, debit, PayPal, Apple Pay on iPhone, etc.)

   Is this on auto-renew?   Yes or No
   Payment method: Monthly or Annually
   Amount $ _____ Renewal month: _____

6. App name: _____
   Name(s) on subscription: _____
   _____

   Email used: _____
   How do you pay? _____
   (Credit card, debit, PayPal, Apple Pay on iPhone, etc.)

   Is this on auto-renew?   Yes or No
   Payment method: Monthly or Annually
   Amount $ _____ Renewal month: _____

7. App name: _____
   Name(s) on subscription: _____
   _____

   Email used: _____
   How do you pay? _____
   (Credit card, debit, PayPal, Apple Pay on iPhone, etc.)

   Is this on auto-renew?   Yes or No
   Payment method: Monthly or Annually
   Amount $ _____ Renewal month: _____

7. App name: _____
   Name(s) on subscription: _____
   _____

   Email used: _____
   How do you pay? _____
   (Credit card, debit, PayPal, Apple Pay on iPhone, etc.)

   Is this on auto-renew?   Yes or No
   Payment method: Monthly or Annually
   Amount $ _____ Renewal month: _____

8. App name: _____
   Name(s) on subscription: _____
   _____

   Email used: _____
   How do you pay? _____
   (Credit card, debit, PayPal, Apple Pay on iPhone, etc.)

   Is this on auto-renew?   Yes or No
   Payment method: Monthly or Annually
   Amount $ _____ Renewal month: _____

8. App name: _____
   Name(s) on subscription: _____
   _____

   Email used: _____
   How do you pay? _____
   (Credit card, debit, PayPal, Apple Pay on iPhone, etc.)

   Is this on auto-renew?   Yes or No
   Payment method: Monthly or Annually
   Amount $ _____ Renewal month: _____

Additional details: _____
_____
_____
_____
_____
_____

Do you have any Social Networking/Social Media accounts?   Yes or No

(Facebook, Twitter, Instagram, LinkedIn, Snapchat, TikTok, Blog, etc.)

Note: Each social networking/media site has particulars regarding how to shut down or memorialize the profile to preserve the account after death. List all your accounts to help your loved ones prevent unwanted spam and RIP trolling and to protect your legacy.

Social Site Name	Username Password	Just In Case of Death Do you want this account shut down/deleted or memorialized?	Who is your legacy contact? Social media executor
1.			
2.			
3.			
4.			
5.			
6.			
7.			
8.			
9.			

Additional details: _____

_____

_____

_____

_____

_____

Secondary User   Social Networking/Social Media Sites

Do you have any Social Networking/Social Media accounts?   Yes or No

(Facebook, Twitter, Instagram, LinkedIn, Snapchat, TikTok, Blog, etc.)

Note: Each social networking/media site has particulars regarding how to shut down or memorialize the profile to preserve the account after death. List all your accounts to help your loved ones prevent unwanted spam and RIP trolling and to protect your legacy.

Social Site Name	Username / Password	Just In Case of Death Do you want this account shut down/deleted or memorialized?	Who is your Legacy Contact? Social media executor
1.			
2.			
3.			
4.			
5.			
6.			
7.			
8.			
9.			

Additional details: _____

_____

_____

_____

_____

_____

Step 1: Personal Details and Technology
(Primary User and Secondary User)

 Date Completed: _____

Fun Memory

Way to go! You have completed Step 1!

Did a fun or interesting fact from your past come to mind while you were working on this Step?

Use the space below to share a memory with your loved ones. It could be a funny story about yourself, a loving memory, or a fascinating fact about a moment in your past. This will bring joy and a smile during challenging times. Instead of writing, share your favorite song, poem, or insert a picture!

Need ideas? Here are some suggestions to write about for Step 1:

Share the age you enjoyed most during your childhood and why, a funny story about learning to drive, the favorite place you lived, where was your first kiss and with whom, a special wedding moment, the best event or concert you've been to, your pet peeves, favorite food or drink, etc.

_____
_____
_____
_____
_____
_____
_____
_____
_____
_____
_____
_____
_____
_____
_____
_____
_____
_____

Step 2

Family, Friends, and Pets

In Step 2, you will complete information about your family, friends, neighbors, and pets. There are many Just In Case scenarios in which your loved ones might need to contact someone or understand details about a specific person – or even your dog.

Ask Yourself, have you designated someone to care for your children and/or beloved pets in case of your death?

Every family has different dynamics. Some families are close with few issues, while others are not so fortunate. And some families seem to get smaller as we age, causing anxiety about who will take care of details in case of a crisis. If you know someone outside the immediate family who will be able to step in and help, have a conversation with them in advance and tell them about this workbook.

If you have no children or family, simply cross out the irrelevant sections and provide other necessary details for your designated personal representative or entity.

Here are some other ways Step 2 can be helpful:

- If there are young children who will need assistance in case of an accident, illness, or death, include contact and details of a close friend or neighbor who might be willing to step in and help. Also include the names of daycare, teachers and/or favorite babysitters, and others who can keep life as normal as possible for children.

- Provide a list of any allergies, medications, and special needs that may be relevant for caretakers to know for your children, including contact information for their doctors. This will help ensure their well-being while under the care of someone else.

- Write down where to locate family paperwork, such as custody agreements or adoption papers. This might include how to contact a caseworker or whether you have guardianship for a grandchild.

- If applicable, include contact information of stepparents or stepchildren.

- If you have an adult child with a special need, write down imperative information family and friends will need to know in the case of your death.

  - You may want to complete a separate Just In Case Solutions workbook for your adult child with a special need, which will serve as a comprehensive guide for their future caregiver to reference, covering all aspects of their life.

Pets: Do not forget about your beloved pets!

Ask Yourself, what would your pet caretaker need to know?

- Record the details about all your pets: diet, medications, fears, favorite toys or activities, and if they have microchip identification.

- List the names of your veterinarian, groomer, and pet sitter. Note the location of paperwork such as vaccination records, pedigree registration, and pet insurance.

Please take a moment to review what's included in this Step:

Step 2: NOTE TO LOVED ONES

In Step 2, your loved one has prepared you with details about their family, close friends, neighbors, and pets. This Step will help you with family contacts as well as other people who can help or whom you need to contact in the case of illness or death.

How can Step 2 be helpful?

- If you are an assigned executor and not a family member, it will help you to understand family dynamics. Some families have multiple children or difficult personalities. This Step will assist you with the names and contact details along with their relationships.

- If you need to understand a family's legal situation, this section can help you locate documents such as custody or guardianship arrangements.

- If you find yourself responsible for taking care of a pet while a loved one is undergoing rehabilitation, this resource will provide you or any other caretaker with the necessary details to ensure proper care.

- If you are in charge of writing your loved one's obituary, this section will be helpful because it lists all parents, siblings, children, and grandchildren. Please also refer to the obituary writing assistance section in Step 10.

2

Primary User Mother:

What is your mother's full legal name? _____

Mother's maiden name: _____ Date of Birth: _____

Is your mother living or deceased? _____ Date of Death: _____

Address and contact information:

_____

_____

Do you have a stepmother?   Yes or No

    If yes: Stepmother's name and contact information: _____

_____

Additional details about mother and/or stepmother: _____

_____

_____

Primary User Father:

What is your father's full legal name? _____

Father's Date of Birth: _____

Is your father living or deceased? _____ Date of Death: _____

Address and contact information:

_____

_____

Do you have a stepfather?   Yes or No

    If yes: Stepfather's name and contact information: _____

_____

Additional details about father and/or stepfather: _____

_____

_____

Primary User Siblings:

Do you have any siblings?   Yes or No   If yes: How many # _____

Do you have any stepsiblings?   Yes or No   If yes: How many # _____

Sibling Full Name	Type of Sibling (Biological, step, half)	Contact Information

Additional details about siblings: _____

_____

_____

Secondary User   Parents and Siblings

Secondary User Mother:

What is your mother's full legal name? _____

Mother's maiden name: _____   Date of Birth: _____

Is your mother living or deceased? _____   Date of Death: _____

Address and contact information:

_____

_____

Do you have a stepmother?   Yes or No

    If yes: Stepmother's name and contact information: _____

_____

Additional details about mother and/or stepmother: _____

_____

_____

Secondary User Father:

What is your father's full legal name? _____

Father's Date of Birth: _____

Is your father living or deceased? _____   Date of Death: _____

Address and contact information:

_____

_____

Do you have a stepfather?   Yes or No

    If yes: Stepfather's name and contact information: _____

_____

Additional details about father and/or stepfather: _____

_____

_____

Secondary User Siblings:

Do you have any siblings?   Yes or No   If yes: How many # _____

Do you have any stepsiblings?   Yes or No   If yes: How many # _____

Sibling Full Name	Type of Sibling (Biological, step, half)	Contact Information

Additional details about siblings: _____

_____

_____

_____

Children	Primary and Secondary

Do you have any **children under the age of 18**?
    If yes: How many minor children?

Yes or No   **Together #** _____
Primary User #_____**Secondary User #** _____

Do you have any **adult children aged 18 or older**?
    If yes: How many adult children?

Yes or No   **Together #** _____
Primary User #_____**Secondary User #** _____

Do you have any **grandchildren**?
    If yes: How many grandchildren?

Yes or No   **Together #** _____
Primary User #_____**Secondary User #** _____

Do you have any **great-grandchildren**?
    If yes: How many great-grandchildren?

Yes or No   **Together #** _____
Primary User #_____**Secondary User #** _____

Adoption

Are any of your children adopted?
    If yes: How many adopted children?
    Where are the adoption papers located?

Yes or No   **Together #** _____
Primary User #_____**Secondary User #** _____
_____
_____

Additional details: Agency name/Documentation/Family medical history/Ethnic background/etc.

_____
_____
_____
_____

Note: If you have adult children, it may be beneficial to give them any adoption information that you have.

Foster

Do you have a foster child/children?
    If yes: How many foster children?

Yes or No   **Together #** _____
Primary User #_____**Secondary User #** _____

Name/Contact information for the agency, caseworker, and other important information:

_____
_____
_____
_____

Stepchildren

Do you have any stepchildren?
    If yes: How many stepchildren?

Yes or No   **Together #** _____
Primary User #_____**Secondary User #** _____

Name/Contact information of biological parent(s) or relative:

_____
_____
_____

2

Children	Primary and Secondary

Birth Certificates for Children
Do you have your children's birth certificate(s)?   Yes or No
     If yes: Do you have a copy or original?   Copy or Original
         Where are they located?   _____
Additional details: _____

_____

_____

Note: If you have adult children, it may be beneficial to give them any original birth certificates that you have.

Co-Parenting
Do you co-parent with another person?   Yes or No
If yes: Name/Contact information of co-parent   _____
     and their relationship to you: _____

_____

_____

_____

Custody Agreement(s)/Child Support Order
Do you have any custody agreements in place?   Yes or No
Do you have a child support order in place?   Yes or No
     If yes: Where are the documents located?   _____

_____

Additional details: *(Important information regarding the custody agreement and/or child support order you want your loved ones to know.)*
_____
_____
_____

Guardianship for Child(ren)
Do you have guardianship for a child or children?   Yes or No
Are you a grandparent who has guardianship for a grandchild?   Yes or No
     Details:

Please note that this workbook is not legally binding. However, in case of an accident, illness, or death, you can write your intentions with the hope that someone will follow them.

Name/Contact information of the person you **WANT** to be appointed as guardian for your child/children:
_____
_____

Name and details for the person(s) you **DO NOT WANT** to be appointed as guardian:
_____
_____

Minor Children (Under Age 18)   (If you do not have minor children skip this section)

Today's Date: _____

1. **Full Legal Name of Minor Child:** _____

   Nickname:_____Date of birth: _____

   Hospital, City/State where this child was born: _____

   Circle your relationship with this child: Biological child or Stepchild or Adopted Other: _____

   Does this child have a cell phone?   Yes or No   If yes: Phone number: _____

   Does this child have any allergies?   Yes or No
      If yes: What allergy and how is it treated? _____
      _____
      _____

   Does this child take any medications or vitamins?   Yes or No
      If yes: What is the medication or vitamin and dosage? _____
      _____
      _____

   Does this child go to daycare?   Yes or No
      If yes: Name/Contact information: _____
      _____

   Does this child have a favorite babysitter?   Yes or No
      If yes: Name/Contact information: _____
      _____

   Child's school name/Contact information: _____
   _____

   Pediatrician name/Contact information: _____
   _____

   Specialty doctor's name/Contact information/Frequency: *(Neurologist, dentist, allergist, eye, orthopedic, etc.)*
   _____
   _____
   _____

   Does this minor child have any special needs?   Yes or No
      If yes: What are the special needs and information someone would need to know: _____
      _____
      _____
      _____
      _____
      _____
      _____

   Does this child have any aversions?   Yes or No
      If yes: Describe: _____
   Child's best friend's name/Contact information: _____
   _____

   Additional details: Activities/Hobbies/Sports/Other issues
   (Sports team/coaches contact information, child has anxiety around lots of people, member of the school band, afraid of dogs, etc.)

Minor Children (Under Age 18)

Today's Date: _____

2. **Full Legal Name of Minor Child:** _____

Nickname:_____Date of birth: _____

Hospital, City/State where this child was born: _____

Circle your relationship with this child: Biological child or Stepchild or Adopted Other: _____

Does this child have a cell phone?   Yes or No   If yes: Phone number: _____

Does this child have any allergies?   Yes or No
   If yes: What allergy and how is it treated? _____
_____
_____

Does this child take any medications or vitamins?   Yes or No
   If yes: What is the medication or vitamin and dosage? _____
_____
_____

Does this child go to daycare?   Yes or No
   If yes: Name/Contact information: _____
_____

Does this child have a favorite babysitter?   Yes or No
   If yes: Name/Contact information: _____
_____

Child's school name/Contact information: _____
_____

Pediatrician name/Contact information: _____
_____

Specialty doctor's name/Contact information/Frequency: *(Neurologist, dentist, allergist, eye, orthopedic, etc.)*
_____
_____
_____

Does this minor child have any special needs?   Yes or No
   If yes: What are the special needs and information someone would need to know: _____
_____
_____
_____
_____
_____
_____

Does this child have any aversions?   Yes or No
   If yes: Describe: _____
Child's best friend's name/Contact information: _____
_____

Additional details: Activities/Hobbies/Sports/Other issues
(Sports team/coaches contact information, child has anxiety around lots of people, member of the school band, afraid of dogs, etc.)

Minor Children (Under Age 18)

Today's Date: _____

3. **Full Legal Name of Minor Child:** _____

Nickname:_____Date of birth: _____

Hospital, City/State where this child was born: _____

Circle your relationship with this child: Biological child or Stepchild or Adopted Other: _____

Does this child have a cell phone?   Yes or No   If yes: Phone number: _____

Does this child have any allergies?   Yes or No
   If yes: What allergy and how is it treated? _____

_____

_____

Does this child take any medications or vitamins?   Yes or No
   If yes: What is the medication or vitamin and dosage? _____

_____

_____

Does this child go to daycare?   Yes or No
   If yes: Name/Contact information: _____

_____

Does this child have a favorite babysitter?   Yes or No
   If yes: Name/Contact information: _____

_____

Child's school name/Contact information: _____

_____

Pediatrician name/Contact information: _____

_____

Specialty doctor's name/Contact information/Frequency: *(Neurologist, dentist, allergist, eye, orthopedic, etc.)*

_____

_____

_____

Does this minor child have any special needs?   Yes or No
   If yes: What are the special needs and information someone would need to know: _____

_____

_____

_____

_____

_____

_____

Does this child have any aversions?   Yes or No
   If yes: Describe: _____

Child's best friend's name/Contact information: _____

Additional details: Activities/Hobbies/Sports/Other issues
(Sports team/coaches contact information, child has anxiety around lots of people, member of the school band, afraid of dogs, etc.)

Minor Children (Under Age 18)

4. **Full Legal Name of Minor Child:** _____

   Nickname:_____Date of birth: _____

   Hospital, City/State where this child was born: _____

   Circle your relationship with this child: Biological child or Stepchild or Adopted Other: _____

   Does this child have a cell phone?   Yes or No   If yes: Phone number: _____

   Does this child have any allergies?   Yes or No
      If yes: What allergy and how is it treated? _____
      _____
      _____

   Does this child take any medications or vitamins?   Yes or No
      If yes: What is the medication or vitamin and dosage? _____
      _____
      _____

   Does this child go to daycare?   Yes or No
      If yes: Name/Contact information: _____
      _____

   Does this child have a favorite babysitter?   Yes or No
      If yes: Name/Contact information: _____
      _____

   Child's school name/Contact information: _____
   _____

   Pediatrician name/Contact information: _____
   _____

   Specialty doctor's name/Contact information/Frequency: *(Neurologist, dentist, allergist, eye, orthopedic, etc.)*
   _____
   _____
   _____

   Does this minor child have any special needs?   Yes or No
      If yes: What are the special needs and information someone would need to know: _____
      _____
      _____
      _____
      _____
      _____
      _____

   Does this child have any aversions?   Yes or No
      If yes: Describe: _____
   Child's best friend's name/Contact information: _____
   _____

   Additional details: Activities/Hobbies/Sports/Other issues
   (Sports team/coaches contact information, child has anxiety around lots of people, member of the school band, afraid of dogs, etc.)

Today's Date: _____

5. **Full Legal Name of Minor Child:** _____

Nickname:_____Date of birth: _____

Hospital, City/State where this child was born: _____

Circle your relationship with this child: Biological child or Stepchild or Adopted Other: _____

Does this child have a cell phone?   Yes or No   If yes: Phone number: _____

Does this child have any allergies?   Yes or No
    If yes: What allergy and how is it treated? _____
    _____
    _____

Does this child take any medications or vitamins?   Yes or No
    If yes: What is the medication or vitamin and dosage? _____
    _____
    _____

Does this child go to daycare?   Yes or No
    If yes: Name/Contact information: _____
    _____

Does this child have a favorite babysitter?   Yes or No
    If yes: Name/Contact information: _____
    _____

Child's school name/Contact information: _____
_____

Pediatrician name/Contact information: _____
_____

Specialty doctor's name/Contact information/Frequency: *(Neurologist, dentist, allergist, eye, orthopedic, etc.)*
_____
_____

Does this minor child have any special needs?   Yes or No
    If yes: What are the special needs and information someone would need to know: _____
    _____
    _____
    _____
    _____
    _____

Does this child have any aversions?   Yes or No
    If yes: Describe: _____
Child's best friend's name/Contact information: _____
_____

Additional details: Activities/Hobbies/Sports/Other issues
(Sports team/coaches contact information, child has anxiety around lots of people, member of the school band, afraid of dogs, etc.)

Minor Children (Under Age 18)

Today's Date: _____

6. **Full Legal Name of Minor Child:** _____

Nickname:_____Date of birth: _____

Hospital, City/State where this child was born: _____

Circle your relationship with this child: Biological child or Stepchild or Adopted Other: _____

Does this child have a cell phone?   Yes or No   If yes: Phone number: _____

Does this child have any allergies?   Yes or No
   If yes: What allergy and how is it treated? _____
   _____
   _____

Does this child take any medications or vitamins?   Yes or No
   If yes: What is the medication or vitamin and dosage? _____
   _____
   _____

Does this child go to daycare?   Yes or No
   If yes: Name/Contact information: _____
   _____

Does this child have a favorite babysitter?   Yes or No
   If yes: Name/Contact information: _____
   _____

Child's school name/Contact information: _____
_____

Pediatrician name/Contact information: _____
_____

Specialty doctor's name/Contact information/Frequency: *(Neurologist, dentist, allergist, eye, orthopedic, etc.)*
_____
_____
_____

Does this minor child have any special needs?   Yes or No
   If yes: What are the special needs and information someone would need to know: _____
   _____
   _____
   _____
   _____
   _____
   _____

Does this child have any aversions?   Yes or No
   If yes: Describe: _____
Child's best friend's name/Contact information: _____
_____

Additional details: Activities/Hobbies/Sports/Other issues
(Sports team/coaches contact information, child has anxiety around lots of people, member of the school band, afraid of dogs, etc.)

Adult Children   (Over Age 18)   (If you do not have adult children, skip this section)

Today's Date: _____

1. **Full Legal Name of Minor Child:** _____

    Nickname:_____Date of birth: _____

    Hospital, City/State where this child was born: _____

    Circle your relationship with this child: Biological child or Stepchild or Adopted Other: _____

    Does this adult child live with you?   Yes or No
        Telephone Number(s): _____
        Address and other contact information: _____
    _____

    Does this adult child attend high school or college?   Yes or No
        If yes: School name/Contact information: _____
    _____

    Current marital status for this adult child: Single   Married   Divorced   Widowed   Other: _____
        If married: Spouse's name/Telephone: _____
    Does this adult child have any children?   Yes or No   If yes: How many? # _____
    Does this adult child have any stepchildren?   Yes or No   If yes: How many? # _____
    Does this adult child have any grandchildren?   Yes or No   If yes: How many? # _____

    Does this adult child have any special needs?   Yes or No
        If yes: What are the special needs and information someone would need to know: _____

    Does this child have any aversions?   Yes or No
        If yes: Describe: _____
    _____

    Does this adult child attend an adult daycare program?   Yes or No
        If yes: Name/Contact information: _____
    _____

    Medical: Adult child's primary care physician's name/contact information: _____
    _____

    Specialty doctor's name/Contact information/Frequency: *(Neurologist, dentist, allergist, eye, orthopedic, etc.)*
    _____
    _____
    _____

    Additional details: *(Information about this adult child someone may need to know)*

Adult Children   (Over Age 18)

2. **Full Legal Name of Minor Child:** _____

Nickname:_____Date of birth: _____

Hospital, City/State where this child was born: _____

Circle your relationship with this child: Biological child or Stepchild or Adopted Other: _____

Does this adult child live with you?   Yes or No
   Telephone Number(s): _____
   Address and other contact information: _____
_____

Does this adult child attend high school or college?   Yes or No
   If yes: School name/Contact information: _____
_____

Current marital status for this adult child: Single   Married   Divorced   Widowed   Other: _____
   If married: Spouse's name/Telephone: _____
Does this adult child have any children?   Yes or No   If yes: How many? # _____
Does this adult child have any stepchildren?   Yes or No   If yes: How many? # _____
Does this adult child have any grandchildren?   Yes or No   If yes: How many? # _____

Does this adult child have any special needs?   Yes or No
   If yes: What are the special needs and information someone would need to know: _____

Does this child have any aversions?   Yes or No
   If yes: Describe: _____
_____

Does this adult child attend an adult daycare program?   Yes or No
   If yes: Name/Contact information: _____
_____

Medical: Adult child's primary care physician's name/contact information: _____
_____

Specialty doctor's name/Contact information/Frequency: *(Neurologist, dentist, allergist, eye, orthopedic, etc.)*
_____
_____
_____

Additional details: *(Information about this adult child someone may need to know)*

Adult Children   (Over Age 18)

Today's Date: _____

3. **Full Legal Name of Minor Child:** _____

Nickname:_____Date of birth: _____

Hospital, City/State where this child was born: _____

Circle your relationship with this child: Biological child or Stepchild or Adopted Other: _____

Does this adult child live with you?   Yes or No
    Telephone Number(s): _____
    Address and other contact information: _____
    _____

Does this adult child attend high school or college?   Yes or No
    If yes: School name/Contact information: _____
    _____

Current marital status for this adult child: Single   Married   Divorced   Widowed   Other: _____
    If married: Spouse's name/Telephone: _____
Does this adult child have any children?   Yes or No   If yes: How many? # _____
Does this adult child have any stepchildren?   Yes or No   If yes: How many? # _____
Does this adult child have any grandchildren?   Yes or No   If yes: How many? # _____

Does this adult child have any special needs?   Yes or No
    If yes: What are the special needs and information someone would need to know: _____

Does this child have any aversions?   Yes or No
    If yes: Describe: _____
    _____

Does this adult child attend an adult daycare program?   Yes or No
    If yes: Name/Contact information: _____
    _____

Medical: Adult child's primary care physician's name/contact information: _____
_____

Specialty doctor's name/Contact information/Frequency: *(Neurologist, dentist, allergist, eye, orthopedic, etc.)*
_____
_____
_____

Additional details: *(Information about this adult child someone may need to know)*

Today's Date: _____

4.   **Full Legal Name of Minor Child:** _____

Nickname:_____Date of birth: _____

Hospital, City/State where this child was born: _____

Circle your relationship with this child: Biological child or Stepchild or Adopted Other: _____

Does this adult child live with you?   Yes or No
   Telephone Number(s): _____
   Address and other contact information: _____
   _____

Does this adult child attend high school or college?   Yes or No
   If yes: School name/Contact information: _____
   _____

Current marital status for this adult child: Single   Married   Divorced   Widowed   Other: _____
   If married: Spouse's name/Telephone: _____
Does this adult child have any children?   Yes or No   If yes: How many? # _____
Does this adult child have any stepchildren?   Yes or No   If yes: How many? # _____
Does this adult child have any grandchildren?   Yes or No   If yes: How many? # _____

Does this adult child have any special needs?   Yes or No
   If yes: What are the special needs and information someone would need to know: _____

Does this child have any aversions?   Yes or No
   If yes: Describe: _____
   _____

Does this adult child attend an adult daycare program?   Yes or No
   If yes: Name/Contact information: _____
   _____

Medical: Adult child's primary care physician's name/contact information: _____
_____

Specialty doctor's name/Contact information/Frequency: *(Neurologist, dentist, allergist, eye, orthopedic, etc.)*
_____
_____
_____

Additional details: *(Information about this adult child someone may need to know)*

2

Today's Date: _____

5. **Full Legal Name of Minor Child:** _____

   Nickname:_____Date of birth: _____

   Hospital, City/State where this child was born: _____

   Circle your relationship with this child: Biological child or Stepchild or Adopted Other: _____

   Does this adult child live with you?   Yes or No
      Telephone Number(s): _____

      Address and other contact information: _____

   _____

   Does this adult child attend high school or college?   Yes or No
      If yes: School name/Contact information: _____

   _____

   Current marital status for this adult child: Single   Married   Divorced   Widowed   Other: _____
      If married: Spouse's name/Telephone: _____

   Does this adult child have any children?   Yes or No   If yes: How many? # _____

   Does this adult child have any stepchildren?   Yes or No   If yes: How many? # _____

   Does this adult child have any grandchildren?   Yes or No   If yes: How many? # _____

   Does this adult child have any special needs?   Yes or No
      If yes: What are the special needs and information someone would need to know: _____

   Does this child have any aversions?   Yes or No
      If yes: Describe: _____

   _____

   Does this adult child attend an adult daycare program?   Yes or No
      If yes: Name/Contact information: _____

   _____

   Medical: Adult child's primary care physician's name/contact information: _____

   _____

   Specialty doctor's name/Contact information/Frequency: *(Neurologist, dentist, allergist, eye, orthopedic, etc.)*

   _____

   _____

   _____

   Additional details: *(Information about this adult child someone may need to know)*

Adult Children   (Over Age 18)   (If you do not have adult children, skip this section)

6.   **Full Legal Name of Minor Child:** _____

Nickname:_____Date of birth: _____

Hospital, City/State where this child was born: _____

Circle your relationship with this child: Biological child or Stepchild or Adopted Other: _____

Does this adult child live with you?   Yes or No
   Telephone Number(s): _____
   Address and other contact information: _____
_____

Does this adult child attend high school or college?   Yes or No
   If yes: School name/Contact information: _____
_____

Current marital status for this adult child: Single Married Divorced Widowed Other: _____
   If married: Spouse's name/Telephone: _____
Does this adult child have any children?   Yes or No   If yes: How many? # _____
Does this adult child have any stepchildren?   Yes or No   If yes: How many? # _____
Does this adult child have any grandchildren?   Yes or No   If yes: How many? # _____

Does this adult child have any special needs?   Yes or No
   If yes: What are the special needs and information someone would need to know: _____

Does this child have any aversions?   Yes or No
   If yes: Describe: _____
_____

Does this adult child attend an adult daycare program?   Yes or No
   If yes: Name/Contact information: _____
_____

Medical: Adult child's primary care physician's name/contact information: _____
_____

Specialty doctor's name/Contact information/Frequency: *(Neurologist, dentist, allergist, eye, orthopedic, etc.)*
_____
_____
_____

Additional details: *(Information about this adult child someone may need to know)*

Grandchildren

2

1. Full Legal Name of Grandchild
Date of birth
Grandchild's contact information
Biological or Step-grandchild or Adopted Grandchild's parent(s) name(s)

2. Full Legal Name of Grandchild
Date of birth
Grandchild's contact information
Biological or Step-grandchild or Adopted Grandchild's parent(s) name(s)

3. Full Legal Name of Grandchild
Date of birth
Grandchild's contact information
Biological or Step-grandchild or Adopted Grandchild's parent(s) name(s)

4. Full Legal Name of Grandchild
Date of birth
Grandchild's contact information
Biological or Step-grandchild or Adopted Grandchild's parent(s) name(s)

5. Full Legal Name of Grandchild
Date of birth
Grandchild's contact information
Biological or Step-grandchild or Adopted Grandchild's parent(s) name(s)

6. Full Legal Name of Grandchild
Date of birth
Grandchild's contact information
Biological or Step-grandchild or Adopted Grandchild's parent(s) name(s)

Additional details:

Grandchildren

2

7. Full Legal Name of Grandchild
Date of birth
Grandchild's contact information
Biological or Step-grandchild or Adopted Grandchild's parent(s) name(s)

8. Full Legal Name of Grandchild
Date of birth
Grandchild's contact information
Biological or Step-grandchild or Adopted Grandchild's parent(s) name(s)

9. Full Legal Name of Grandchild
Date of birth
Grandchild's contact information
Biological or Step-grandchild or Adopted Grandchild's parent(s) name(s)

10. Full Legal Name of Grandchild
Date of birth
Grandchild's contact information
Biological or Step-grandchild or Adopted Grandchild's parent(s) name(s)

11. Full Legal Name of Grandchild
Date of birth
Grandchild's contact information
Biological or Step-grandchild or Adopted Grandchild's parent(s) name(s)

12. Full Legal Name of Grandchild
Date of birth
Grandchild's contact information
Biological or Step-grandchild or Adopted Grandchild's parent(s) name(s)

Additional details:

Great-grandchildren

Today's Date:_____

1. Full Legal Name of Great-grandchild
Date of birth
Great-grandchild's contact information
Biological or Step-great-grandchild or Adopted Great-grandchild's parent(s) name(s)

2. Full Legal Name of Great-grandchild
Date of birth
Great-grandchild's contact information
Biological or Step-great-grandchild or Adopted Great-grandchild's parent(s) name(s)

3. Full Legal Name of Great-grandchild
Date of birth
Great-grandchild's contact information
Biological or Step-great-grandchild or Adopted Great-grandchild's parent(s) name(s)

4. Full Legal Name of Great-grandchild
Date of birth
Great-grandchild's contact information
Biological or Step-great-grandchild or Adopted Great-grandchild's parent(s) name(s)

5. Full Legal Name of Great-grandchild
Date of birth
Great-grandchild's contact information
Biological or Step-great-grandchild or Adopted Great-grandchild's parent(s) name(s)

6. Full Legal Name of Great-grandchild
Date of birth
Great-grandchild's contact information
Biological or Step-great-grandchild or Adopted Great-grandchild's parent(s) name(s)

Additional details:

Aunts and Uncles

Full Name	Contact Information

Nieces and Nephews

Full Name	Contact Information

Close Friends and/or Neighbors

Your loved ones may need to contact your friends and neighbors for assistance or to inform them of your situation. Provide the names of your close friends and neighbors for this purpose.

Name	Relationship to You	Contact Information

Family Dynamics

Each family has unique dynamics. Some families have a close, affectionate bond with no complications, while others have complications. Some family members may not have communicated in years or may cause issues during tough times. In a Just In Case scenario, these family dynamics may add to the stress, causing more anxiety and heartache for your loved ones.

Do you have any significant family relationship problems?   Yes or No

The purpose of this section is not to revisit or dwell on the past but to offer guidance on how to facilitate and assist those who will sincerely help with your situation.

(What/who may cause a problem, what/who may help or intervene, or suggest a solution)

_____

_____

_____

_____

Pet(s)	Primary and Secondary

Do you have a pet?   Yes   or   No

   If yes: How many pets do you have?   **Primary User #**_____**Secondary User #** _____

2

Who will take care of your pet(s) if you are unable? Name/telephone and other contact information:

_____

_____

_____

_____

Who will acquire ownership of your pet(s)? Name/telephone and other contact information:

_____

_____

_____

_____

Note: Transferring ownership of a pet may differ depending on the state/country.
Please contact a professional for help!

Pet Details

1. Name of pet:_____ Date of birth:_____

  What kind of pet? *(Dog, cat, horse, parrot, etc.)* _____

  Does this pet have: Registered papers?   Yes or No   If yes: Papers location: _____

    Microchip?   Yes or No   If yes: # _____ Paperwork location:_____

    License?   Yes or No   If yes: # _____ Paperwork location: _____

    Passport?   Yes or No   If yes: Country: _____ Passport location:_____

Food: What type of food does this pet eat? Brand:_____

Dietary restrictions: _____

How many meals per day? #_____What time(s) of day? _____

Does this pet have any **allergies or skin irritations**?   Yes or No

  If yes: List allergies and/or skin irritations and what treatment works: _____

_____

Medical Conditions/Medications: Does this pet have a medical condition or take medication?   Yes or No

  If yes: Medical issue details, name of medication(s), dosage, any tips on how to administer medication to this pet, etc.

_____

_____

Equipment: _____

_____

Additional details: *(Dog is afraid of the rain, Cat is not good with children, Horse requires hours of exercise, etc.)*

Pet Details

2. Name of pet:_____ Date of birth:_____

What kind of pet? *(Dog, cat, horse, parrot, etc.)* _____

Does this pet have: Registered papers?   Yes or No   If yes: Papers location: _____

   Microchip?   Yes or No   If yes: # _____   Paperwork location:_____

   License?   Yes or No   If yes: # _____   Paperwork location: _____

   Passport?   Yes or No   If yes: Country: _____ Passport location:_____

Food: What type of food does this pet eat? Brand:_____

Dietary restrictions: _____

How many meals per day? #_____ What time(s) of day? _____

Does this pet have any **allergies or skin irritations**?   Yes or No

   If yes: List allergies and/or skin irritations and what treatment works: _____

   _____

Medical Conditions/Medications: Does this pet have a medical condition or take medication?   Yes or No

   If yes: Medical issue details, name of medication(s), dosage, any tips on how to administer medication to this pet, etc.

   _____

   _____

Equipment: _____

   _____

Additional details: *(Dog is afraid of the rain, Cat is not good with children, Horse requires hours of exercise, etc.)*

---

3. Name of pet:_____ Date of birth:_____

What kind of pet? *(Dog, cat, horse, parrot, etc.)* _____

Does this pet have: Registered papers?   Yes or No   If yes: Papers location: _____

   Microchip?   Yes or No   If yes: # _____   Paperwork location:_____

   License?   Yes or No   If yes: # _____   Paperwork location: _____

   Passport?   Yes or No   If yes: Country: _____ Passport location:_____

Food: What type of food does this pet eat? Brand:_____

Dietary restrictions: _____

How many meals per day? #_____ What time(s) of day? _____

Does this pet have any **allergies or skin irritations**?   Yes or No

   If yes: List allergies and/or skin irritations and what treatment works: _____

   _____

Medical Conditions/Medications: Does this pet have a medical condition or take medication?   Yes or No

   If yes: Medical issue details, name of medication(s), dosage, any tips on how to administer medication to this pet, etc.

   _____

   _____

Equipment: _____

   _____

Additional details: *(Dog is afraid of the rain, Cat is not good with children, Horse requires hours of exercise, etc.)*

Pet Details

4. Name of pet:_____ Date of birth:_____

What kind of pet? *(Dog, cat, horse, parrot, etc.)* _____

Does this pet have: Registered papers?　　Yes　or　No　　If yes: Papers location: _____

　Microchip?　Yes　or　No　　　If yes: # _____　Paperwork location:_____

　License?　　Yes　or　No　　　If yes: # _____　Paperwork location: _____

　Passport?　　Yes　or　No　　　If yes: Country: _____Passport location:_____

Food: What type of food does this pet eat?　Brand:_____

Dietary restrictions: _____

How many meals per day?　#_____What time(s) of day? _____

Does this pet have any **allergies or skin irritations**?　Yes　or　No

　If yes: List allergies and/or skin irritations and what treatment works: _____

　_____

Medical Conditions/Medications: Does this pet have a medical condition or take medication?　Yes　or　No

　If yes: Medical issue details, name of medication(s), dosage, any tips on how to administer medication to this pet, etc.

　_____

　_____

Equipment: _____

_____

Additional details: *(Dog is afraid of the rain, Cat is not good with children, Horse requires hours of exercise, etc.)*

---

5. Name of pet:_____ Date of birth:_____

What kind of pet? *(Dog, cat, horse, parrot, etc.)* _____

Does this pet have: Registered papers?　　Yes　or　No　　If yes: Papers location: _____

　Microchip?　Yes　or　No　　　If yes: # _____　Paperwork location:_____

　License?　　Yes　or　No　　　If yes: # _____　Paperwork location: _____

　Passport?　　Yes　or　No　　　If yes: Country: _____Passport location:_____

Food: What type of food does this pet eat?　Brand:_____

Dietary restrictions: _____

How many meals per day?　#_____What time(s) of day? _____

Does this pet have any **allergies or skin irritations**?　Yes　or　No

　If yes: List allergies and/or skin irritations and what treatment works: _____

　_____

Medical Conditions/Medications: Does this pet have a medical condition or take medication?　Yes　or　No

　If yes: Medical issue details, name of medication(s), dosage, any tips on how to administer medication to this pet, etc.

　_____

　_____

Equipment: _____

_____

Additional details: *(Dog is afraid of the rain, Cat is not good with children, Horse requires hours of exercise, etc.)*

Pet Details

6. Name of pet:_____ Date of birth:_____

What kind of pet? *(Dog, cat, horse, parrot, etc.)* _____

Does this pet have: Registered papers?   Yes or No   If yes: Papers location: _____

  Microchip?   Yes or No   If yes: # _____ Paperwork location:_____

  License?   Yes or No   If yes: # _____ Paperwork location: _____

  Passport?   Yes or No   If yes: Country: _____Passport location:_____

Food: What type of food does this pet eat? Brand:_____

Dietary restrictions: _____

How many meals per day? #_____What time(s) of day? _____

Does this pet have any **allergies or skin irritations**?   Yes or No

  If yes: List allergies and/or skin irritations and what treatment works: _____

_____

Medical Conditions/Medications: Does this pet have a medical condition or take medication?   Yes or No

  If yes: Medical issue details, name of medication(s), dosage, any tips on how to administer medication to this pet, etc.

_____

_____

Equipment: _____

_____

Additional details: *(Dog is afraid of the rain, Cat is not good with children, Horse requires hours of exercise, etc.)*

---

7. Name of pet:_____ Date of birth:_____

What kind of pet? *(Dog, cat, horse, parrot, etc.)* _____

Does this pet have: Registered papers?   Yes or No   If yes: Papers location: _____

  Microchip?   Yes or No   If yes: # _____ Paperwork location:_____

  License?   Yes or No   If yes: # _____ Paperwork location: _____

  Passport?   Yes or No   If yes: Country: _____Passport location:_____

Food: What type of food does this pet eat? Brand:_____

Dietary restrictions: _____

How many meals per day? #_____What time(s) of day? _____

Does this pet have any **allergies or skin irritations**?   Yes or No

  If yes: List allergies and/or skin irritations and what treatment works: _____

_____

Medical Conditions/Medications: Does this pet have a medical condition or take medication?   Yes or No

  If yes: Medical issue details, name of medication(s), dosage, any tips on how to administer medication to this pet, etc.

_____

_____

Equipment: _____

_____

Additional details: *(Dog is afraid of the rain, Cat is not good with children, Horse requires hours of exercise, etc.)*

Pet(s)	Primary and Secondary

Veterinarian

1. Veterinarian Name:_____Telephone:_____
   Address: _____

2. Veterinarian Name:_____Telephone:_____
   Address: _____

Animal Hospital

Animal Hospital Name:_____Telephone:_____
Address: _____

Groomer Name:_____Telephone: _____

Pet sitter or Daycare Name:_____Telephone: _____
Pet sitter or Daycare Name:_____Telephone: _____

Pet Insurance:

Do you have pet insurance?   Yes   or   No   If yes: How many policies? # _____

1. Company name:_____Telephone:_____
   Policy number:_____Covered pet's name(s): _____
   Where is the policy located?_____Policy Date: _____
   Benefits:_____
   How do you pay the premium and frequency of payment? _____
   (Monthly/automatic from checking, annual/handwritten check, quarterly/deducted from money market, etc.)
   Any claims against this animal?   Yes or No   If yes: Details: _____
   Additional details:

2. Company name:_____Telephone:_____
   Policy number:_____Covered pet's name(s): _____
   Where is the policy located?_____Policy Date: _____
   Benefits:_____
   How do you pay the premium and frequency of payment? _____
   (Monthly/automatic from checking, annual/handwritten check, quarterly/deducted from money market, etc.)
   Any claims against this animal?   Yes or No   If yes: Details: _____
   Additional details:

Step 2: Family, Friends, and Pets

Date Completed: _____

2

Fun Memory

Way to go! You have completed Step 2!

Did a fun or interesting fact from your past come to mind while you were working on this Step?

Use the space below to share a memory with your loved ones. It could be a funny story about yourself, a loving memory, or a fascinating fact about a moment in your past. This will bring joy and a smile during challenging times. Instead of writing, share your favorite song, poem, or insert a picture!

Need ideas? Here are some suggestions to write about for Step 2:
Share a fond or funny memory from your childhood, a cherished moment from the birth of your child, what lifts your spirit when you're feeling down, a memorable family gathering, what family means to you, a highlight from your life that you feel proud of, your favorite pet, a loved story about your furry friend, etc.

_____
_____
_____
_____
_____
_____
_____
_____
_____
_____
_____
_____
_____
_____
_____
_____
_____
_____
_____
_____
_____
_____

Step 3

Health, Medical, and Health Insurance

In Step 3, you will complete information about your medical professionals, including any specialists; the medications you take; your medical conditions and history; health insurance; and much more.

This information will be important in the case of an accident, illness, or even your death. Your loved ones might need to communicate on your behalf, assist with your ongoing care, arrange for someone to help you or work with you and a hospital to arrange a stay in a rehabilitation or long-term nursing center.

It's important to complete this information, but it's also highly recommended to have a health care proxy, which assigns someone to make medical decisions on your behalf in case you become unable to do so. You should also consider the necessity of having a living will, which communicates your wishes for extreme health measures or end-of-life care. You'll have a chance to record if you have an advance directive, a living will, DNR, and/or a health-care proxy in the legal documents section in Step 5. Please contact an attorney should you have any questions.

Ask Yourself, what do your loved ones need to know to best help with your health care?

Here are some things that are important in Step 3:

- Assemble a list of your prescription drugs, dosages, over-the-counter medications, and supplements. A place to record all of these is provided to you at the end of this workbook in EXTRAS. Take a photo of this list with your mobile device or make a photocopy to have it easily accessible when talking with your doctor, hospital, or caretaker. If you live alone, consider placing the prescription drug list in a highly visible area, perhaps on your refrigerator door, and keep a copy with you. Don't forget to share the location of this list and/or the photograph you took with your loved ones or your designated personal representative.

- Share information about your medical history, allergies, hearing aids, glasses, medical devices, and anything else that will be helpful to loved ones who need to help maintain the quality of your care.

- This Step gives you a chance to state your preference for a rehabilitation or nursing facility. But, be aware that where you go may depend on available beds and what kind of health or long-term care insurance you may have.

- List the name of your health insurance company, other supplemental coverage, as well as the company that holds your long-term care insurance if you have it. This includes Medicare and/or Medicaid. Your loved ones will need to know how you pay the premiums so coverage does not lapse or get canceled for nonpayment while you recover or are unable to handle your bills.

Ask Yourself, do your loved ones know your wishes for end-of-life care or medical measures such as intubation? It's a good idea to start thinking about this now. In Step 5, you will have the opportunity to indicate which legal documents you have that convey your intentions.

Understand this may be an emotional and stressful time for you and your loved ones. Some of this information may change after you initially complete it, so follow through with your annual review to make any adjustments. If you do not want to share all these details at this moment, that's OK. At least let your loved ones know that you have written them down for their future reference.

STEP 3: HEALTH, MEDICAL, AND HEALTH INSURANCE
- Medical Professionals
  - Primary Care Physician, Dentist, Optometrist/Ophthalmologist/Optician
  - Medical Specialists
  - Patient Portal or Gateway
  - Health Advocate
- Facility Preferences (Preferred and Not Preferred)
  - Hospital, Rehabilitation, Nursing Home
- Pharmacy
- List of Medications
- Prescription Drugs
- Over-the-Counter Medication/Supplements
  - Aspirin, Ibuprofen, Acetaminophen, Vitamins, Other
- Medical Conditions
  - Allergies, Asthma: Symptoms, Relief, EpiPen, Inhaler
  - Diabetes, Blood Type, Cholesterol, Blood Pressure
  - Tobacco, Alcohol, and Substance Abuse
  - Medical Device(s), Hearing Aid, Captioned Telephone
  - Medical Conditions and History (Vaccinations, Immunizations, Surgeries)
  - Family Medical History
- Medical Coverage
  - Medicare and Medicaid
  - Health Insurance, Dental Insurance, Vision Insurance
  - Long-Term Care Insurance
  - Other Supplemental Insurance Coverage or Policies
- Flexible Spending Account (FSA), Health Savings Account (HSA)
- Step 3 Completion Date and Fun Memory!

Step 3: NOTE TO LOVED ONES

In Step 3, your loved ones have shared the names of their medical professionals, the medications they are taking, any critical medical conditions, and their medical history.

You will also learn where to find their medical insurance cards or other health insurance information you will need to assist with the expenses associated with their health care.

How can Step 3 be helpful?

- You need to tell the emergency room doctors if your loved one has allergies and what medications they are taking.

- Your loved one has been diagnosed with a terminal illness or a progressive form of dementia that alters the way they can live, and you need to help determine the next course of action. This may involve collecting relevant legal documents in Step 5 in order to make medical decisions on their behalf.

- You need to know where to pick up their prescriptions.

- You are now in charge of various tasks such as scheduling doctors' appointments, tracking blood pressure, providing the necessary medical devices, or replacing a lost hearing aid. Whatever it might be, your loved one has supplied you with a resource to help!

This is when you need to be the advocate for your loved one. Try to have patience, kindness, and compassion. Try not to show your frustration. This is a hard time for both you and your loved one. Feel grateful and appreciate everything your loved one has done to provide you with details to help you struggle less.

Medical Professionals

Primary User	Secondary User

Primary Care Physician (PCP)

Do you have a primary care physician (PCP)?

Yes or No

If yes: Name:
        Telephone:
        Address:

Primary Care Physician (PCP)

Do you have a primary care physician (PCP)?

Yes or No

If yes: Name:
        Telephone:
        Address:

Dentist

Do you have a dentist? Yes or No

If yes: Name:
        Telephone:
        Address:

Do you wear dentures? Yes or No

List any major dental concerns:

_____

_____

Dentist

Do you have a dentist? Yes or No

If yes: Name:
        Telephone:
        Address:

Do you wear dentures? Yes or No

List any major dental concerns:

_____

_____

Optometrist/Ophthalmologist/Optician

Do you have an eye doctor? Yes or No

If yes: Name:
        Telephone:
        Address:

Do you wear glasses? Yes or No
Do you need reading glasses? Yes or No

If yes: Where do you purchase your glasses?

_____

If purchased over the counter, what strength is best?
(+1.00, +1.25, +1.50, etc.)

_____

Do you wear contacts? Yes or No

If yes: What kind do you wear?
      What kind of solution do you use?

_____

_____

List any major vision concerns:
(Glaucoma, macular degeneration, etc.)

_____

_____

Optometrist/Ophthalmologist/Optician

Do you have an eye doctor? Yes or No

If yes: Name:
        Telephone:
        Address:

Do you wear glasses? Yes or No
Do you need reading glasses? Yes or No

If yes: Where do you purchase your glasses?

_____

If purchased over the counter, what strength is best?
(+1.00, +1.25, +1.50, etc.)

_____

Do you wear contacts? Yes or No

If yes: What kind do you wear?
      What kind of solution do you use?

_____

_____

List any major vision concerns:
(Glaucoma, macular degeneration, etc.)

_____

_____

3

Medical Professionals

(Dermatologist, neurologist, cardiologist, physical therapist, urologist, psychiatrist, OB/GYN, oncologist, gastroenterologist, infectious disease specialist, plastic surgeon, thoracic surgeon, vascular surgeon, etc.)

Primary User	**Secondary User**
Do you have a medical specialist? Yes or No	Do you have a medical specialist? Yes or No

Medical Specialist

Name:

Specialty:

Telephone:

Address:

List any major concerns:

_____

_____

Medical Specialist

Name:

Specialty:

Telephone:

Address:

List any major concerns:

_____

_____

Medical Specialist

Name:

Specialty:

Telephone:

Address:

List any major concerns:

_____

_____

Medical Specialist

Name:

Specialty:

Telephone:

Address:

List any major concerns:

_____

_____

Medical Specialist

Name:

Specialty:

Telephone:

Address:

List any major concerns:

_____

_____

Medical Specialist

Name:

Specialty:

Telephone:

Address:

List any major concerns:

_____

_____

Medical Specialist

Name:

Specialty:

Telephone:

Address:

List any major concerns:

_____

_____

Medical Specialist

Name:

Specialty:

Telephone:

Address:

List any major concerns:

_____

_____

3

Primary User	Secondary User

Medical Specialist

Name:

Specialty:

Telephone:

Address:

List any major concerns:

_____

_____

Medical Specialist

Name:

Specialty:

Telephone:

Address:

List any major concerns:

_____

_____

Medical Specialist

Name:

Specialty:

Telephone:

Address:

List any major concerns:

_____

_____

Medical Specialist

Name:

Specialty:

Telephone:

Address:

List any major concerns:

_____

_____

Patient Portal or Gateway	Primary User	Secondary User

Do you have a portal to access your health records, manage your appointments, etc.?

Primary User: Yes or No   Secondary User: Yes or No

1. Website/App: _____ _____

   Username: _____ _____

   Password: _____ _____

2. Website/App: _____ _____

   Username: _____ _____

   Password: _____ _____

Additional details: _____

_____

Health Advocate	Primary User	Secondary User

Do you have a health advocate?

Primary User: Yes or No   Secondary User: Yes or No

If yes: Name:

Telephone: _____ _____

Relationship to you: _____ _____

If health advocate is not a family member or friend, do you have a hired professional?

Primary User: Yes or No   Secondary User: Yes or No

Details: _____ _____ _____

_____

Preferred and NOT Preferred Facilities

Your loved ones may need to assist you in making a decision (or decide for you) about a hospital, rehabilitation facility, or nursing home. Below you can provide your preferred or NOT preferred facilities to offer guidance; however, keep in mind that your insurance may be a factor, so please contact a professional for advice.

Location Preferences	Primary User	Secondary User

Do you have a **preferred hospital**?
If yes: Preferred hospital: _____
       Address: _____
 	
       Preferred hospital: _____
       Address: _____
	Yes or No	Yes or No

Do you have a **preferred rehabilitation facility**?
If yes: Rehabilitation facility: _____
       Address: _____
 	
       Rehabilitation facility: _____
       Address: _____
	Yes or No	Yes or No

Do you have a **preferred nursing home**?
If yes: Nursing Home: _____
       Address: _____
 	
       Nursing Home: _____
       Address: _____
	Yes or No	Yes or No

NOT Preferred Facility(s):
Do you have a facility that you definitely **DO NOT** want to go to?
If yes: Name of the facility/facilities you **DO NOT** want to go to:
    _____
    _____
    _____
	Yes or No	Yes or No

Pharmacy

Pharmacy/Prescription Delivery	Primary User	Secondary User
Do you have a **preferred pharmacy**?	Yes or No	Yes or No
Pharmacy name: _____	Address: _____	
Pharmacy name: _____	Address: _____	
Telephone:_____	Telephone: _____	
Do you have a **prescription delivery service**?	Yes or No	Yes or No
Name/Website: _____	Name/Website:_____	
Email used: _____	Email used: _____	
Username: _____ Password: _____	Username: _____ Password:_____	

3

STOP!

Primary and Secondary Users

If you haven't already created a **LIST OF YOUR MEDICATIONS**,
you will find these charts in the EXTRAS section at the back of this workbook.

Prescription Drugs and Over-the-Counter Medication / Supplements

It's important to date your completed lists, as medications and dosages may change over time.
(Dosage: 5mg, 10mg, 200mg, 250mg, 500mg, etc.)
(Frequency: daily with breakfast, twice a day at 9 a.m. & 9 p.m., before bedtime, etc.)

> **Note:** Once you have compiled your medications and supplements lists,
> take a photo using your mobile device or make a photocopy.
> This way, you will have it easily accessible when it's needed!

Prescription Drugs	Primary User	Secondary User
Do you take any prescription drugs?	Yes or No	Yes or No
Where is your list of medications located?		

Over-the-Counter (OTC)	Primary User	Secondary User
Aspirin, Ibuprofen, Acetaminophen		
Do you take a daily aspirin?	Yes or No	Yes or No
If yes: Brand name and dosage		
Do you take ibuprofen daily or as needed?	Daily or As Needed or Never	Daily or As Needed or Never
Do you take acetaminophen daily or as needed?	Daily or As Needed or Never	Daily or As Needed or Never
Vitamins and/or Supplements		
Do you take vitamins or supplements?	Yes or No	Yes or No
Other		
Do you take any other over-the-counter items? *(Antacids, laxatives, diarrhea remedy, nasal spray, etc.)*	Yes or No	Yes or No

Medical Conditions

Allergies, Asthma	Primary User	Secondary User
Do you have any allergies?	Yes or No	Yes or No
If yes: Are you allergic to a medication?	Yes or No	Yes or No
What medications are you allergic to? _(Penicillin, aspirin, chemotherapy drug, etc.)_	_____ _____ _____	_____ _____ _____
Are you allergic to any food?	Yes or No	Yes or No
What food(s) are you allergic to? _(Peanuts, tomatoes, shellfish, eggs, etc.)_	_____ _____ _____	_____ _____ _____
What else are you allergic to? _(Seasonal/pine, pollen, latex, etc.)_	_____ _____ _____	_____ _____ _____

Symptoms and Relief

	Primary User	Secondary User
What happens when you're having an allergic reaction?	_____ _____ _____	_____ _____ _____
What over-the-counter item helps with allergy relief?	_____ _____	_____ _____
Do you have an **EpiPen**?	Yes or No	Yes or No
If yes: Where do you keep/store your EpiPen?	_____	_____
Do you have **asthma**?	Yes or No	Yes or No
Do you have an **inhaler**?	Yes or No	Yes or No
If yes: Where do you keep/store your inhaler?	_____	_____

Additional details:_____
_____
_____

Diabetes	Primary User	Secondary User
Do you have diabetes?	Yes or No	Yes or No
If yes: What type of diabetes do you have?	_____	_____
Are you on insulin?	Yes or No	Yes or No
If yes: What type of insulin do you take?	_____	_____

Provide details regarding your diabetes that someone may need to know:_____
_____
_____

3

Blood Type, Cholesterol, Blood Pressure	Primary User	Secondary User

What is your blood type? *(A positive, B negative, AB -, O + , etc.)* _____ _____

Do you have **high cholesterol**?   Yes or No   Yes or No

Do you track your cholesterol levels?   Yes or No   Yes or No

If yes: Why do you track your cholesterol? _____

Name	Date	Triglycerides	HDL	LDL	Total Cholesterol

Do you have **high blood pressure**?   Yes or No   Yes or No

Do you track your blood pressure?   Yes or No   Yes or No

If yes: Why do you track your blood pressure? _____

Name	Date/Time	Blood Pressure (120/80)	Comments

Provide details regarding your cholesterol or blood pressure that someone may need to know: _____

_____

_____

Tobacco, Alcohol, Substance Abuse	Primary User	Secondary User

Do you **smoke**?   Yes or No   Yes or No

  If yes: how many packs per day?

Do you have a history or **alcoholism**?   Yes or No   Yes or No

Do you have a history of **substance abuse**?   Yes or No   Yes or No

Details/Concerns your loved ones may need to know:_____

_____

Medical Device(s)	Primary User	Secondary User
Do you have/use a **medical device**? (Oxygen tank, wheelchair, hospital bed, dialysis *equipment, inhaler, monitor, walker, scooter, lift equipment, etc.)*	Yes or No	Yes or No
If yes: How many?	#_____	#_____
Do you rent or have a payment plan?	Yes or No	Yes or No
Device name: _____	_____	_____
Payment details: _____	_____	_____
_____	_____	_____
Device name: _____	_____	_____
Payment details: _____	_____	_____
_____	_____	_____
Device name: _____	_____	_____
Payment details: _____	_____	_____
Device name: _____	_____	_____
Payment details: _____	_____	_____
_____	_____	_____

Additional details: _____

_____

_____

_____

Hearing Aid, Captioned Telephone	Primary User	Secondary User
Do you have/wear a **hearing aid?**	Yes or No	Yes or No
If yes: What type of hearing aid?	_____	_____
	_____	_____
Where do you keep your hearing aid when you are not wearing it?	_____	_____
Where did you purchase the hearing aid?	_____	_____
Is hearing aid synched to your cell phone?	Yes or No	Yes or No
Do you have a **captioned telephone**?	Yes or No	Yes or No
If yes: Do you rent or own the telephone?	Rent or Own	Rent or Own
If Rent: Payment details:	_____	_____
Do you have a service plan?	Yes or No	Yes or No
Service plan/Payment details:		

_____

Additional details: _____

_____

_____

HELPFUL FOR EMERGENCY

In an emergency, your loved ones may need to know about any significant medical conditions, past surgeries, and relevant family medical history that could help emergency responders.

This information can also be helpful for your loved ones to provide ongoing care.

Medical Conditions and History	Primary User	Secondary User
Have you received all your vaccinations?	Yes or No	Yes or No
Have you received all your immunizations?	Yes or No	Yes or No

Write your important **medical condition(s), any previous surgeries, heart conditions, and relevant history**.
(Seizures, asthma, stroke one year ago, cancer, metal plate in arm, dementia, diabetes, arthritis in knees, right hip replacement, heart valve replacement, etc.)

Primary User	
Secondary User	

Family Medical History

Write your important, **relevant family medical history**. Provide relative relationship and medical history.
(Mother/breast cancer, father/diabetes, uncle/Alzheimer's, sister/heart disease, etc.)

Primary User	
Secondary User	

Medical Coverage under Medicare (If you do not have Medicare skip this section)

> Please contact a health care professional, attorney, and/or a Medicare (or Medicaid) specialist with any questions or concerns!
>
> **Note for Loved Ones:** Just In Case scenario of death, locate Social Security Number and report the death to Social Security for Medicare/Medicaid.

Medicare - Primary User	Primary User

Are you on **Medicare**?   Yes or No

    If yes: Where do you keep your Medicare card? _____

              What is your Medicare number? _____

Primary User - Medicare

Do you have original **Medicare Part A**? *(Hospital Insurance)*   Yes or No

Do you have **Medicare Part B**? *(Medical Insurance)*   Yes or No
    If yes: How do you pay for your Part B premium? _____

Do you have **Medicare Part C**?   Yes or No
(Medicare Advantage/Supplemental policy with a private health insurance company)
    If yes: Insurance company name: _____
           Telephone:_____
           Policy number:_____
           Type of policy: _____
                  (Stand-alone MA, MAPD, EGWP, etc.)
           Where do you keep your card? _____
           How do you pay your premium?/Frequency of payment: _____
           (Monthly/automatic from checking, annual/handwritten check, quarterly/deducted from money market, etc.)

Do you have **Medicare Part D**? *(An additional prescription drug policy)*   Yes or No
    If yes: Insurance company name: _____
           Telephone: _____
           Policy number: _____
           Type of policy: *(Stand-alone PDP, etc.)* _____
           Where do you keep your card? _____
           How do you pay your premium?/Frequency of payment: _____
           (Monthly/automatic from checking, annual/handwritten check, quarterly/deducted from money market, etc.)

Additional details: _____
_____
_____
_____
_____
_____

Medicare - Secondary User	Secondary User

Are you on **Medicare**?   Yes or No

    If yes: Where do you keep your Medicare card?   _____

        What is your Medicare number?   _____

Secondary User - Medicare

Do you have original **Medicare Part A**? *(Hospital Insurance)*   Yes or No

Do you have **Medicare Part B**? *(Medical Insurance)*   Yes or No
    If yes: How do you pay for your Part B premium? _____

Do you have **Medicare Part C**?   Yes or No
(Medicare Advantage/Supplemental policy with a private health insurance company)
      If <u>yes</u>: Insurance company name: _____
      Telephone:_____
      Policy number:_____
      Type of policy: *(Stand-alone MA, MAPD, EGWP, etc.)* _____
      Where do you keep your card? _____
      How do you pay your premium?/Frequency of payment: _____
      (Monthly/automatic from checking, annual/handwritten check, quarterly/deducted from money market, etc.)

Do you have **Medicare Part D**? *(An additional prescription drug policy)*   Yes or No
    If yes: Insurance company name: _____
      Telephone: _____
      Policy number: _____
      Type of policy: *(Stand-alone PDP, etc.)* _____
      Where do you keep your card? _____
      How do you pay your premium?/Frequency of payment: _____
      (Monthly/automatic from checking, annual/handwritten check, quarterly/deducted from money market, etc.)

Additional details: _____
_____
_____
_____
_____
_____
_____

Primary and/or Secondary User – Additional Medicare Notes:

_____
_____
_____
_____

3

Medical Coverage under Medicaid (If you do not have Medicaid skip this section)

Medicaid is different from Medicare. **Medicaid is a program for people with limited income.**

Medicaid	Primary User	Secondary User
Are you on **Medicaid**?	Yes or No	Yes or No
If yes: Where do you keep your Medicaid card?	_____	_____
What is your Medicaid number?	_____	_____

Primary User - Medicaid

Plan you are enrolled in: _____
Insurance company name: _____
Telephone: _____
Policy number: _____
Where do you keep your card? _____
How do you pay your premium?/Frequency of payment: _____
(Subsidized, monthly/automatic from checking, annual/handwritten check, quarterly, etc.)

Additional details: *(Insurance for long term support or behavioral health, etc.)* _____

_____

_____

_____

_____

Secondary User - Medicaid

Plan you are enrolled in: _____
Insurance company name: _____
Telephone: _____
Policy number: _____
Where do you keep your card? _____
How do you pay your premium?/Frequency of payment: _____
(Subsidized, monthly/automatic from checking, annual/handwritten check, quarterly, etc.)

Additional details: *(Insurance for long term support or behavioral health, etc.)* _____

_____

_____

_____

_____

3

Health Insurance

Health Insurance	Primary User	Secondary User
Do you have health insurance?	Yes or No	Yes or No
Military: Do you have VA health care benefits?	Yes or No	Yes or No

If yes: Complete below and also reference Step 4 Military

Primary User

Health insurance company name: _____

Telephone:_____ Member ID:_____

Policy number:_____ Group # _____

Type of plan: *(HMO PPO, etc.)* _____

Is this an individual or family policy? _____

    If family: Who else is on the policy? _____

Who is the primary holder of this insurance: *(You, your spouse)* _____

    If spouse: Name/Date of birth/Employer: _____

How do you pay your premium?/Frequency of payment: _____

(Payroll deduction, private pay, annual handwritten check, monthly automatic payment, etc.)

Where do you keep your insurance card? _____

Website:_____

Username:_____ Password: _____

Secondary User

Health insurance company name: _____

Telephone:_____ Member ID:_____

Policy number:_____ Group # _____

Type of plan: *(HMO PPO, etc.)* _____

Is this an individual or family policy? _____

    If family: Who else is on the policy? _____

Who is the primary holder of this insurance: *(You, your spouse)* _____

    If spouse: Name/Date of birth/Employer: _____

How do you pay your premium?/Frequency of payment: _____

(Payroll deduction, private pay, annual handwritten check, monthly automatic payment, etc.)

Where do you keep your insurance card? _____

Website:_____

Username:_____ Password: _____

Additional details: (benefits, deductible, coinsurance amounts, copays, etc.)
(Favorite doctor is out-of-network, deductible amount if high deductible plan, walk-in clinic that accepts insurance, coinsurance amount, etc.)

_____

_____

_____

_____

_____

Dental Insurance

Dental Insurance	Primary User	Secondary User
Do you have dental insurance?	Yes or No	Yes or No

Primary User

Dental insurance company name: _____

Telephone:_____ Member ID:_____

Policy number:_____ Group # _____

Type of plan: *(HMO PPO, etc.)* _____

Is this an individual or family policy? _____

   If family: Who else is on the policy? _____

Who is the primary holder of this insurance: *(You, your spouse)* _____

   If spouse: Name/Date of birth/Employer: _____

How do you pay your premium?/Frequency of payment: _____

(Payroll deduction, private pay, annual handwritten check, monthly automatic payment, etc.)

Where do you keep your insurance card? _____

Website:_____

Username:_____Password: _____

3

Secondary User

Dental insurance company name: _____

Telephone:_____ Member ID:_____

Policy number:_____ Group # _____

Type of plan: *(HMO PPO, etc.)* _____

Is this an individual or family policy? _____

   If family: Who else is on the policy? _____

Who is the primary holder of this insurance: *(You, your spouse)* _____

   If spouse: Name/Date of birth/Employer: _____

How do you pay your premium?/Frequency of payment: _____

(Payroll deduction, private pay, annual handwritten check, monthly automatic payment, etc.)

Where do you keep your insurance card? _____

Website:_____

Username:_____Password: _____

Additional details: (benefits, deductible, coinsurance amounts, copays, etc.)

(Favorite doctor is out-of-network, deductible amount if high deductible plan, walk-in clinic that accepts insurance, coinsurance amount, etc.)

_____

_____

_____

_____

_____

_____

_____

_____

Vision Insurance

Vision Insurance	Primary User	Secondary User
Do you have vision insurance?	Yes or No	Yes or No

Primary User

Vision insurance company name: _____

Telephone:_____ Member ID:_____

Policy number:_____ Group # _____

Type of plan: *(HMO PPO, etc.)* _____

Is this an individual or family policy? _____

   If family: Who else is on the policy? _____

Who is the primary holder of this insurance: *(You, your spouse)* _____

   If spouse: Name/Date of birth/Employer: _____

How do you pay your premium?/Frequency of payment: _____

(Payroll deduction, private pay, annual handwritten check, monthly automatic payment, etc.)

Where do you keep your insurance card? _____

Website:_____

Username:_____Password: _____

Secondary User

Vision insurance company name: _____

Telephone:_____ Member ID:_____

Policy number:_____ Group # _____

Type of plan: *(HMO PPO, etc.)* _____

Is this an individual or family policy? _____

   If family: Who else is on the policy? _____

Who is the primary holder of this insurance: *(You, your spouse)* _____

   If spouse: Name/Date of birth/Employer: _____

How do you pay your premium?/Frequency of payment: _____

(Payroll deduction, private pay, annual handwritten check, monthly automatic payment, etc.)

Where do you keep your insurance card? _____

Website:_____

Username:_____Password: _____

Additional details: (benefits, deductible, coinsurance amounts, copays, etc.)
(Favorite doctor is out-of-network, deductible amount if high deductible plan, walk-in clinic that accepts insurance, coinsurance amount, etc.)

_____

_____

_____

_____

_____

_____

_____

Long-Term Care Insurance

Long-Term Care (LTC) Insurance	Primary User	Secondary User
Do you have long-term care (LTC) insurance?	Yes or No	Yes or No
If yes: How many?	# _____	# _____
Do you have a traditional (standalone) LTC policy?	Yes or No	Yes or No
Do you have LTC coverage linked to life insurance?	Yes or No	Yes or No
Do you have LTC coverage linked to an annuity? (LTC Rider)	Yes or No	Yes or No

Note: Life Insurance and Annuity details are referenced in Step 6, Financials and Insurance.

Circle: Primary User   or   Secondary User

1. **Long-Term Care Company:** _____
   - Website:_____ Telephone: _____
   - Contract/Policy number: _____
   - Name(s) on policy: _____
   - Primary beneficiary and % *(% totals 100%)*
     - _____ % _____ _____ % _____
     - _____ % _____ _____ % _____
   - Contingent beneficiary and % *(% totals 100%)*
     - _____ % _____ _____ % _____
     - _____ % _____ _____ % _____
   - Where is the policy located? _____
   - How do you receive the bill to pay premium? *(Paper via mail or paperless via electronic delivery)* _____
     - If electronic delivery: Where? *(Email, online banking, etc.)* _____
   - How do you make payments? *(Check, online banking manual, automatic recurring payment, etc.)* _____
   - Payment amount is $_____ Due date is _____
   - Additional details/Benefit limitations:_____

Circle: Primary User   or   Secondary User

2. **Long-Term Care Company:** _____
   - Website:_____ Telephone: _____
   - Contract/Policy number: _____
   - Name(s) on policy: _____
   - Primary beneficiary and % *(% totals 100%)*
     - _____ % _____ _____ % _____
     - _____ % _____ _____ % _____
   - Contingent beneficiary and % *(% totals 100%)*
     - _____ % _____ _____ % _____
     - _____ % _____ _____ % _____
   - Where is the policy located? _____
   - How do you receive the bill to pay premium? *(Paper via mail or paperless via electronic delivery)* _____
     - If electronic delivery: Where? *(Email, online banking, etc.)* _____
   - How do you make payments? *(Check, online banking manual, automatic recurring payment, etc.)* _____
   - Payment amount is $_____ Due date is _____
   - Additional details/Benefit limitations:_____

Other Supplemental Insurance Coverage or Policies

(Supplemental health policy, trauma or critical illness, hospital, cancer insurance, etc.)

Other Insurance Coverage or Policies	Primary User	Secondary User
Do you have any other policies that provide a benefit?	Yes or No	Yes or No

1. Circle: Primary User or Secondary User

Company name: _____

Telephone:_____

Policy/Account number: _____

Type of plan:_____

Is this an individual or family policy?   Individual or Family

　　　If family: Who else is on the policy: _____

　　　　　Primary account holder: _____

Where do you keep your card? _____

How do you pay your premium?/Frequency of payment: _____

(Monthly/automatic from checking, annual/handwritten check, quarterly/deducted from money market, etc.)

Benefit details: _____

_____

2. Circle: Primary User or Secondary User

Company name: _____

Telephone:_____

Policy/Account number: _____

Type of plan:_____

Is this an individual or family policy?   Individual or Family

　　　If family: Who else is on the policy: _____

　　　　　Primary account holder: _____

Where do you keep your card? _____

How do you pay your premium?/Frequency of payment: _____

(Monthly/automatic from checking, annual/handwritten check, quarterly/deducted from money market, etc.)

Benefit details: _____

_____

3. Circle: Primary User or Secondary User

Company name: _____

Telephone:_____

Policy/Account number: _____

Type of plan:_____

Is this an individual or family policy?   Individual or Family

　　　If family: Who else is on the policy: _____

　　　　　Primary account holder: _____

Where do you keep your card? _____

How do you pay your premium?/Frequency of payment: _____

(Monthly/automatic from checking, annual/handwritten check, quarterly/deducted from money market, etc.)

Benefit details: _____

_____

Flexible Spending Account (FSA) - Health Savings Account (HSA)

If you have any questions regarding your FSA/HSA account(s), please contact your employer, financial advisor, accountant, or another professional for assistance.

FSA and/or HSA	Primary User	Secondary User
Do you have a Flexible Spending Account (FSA)?	Yes or No	Yes or No
Do you have a Health Savings Account (HSA)?	Yes or No	Yes or No

Primary User

Company name:_____
Telephone: _____
Account number: _____
Type of card: *(HSA VISA, Name/Debit card, etc.)* _____
Where do you keep your card? _____
Who is able to use the card? *(Only you, spouse, dependent, etc.)* _____

What happens to account upon death? _____
Primary beneficiary and % *(% totals 100%)*
_____ % _____   _____ % _____
Contingent beneficiary and % *(% totals 100%)*
_____ % _____   _____ % _____

Website: _____
Username:_____Password: _____

Secondary User

Company name:_____
Telephone: _____
Account number: _____
Type of card: *(HSA VISA, Name/Debit card, etc.)* _____
Where do you keep your card? _____
Who is able to use the card? *(Only you, spouse, dependent, etc.)* _____

What happens to account upon death? _____
Primary beneficiary and % *(% totals 100%)*
_____ % _____   _____ % _____
Contingent beneficiary and % *(% totals 100%)*
_____ % _____   _____ % _____

Website: _____
Username:_____Password: _____

Additional details: *(HSA account still has money in it to use, etc.)*

_____

_____

3

Just In Case
SOLUTIONS

3

> # Step 3: Health, Medical, and Health Insurance
>
> ## Date Completed: _____

Fun Memory

Way to go! You have completed Step 3!

Did a fun or interesting fact from your past come to mind while you were working on this Step?

Use the space below to share a memory with your loved ones. It could be a funny story about yourself, a loving memory, or a fascinating fact about a moment in your past. This will bring joy and a smile during challenging times. Instead of writing, share your favorite song, poem, or insert a picture!

Need ideas? Here are some suggestions to write about for Step 3:

Share what instantly makes you feel better when you're not feeling well, your most embarrassing funny medical moment, your favorite doctor, any unexpected memorable trips to the emergency room, etc.

_____

_____

_____

_____

_____

_____

_____

_____

_____

_____

_____

_____

_____

_____

_____

_____

_____

_____

_____

_____

_____

_____

_____

Step 4

Employment, Business Owner, and Military

In Step 4, you will complete details about your employment and military service. Depending on your situation, someone may need to communicate with your employer, act on your behalf with the union, or be a liaison to assist with your military benefits.

Share the contact information for your current employer and/or union, along with any benefits the employer offers. Provide specific actions that may need to be taken in a Just In Case scenario.

Ask Yourself, do you have any previous employers who offered retirement accounts? Many people forget about these accounts over time, resulting in millions of forgotten retirement accounts every year. While you write details regarding your current employer, take a moment to think back on your past employers and see if you can find any older retirement accounts. In Step 6, you can include these accounts along with your other financial details.

Here are some additional ways in which Step 4 can be helpful:

- If you are a business owner, write down the contact information for your partner and/or administrators and the location of any business agreements or any necessary credentials.

- Provide essential details about patents, copyrights, trademarks, or domains.

- It's important to plan for the future of your business in the event of your passing or inability to manage it. Give instructions on how your business should be managed and give clear direction for what happens when the time comes. Also, make sure that your hard-earned business is included in your estate planning documents.

Military members and their loved ones should be able to easily access the information needed to complete a military form. Take a moment to organize and record all details relating to your involvement with the military.

- Locate your discharge documents (your DD214 or equivalent) so loved ones do not have to go searching to find the answers.

- If you have questions about your military service or benefits, contact a professional or visit your local veterans' office. Maybe you want to make sure your spouse is all set with survivorship benefits, or you need to pre-apply at the veteran's cemetery to receive your eligibility certificate. Survivorship benefits may take a while to process, so be proactive and consider getting educated in advance.

- If you are a member of a veteran's organization or have responsibilities at the organization, describe how you are involved.

Ask Yourself, are you ready to share with your family your stories, such as your achievements, challenges, duties, decorations, or awards that you received or experienced during your time in the military? If not, write it down for loved ones to read later. Don't let these stories be lost to future generations.

Please take a moment to review what's included in this Step:

STEP 4: EMPLOYMENT, BUSINESS OWNER, AND MILITARY
- Retired
- Past Employer Notification
- Employment (Primary User and Secondary User)
- Business Owner, Name/Details
- Sale of Business
- Patents, Copyrights, Trademarks, or Domains
- Workers' Compensation
- Union
- Military
  - Active Duty, Veteran, Branch(es) of Service, Service Number, Military Rank, Enlistment/Discharge Dates, Transition, Veteran Eligibility Documentation, Organizations
  - VA File/Claim Number, Veterans Assistance/Military Benefits, VA Local Offices/Contacts
  - Military Awards and Decorations, Military Funeral Service Wishes
- Step 4 Completion Date and Fun Memory!

Step 4: NOTE TO LOVED ONES

In Step 4, your loved ones have provided you with essentials regarding their employment, business, and their military experience.

How can this Step be helpful?

- If your loved one holds a major responsibility at their workplace and the position would require coverage or replacement, prompt notification to their employer so appropriate arrangements can be made would be appreciated.

- It's important to understand any benefits the employer or union was providing and whom you need to contact to access them. The company or union should have someone to assist you with paperwork such as disability forms or preparing your loved one's final paycheck and help with employer-sponsored life insurance, retirement accounts, or pension plans.

  - Keep in mind, many people may have participated in multiple retirement plans over the years. If the funds were never consolidated, you will need to take action on each one of those accounts. All retirement accounts are listed within Step 6, Financial and Insurance.

- If your loved one is an entrepreneur and owns their own business, review the business owner section, contact their business partner if they have one, and locate all the essential documents to learn what their intent is with their business.

- Review all the military details your loved one has provided to you, including their awards and decorations, along with the location of all the essential paperwork, such as service records, discharge documents, and certificates you may need.

- If your loved one is a veteran, contact the VA office or consider visiting your local veteran service officer with any questions. If your veteran has passed away, notify the VA as soon as possible.

- If your loved one requested a military funeral, review details in this military section as well as the information provided to you in Step 10 for what to do in case of death. The VA and the funeral home should be able to assist you with respecting their wishes and with military funeral honors.

Retired	Primary User	Secondary User
Are you retired?	Yes or No	Yes or No

Note: Volunteering during retirement is referenced in Step 9.

Past Employer Notification	Primary User	Secondary User
Just In Case of your death, would you like any of your former employers or colleagues to be informed?	Yes or No	Yes or No

Are there any specific obligations from past employment concerning informing them?

   If yes: Provide the name, contact information, and any necessary details.

_____

_____

_____

_____

_____

_____

_____

_____

_____

_____

_____

_____

_____

_____

_____

Employment	Primary User	Secondary User
Are you employed?	Yes or No	Yes or No
If yes: How many jobs do you have?	#_____	#_____

Primary User – Employment

Primary User - Employer Number 1

Name of your employer: _____

Employer telephone:_____Your work email: _____

Do you work: Part-Time or Full-Time

Does your employer provide any benefits?   Yes or No

When is your annual open enrollment? _____

What benefits do you have?
(Health, dental, vision, 401(k), stock options, deferred compensation, pension, short/long-term disability, life ins., AD&D, etc.)

Human resources contact information or person's name to assist with benefits:

Name:_____Telephone:_____

Address:_____Email: _____

Just In Case of an accident, illness, or death, provide any specific actions that may need to be taken.

Primary User - Employer Number 2

Name of your employer: _____

Employer telephone:_____Your work email: _____

Do you work: Part-Time or Full-Time

Does your employer provide any benefits?   Yes or No

When is your annual open enrollment? _____

What benefits do you have?
(Health, dental, vision, 401(k), stock options, deferred compensation, pension, short/long-term disability, life ins., AD&D, etc.)

Human resources contact information or person's name to assist with benefits:

Name:_____Telephone:_____

Address:_____Email: _____

Just In Case of an accident, illness, or death, provide any specific actions that may need to be taken.

Secondary User – Employment

Secondary User - Employer Number 1

Name of your employer: _____

Employer telephone:_____Your work email: _____

Do you work: Part-Time or Full-Time

Does your employer provide any benefits? Yes or No

When is your annual open enrollment? _____

What benefits do you have?
(Health, dental, vision, 401(k), stock options, deferred compensation, pension, short/long-term disability, life ins., AD&D, etc.)

Human resources contact information or person's name to assist with benefits:

Name:_____Telephone:_____

Address:_____Email: _____

Just In Case of an accident, illness, or death, provide any specific actions that may need to be taken.

Secondary User - Employer Number 2

Name of your employer: _____

Employer telephone:_____Your work email: _____

Do you work: Part-Time or Full-Time

Does your employer provide any benefits? Yes or No

When is your annual open enrollment? _____

What benefits do you have?
(Health, dental, vision, 401(k), stock options, deferred compensation, pension, short/long-term disability, life ins., AD&D, etc.)

Human resources contact information or person's name to assist with benefits:

Name:_____Telephone:_____

Address:_____Email: _____

Just In Case of an accident, illness, or death, provide any specific actions that may need to be taken.

Business Owner	Primary User	Secondary User
Do you own a business?	Yes or No	Yes or No
If yes: How many businesses do you own?	#_____	#_____

1. **Business name**: _____ Website: _____

   Address: _____ Business Telephone: _____

   What is the business type? *(Sole proprietor, partnership, LLC, corporation, or another other business entity)*

   _____

   Do you have a business partner? Yes or No

   If yes: Name of business partner(s): _____

   Email: _____ Telephone: _____

   Do you have a legal buy/sell agreement? Yes or No

   If yes: Attorney/contact person for the buy/sell agreement: _____

   Email: _____ Telephone: _____

   Where are the essential documents, business plans, tax records, ownership details, login credentials stored?

   Details:_____

   _____

   Is this business covered in your estate planning documents? Yes or No

   What is your intent with the business upon your death? _____

   _____

   Additional Details: *(Vendors, networks, etc.)*

2. **Business name**: _____ Website: _____

   Address: _____ Business Telephone: _____

   What is the business type? *(Sole proprietor, partnership, LLC, corporation, or another other business entity)*

   _____

   Do you have a business partner? Yes or No

   If yes: Name of business partner(s): _____

   Email: _____ Telephone: _____

   Do you have a legal buy/sell agreement? Yes or No

   If yes: Attorney/contact person for the buy/sell agreement: _____

   Email: _____ Telephone: _____

   Where are the essential documents, business plans, tax records, ownership details, login credentials stored?

   Details:_____

   _____

   Is this business covered in your estate planning documents? Yes or No

   What is your intent with the business upon your death? _____

   _____

Sale of Business	Primary User	Secondary User
Are you receiving a buyout or distribution from the sale of a business, LLC, stock, partnership, etc.?	Yes or No	Yes or No
If yes: Is there a legal document that specifies the distribution?	Yes or No	Yes or No

User: Where is this legal document located? _____

    Duration:_____Number of years:_____End date: _____

    Is there a beneficiary assigned? Yes   or   No

      If yes: Who is the beneficiary: _____

User: Where is this legal document located? _____

    Duration:_____Number of years:_____End date: _____

    Is there a beneficiary assigned? Yes   or   No

      If yes: Who is the beneficiary: _____

Additional details:

Patents, Copyrights, Trademarks, or Domains	Primary User	Secondary User
Do you own any **patents**?	Yes or No How many? _____	Yes or No How many? _____
Do you own any **copyrights**?	Yes or No How many? _____	Yes or No How many? _____
Do you own any **trademarks**?	Yes or No How many? _____	Yes or No How many? _____
Do you own any website **domains**?	Yes or No How many? _____	Yes or No How many? _____

Additional details: *(Name of domains, where you own them, login credentials, etc.)*

_____

_____

_____

_____

_____

_____

_____

_____

_____

_____

_____

_____

_____

_____

_____

Where are the original documents located? _____

If yes: Are these addressed in your estate plan?	Yes or No	Yes or No

    Additional details:

Workers' Compensation	Primary User	Secondary User
Are you receiving any workers' compensation benefits?	Yes or No	Yes or No

If yes: What is the duration of the payments? _____

      Company name: _____

      Address:_____Telephone: _____

      Main Contact Person: _____

Additional details:

Union	Primary User	Secondary User
Do you belong to a union?	Yes or No	Yes or No
Are you a retired member of a union?	Yes or No	Yes or No

1. **Union name**: _____

   Main contact person:_____Telephone: _____

   Union Rep name/Telephone: _____

   Website: _____ Email used: _____

   Username: _____ Password: _____

   Additional details:

2. **Union name**: _____

   Main contact person:_____Telephone: _____

   Union Rep name/Telephone: _____

   Website: _____ Email used: _____

   Username: _____ Password: _____

   Additional details:

Military	Primary User	Secondary User
Are you on **active duty**?	Yes or No	Yes or No
Are you a **veteran**?	Yes or No	Yes or No

What branch(es) of service? _____ _____

What is your service number? _____ _____

The full/official name you served under:
(Note: it might be a maiden name) _____ _____

Highest military rank you held: *(title)* _____ _____

Enlistment Date: *(Date you entered service)* _____ _____

Discharge Date: *(Date you separated/retired)* _____ _____

Category/Type of discharge?
(Honorable, reserve retirement, disability, entry-level separation, etc.) _____ _____

Transition: How did you leave the military? _____

	Primary User	Secondary User
Retire from the military?	Yes or No	Yes or No
Active duty retired?	Yes or No	Yes or No
Guard or Reserve retired?	Yes or No	Yes or No
Other separation:	_____	_____

Storage: Where are all your military items and documentation located? _____ _____

Veteran Eligibility Documentation

What do you have to show veteran eligibility? _____ _____
(Service record DD 214, NBG 22, *discharge/separation documents, certificate, retirement order or equivalent)* **Note:** *If married, you may need to provide marriage, death, or divorce certificates along with your DD214.*

Veteran Organization(s)

Are you a member of a veterans' organization?	Yes or No	Yes or No

If yes: What organization(s)?
(VFW, American Legion, Disabled Vets, AMVETS, Marine Corps League, etc.) _____ _____

Organization Name _____ _____
Telephone _____ _____

Organization Name _____ _____
Telephone _____ _____

Do you have any responsibilities at the organization?	Yes or No	Yes or No

If yes: What are your responsibilities? _____ _____
_____ _____

Note: VA health care benefits/insurance details are recorded in Step 3.

Military	Primary User	Secondary User

What is your **VA File/Claim Number**? _____   _____

Veteran Assistance / Military Benefits

	Primary User	Secondary User
Are you receiving any veterans' assistance?	Yes or No	Yes or No
If yes: Do you have survivor benefits?	Yes or No	Yes or No
Do you have VA health care benefits?	Yes or No	Yes or No
Do you have the GI Bill?	Yes or No	Yes or No
If yes: Will unused benefits be eligible for transfer?	Yes or No	Yes or No

(Note: Complete paperwork ahead of time in order to pass benefits on)

	Primary User	Secondary User
Are you currently receiving any other military benefits?	Yes or No	Yes or No
If yes: Are your dependents or survivors eligible for continued benefits?	Yes or No	Yes or No

4

Details about the veteran assistance and/or military benefits you receive that someone may need to know. What are the survivorship benefits? Any death benefits? What assistance continues for spouse or dependents?

_____

_____

_____

_____

_____

_____

_____

_____

Local VA Offices and Contacts *(Office names may differ depending on the state/country)*

Your local: Veterans Health Administration Office *(Health)*

   Address:_____Telephone:_____

Your local: Veterans Benefits Administration Office *(All benefits)*

   Address:_____Telephone:_____

Your local: Veteran Service Officer *(Helps with submitting benefit claims)*

   Address:_____Telephone:_____

Your Local: Veterans Transportation Program (VTP)   Telephone:_____

Your local: U.S. Department of Veterans Affairs

   Address:_____Telephone:_____

Your local: Casualty Assistance Office

   Address:_____Telephone:_____

Defense Finance and Accounting Service (DFAS)   Telephone:_____

Defense Enrollment Eligibility Reporting System (DEERS)   Telephone:_____

Other _____   Telephone:_____
    (TRICARE, FEDVIP/BENEFEDS, etc.)

Other _____   Telephone:_____

Military	Primary User	Secondary User

Just In Case of your death, share your military experience with loved ones so they can honor your time in the service and fulfill your wishes. (**More details in Step 10**)

Military Awards and Decorations
Medals, Stars, Cross, Heart,
Unit Citation, etc.

_____ _____
_____ _____
_____ _____
_____ _____
_____ _____
_____ _____
_____ _____

Where is the documentation for all
your awards and decorations located?
_____ _____

Military Funeral Service Wishes:
Do you want a patriotic funeral service?

Yes or No   Yes or No

Honors: Depending on your veteran
status, you may have funeral honors.
(Full military honors, 7-person detail, or standard honor team detail)
Do you want military funeral honors?

Yes or No   Yes or No

If yes: Details

_____ _____
_____ _____

Pallbearers: Do you want military
pallbearers? _(This may need to be requested by family or you as a veteran; be proactive!)_

Yes or No   Yes or No

Interment: Will you be buried in a VA
national, state, or tribal cemetery?

Yes or No   Yes or No

If yes:

National   State   Tribal   National   State   Tribal

Have you completed the burial
eligibility paperwork/application?

Yes or No   Yes or No

Where is your eligibility
certificate/paperwork located?
_____ _____

If no: Contact the Department of Veterans Affairs to complete the appropriate paperwork and/or application to determine your eligibility to be buried in a national cemetery.

If applicable: Will spouse be laid to rest
next to the veteran?

Yes or No   Yes or No

Note: It will make things easier for your loved ones if you, as the veteran, pre-apply.
Complete the necessary paperwork prior to death.

Additional military details: _____
_____
_____

Thank you for your service!
Additional details on Step 10

Just In Case
SOLUTIONS

Step 4: Employment, Business Owner, and Military

Date Completed: _____

Fun Memory

Way to go! You have completed Step 4!

Did a fun or interesting fact from your past come to mind while you were working on this Step?

Use the space below to share a memory with your loved ones. It could be a funny story about yourself, a loving memory, or a fascinating fact about a moment in your past. This will bring joy and a smile during challenging times. Instead of writing, share your favorite song, poem, or insert a picture!

Need ideas? Here are some suggestions to write about for Step 4:

Share a funny work experience, your first job, your first hourly wage, a military story, what inspired you to start your own business, the best or worst career advice you've received, what makes you laugh, etc.

_____
_____
_____
_____
_____
_____
_____
_____
_____
_____
_____
_____
_____
_____
_____
_____
_____
_____
_____
_____
_____
_____
_____

Step 5
Legal Documents and Professionals

In Step 5, you will complete information about the professionals you rely on, including accountants, attorneys, financial advisors, real estate agents, and other specialists your loved ones may need to contact in a Just In Case scenario.

In this Step, you will also note whether you have important legal documents, such as a will or health care proxy, and where they are located.

<u>Please make sure to talk with the appropriate professional in extensive detail regarding what you have, or may need, to ensure you have all the necessary legal paperwork</u>. This will help not only you but prepare in advance the ones who love you the most. Your professional will be able to help you foresee and solve any issues that may arise in the future.

Ask Yourself the probing, important questions listed in Step 5. They may help you or your loved ones avoid sticky situations in the case of a crisis or your death. You can use this as a resource in partnership with your professionals to make sure you have all the appropriate paperwork and plans in place.

Here are some things that are important in Step 5:

- This Step does not ask what is stated in the legal documents. It simply asks whether you have a document, its location, and who is responsible for it.

Ask Yourself, what documents are important? Are there documents I should have that I do not have? For example, regardless of your financial status, a will allows you to allocate your estate according to your wishes.

If your estate planning is done, perhaps it's a good time to review it, especially if you have had a life-changing event.

- Make sure all your documents are legally binding and in good standing, including signatures, dates, witnesses, and filing status. Laws are different in each state/country. Obtaining professional advice is highly recommended to ensure your estate plan and legal documents are properly executed.

- If you have a legal responsibility for a person, organization, or charity, make sure to describe your responsibilities and whom to contact if you are unable to perform these duties.

- If you own any digital assets, make sure a digital executor/executrix is assigned within your legal documents.

Ask Yourself, do your loved ones or your personal representative know where you store your important original documents, valuable possessions, and other essential details?

- Whether you have a file cabinet, a fireproof box/safe, a computer hard drive, or a messy pile on your desk, make sure to list where your original legal documents are kept.

- If you have a safe-deposit box, record the location, the names of those who have access, and where you keep any keys. You may need to talk with someone at the vault about setting up box access so your loved ones can avoid having to file a court petition to get into it.

- Everyone has precious, irreplaceable items. Whether yours have a high dollar value, such as an antique car, jewelry, or painting, or are purely sentimental, like photographs and keepsakes, create an inventory list. It will be extremely helpful to your loved ones.

- Consider scheduling an appointment to discuss your personal property with an estate-planning attorney. The Just In Case Solutions workbook is not a legal document. An attorney can help you in listing specific actions or bequests within a legal document. So, for example, perhaps you want your real estate held in a trust, or you need to specify in your will if you want an item to go to a particular person or organization.

Please take a moment to review what's included in this Step:

STEP 5: LEGAL DOCUMENTS AND PROFESSIONALS
- Important Questions
- Professionals
  - Accountant, Insurance Agent/Agency, Attorney, Financial Advice / Financial Advisor, Fiduciary, Real Estate Agent/Broker, Appraiser, Appraisal Company, Other Professionals
- Health Care Proxy, Advance and/or Personal Directives, Living Will, Do Not Resuscitate
- Power of Attorney
- Last Will and Testament
- Trust(s)
- Storage and Document Storage
  - Safe-Deposit Box, Home Safe, File Cabinet, Document Repository
- Personal Possessions / Valuable Items
  - Inventory List *(Additional Inventory Lists for Personal Possessions are provided in the EXTRAS section)*
- Legal Responsibility for Someone Else, Organization, Charity, or Foundation
- Step 5 Completion Date and Fun Memory!

Step 5: NOTE TO LOVED ONES

In Step 5, your loved one has listed important legal documents and recorded the professionals that they work with. Please do not hesitate to reach out to these professionals and ask for help!

- An accountant or CPA can help with tax filing and estimated payments while your loved one is unable to manage these tasks independently.

- If your loved one is no longer living, a tax or legal professional can help you file the final income tax return and any estate or trust returns. Make sure you are aware of any deadlines regarding when you need to file.

- Financial and insurance professionals will be able to assist with investments, banking, insurance policies, and other accounts.

- A real estate agent or broker will be able to help with the sale or transfer of real estate. They will also be able to suggest what may need to be addressed within the residence or on the property to increase marketability.

This Step includes an inventory list of personal possessions that either have financial or sentimental value. (Additional lists also found in EXTRAS.) We have all heard stories of someone tossing out an item that they thought was worthless to then realize it was worth some money! Take the time to review the list and walk room to room to make sure this does not happen to you!

Here are two other ways Step 5 can be helpful:

- If your loved one is suffering from a terminal illness or unexpected accident, you may need to step in and assist with medical conversations and finances. You will need to know the location of their power of attorney, which allows someone to act legally on their behalf, and their health care proxy, which gives another person the authority to make health care decisions.

- If your loved one has passed on, you will need to locate documents such as the last will and testament, as well as any trust documents.

Important Questions: Please contact an estate planning attorney, financial advisor, accountant, or a relevant professional to obtain advice and answer all your questions.	Primary User	Secondary User
Real Estate: Do you own any real estate?	Yes or No	Yes or No
If yes: Is your real estate held in a trust?	Yes or No	Yes or No
Wishes and Intent for Real Estate: Have you documented what your wishes and intentions are with your property? *(Would you like your heirs to sell your home and move on, not sell your home and have heirs enjoy the property, which heirs, etc.)*	Yes or No	Yes or No
If yes: Where are your written intended wishes for your real estate located?	_____	_____
If no: Talk with a professional and write your intent so your loved ones know.		
Sale of Property/Estate Tax: If real estate needs to be sold upon your death, have you addressed selling your real estate?	Yes or No	Yes or No
Have you discussed how to handle proceeds from an estate sale with a lawyer and tax professional?	Yes or No	Yes or No
Loved Ones and Income/Estate Tax Returns: Have you talked with your accountant and/or attorney to help prepare your loved ones in advance about any estate tax returns?	Yes or No	Yes or No
Capital Gains: Have you talked with a professional about avoiding capital gains?	Yes or No	Yes or No
Estate Planning: Do you have estate planning goals in mind? If yes: Sit down with an estate planning professional to accomplish this. *(Note: Every state is different)*	Yes or No	Yes or No
Trust Funding: Have you discussed with a professional planning to fund your trust during your lifetime?	Yes or No	Yes or No

5

Important Questions:	Primary User	Secondary User
Gifting Cash/Investment: Is cash/investment gifting addressed in your estate plan?	Yes or No	Yes or No
Electronic Fiduciary Powers: Are electronic communication and fiduciary powers for electronic devices and/or online accounts covered in your estate plan?	Yes or No	Yes or No
Digital Executor/Digital Assets: Is accessing your digital assets covered in your estate plan?	Yes or No	Yes or No
• If your life is mainly digital, provide as much direction as possible to ensure your loved ones are prepared.	Yes or No	Yes or No
Joint Bank Account: Do you have a joint bank account with someone you trust who would be able to pay for immediate medical expenses? *(Consider making sure funds are available for monthly expenses and more.)*	Yes or No	Yes or No

If yes: Joint bank account is held with whom?   Name   _____   _____

Telephone   _____   _____

	Primary User	Secondary User
Account Registrations (titled/owned) and Beneficiaries: Have you reviewed *all* your accounts and policies to ensure the accounts are registered/titled, and beneficiaries are listed as you wish?	Yes or No	Yes or No

Important Notes:

- Having beneficiaries listed on all your accounts guarantees that your account/policies will be distributed appropriately.
- As you complete this workbook, look at every account you have, retirement and non-retirement, ensuring your accounts are registered/titled appropriately and have beneficiaries listed.
- Consider adding a TOD (Transfer of Death) to your non-qualified accounts. TOD is an account registration/title type and can also be used on your non-retirement accounts as a beneficiary tool and may help assets avoid probate. Please talk with a professional if you have any questions or need assistance adding a TOD to your individual and joint accounts.
- Life-Changing Moment: If you have a change in your life that affects your current account titles or beneficiaries, make sure to adjust your accounts appropriately before a Just In Case scenario happens!

Last Will and Testament, Executor/Executrix: Have you assigned an executor/executrix/responsible person?	Yes or No	Yes or No

- If you do not choose an executor/executrix, person, or institute, the court will assign one.
  - Do not leave your loved ones having the state determine how your things (property, assets, etc.) are distributed.

Important Questions:	Primary User	Secondary User
Avoiding Probate: Will your estate be able to avoid the probate process?	Yes or No	Yes or No
Avoid Inheritance Issues: Have you talked with a lawyer and tax professional regarding your estate to confirm inheritance issues are covered in your will and/or trust? *(Inheritance tax)*	Yes or No	Yes or No
Health Care Proxy, Advance Directive, Living Will, Do Not Resuscitate (DNR): Have you addressed your wishes for end-of-life care or medical measures such as intubation?	Yes or No	Yes or No
Have you discussed your wishes with your loved ones?	Yes or No	Yes or No
Long-Term Care Planning: Have you discussed long-term care with an estate planning professional?	Yes or No	Yes or No
Have you discussed your wishes with your loved ones?	Yes or No	Yes or No
Health Advocate: Have you selected someone to be your health advocate? *(Someone to accompany you to a doctor's appointment or help better explain a medical situation.)*	Yes or No	Yes or No
Have you had a conversation with them?	Yes or No	Yes or No
Personal Representative Conversation/Responsibilities: Have you had talked with your selected person about how to distribute assets, inheritance, and personal items once alldebts, expenses, and taxes are paid?	Yes or No	Yes or No

- Discuss paying all expenses first. *(Attorney fees,accountant costs, appraisals, taxes, etc.)*
    - You do not want your loved ones to be personally liable for unpaid taxes on your estate.

> **Note:** It's a good idea to ensure sure your personal representative has the skill to keep calm and be fair during a difficult time. If you foresee a problem, consider having someone else assist them or assign a fiduciary to avoid burdening a family member. This person needs to be comfortable with distributing everything from your financials and real estate, paying expenses and taxes, distributing your valuable items, family heirlooms and sentimental things, and so much more!

Estate Plan Discussion with your Loved Ones: Have you talked with your loved ones regarding your *entire* estate plan?	Yes or No	Yes or No

   If no: Have the discussion!

5

Accountant	Primary User	Secondary User
Do you have an accountant/CPA? *(Bookkeeping, tax services, etc.).*	Yes or No	Yes or No
If yes: How many?	#_____	#_____

1. **Accountant name:**_____

   Address_____

   Telephone_____Email _____

2. **Accountant name:**_____

   Address_____

   Telephone_____Email _____

	Primary User	Secondary User
Are estimated tax payments being made?	Yes or No	Yes or No
If yes: Who makes them? *(You personally, financial advisor, etc.)*	_____	_____
How do you make payments? *(Mail physical check, electronically from checking, automatic disbursement from investment account, etc.)*	_____	_____
Where are your past years' tax returns being kept? *(Safe-deposit box, office file cabinet, box in a closet, etc.)*	_____	_____
What is your filing status? *(Single, Married filing jointly or separately, Head of household, a qualifying widow with a dependent child, etc.)*	_____	_____

Additional details: *(Gift tax return, executor duties, etc.)*

Insurance Agent/Agency	Primary User	Secondary User
Do you have an insurance agent/insurance agency?	Yes or No	Yes or No
If yes: How many?	#_____	#_____

1. **Insurance Agency/Agent name:**_____

   Address_____

   Telephone_____Email _____

2. **Insurance Agency/Agent name:**_____

   Address_____

   Telephone_____Email _____

Additional details:

Attorney	Primary User	Secondary User
Do you have an attorney? *(lawyer)*	Yes or No	Yes or No
If yes: How many?	#_____	#_____

1. **Attorney name:** _____

   What type of attorney? _____
   (Estate planning, real estate, civil/personal, criminal, family, etc.)

   Address_____
   Telephone_____Email _____

   Do you have any pending lawsuits or claims against a 3rd party?   Yes or No

   Are there any outstanding legal actions/claims against you or anyone in the household?   Yes or No

   Responsibilities: _____

2. **Attorney name:** _____

   What type of attorney? _____
   (Estate planning, real estate, civil/personal, criminal, family, etc.)

   Address_____
   Telephone_____Email _____

   Do you have any pending lawsuits or claims against a 3rd party?   Yes or No

   Are there any outstanding legal actions/claims against you or anyone in the household?   Yes or No

   Responsibilities: _____

3. **Attorney name:** _____

   What type of attorney? _____
   (Estate planning, real estate, civil/personal, criminal, family, etc.)

   Address_____
   Telephone_____Email _____

   Do you have any pending lawsuits or claims against a 3rd party?   Yes or No

   Are there any outstanding legal actions/claims against you or anyone in the household?   Yes or No

   Responsibilities: _____

Additional details: *(Pending lawsuits, outstanding court fees, executor duties, etc.)*

5

Just In Case of your death: Whether you are married or single, consider talking with your attorney and/or accountant/CPA about any estate tax returns that may need to be filed when you or your spouse pass away to prepare your loved ones in advance.

Financial Advice / Financial Advisor	Primary User	Secondary User
Do you have someone who provides you with financial advice?	Yes or No	Yes or No

If yes:

How many?   # _____   # _____

What type of professional?   _____   _____

(Financial advisor or planner, broker, investment manager, trust officer, banker, etc.)   _____   _____

If no: Who assists you with your investments?   _____   _____

(Bank, financial institution, relative, friend, nobody, etc.)

1. **Financial Advisor Name/Company:** _____
   Address _____
   Telephone _____ Email _____
   Responsibilities: _____

2. **Financial Advisor Name/Company:** _____
   Address _____
   Telephone _____ Email _____
   Responsibilities: _____

3. **Financial Advisor Name/Company:** _____
   Address _____
   Telephone _____ Email _____
   Responsibilities: _____

4. **Financial Advisor Name/Company:** _____
   Address _____
   Telephone _____ Email _____
   Responsibilities: _____

Additional details:

Fiduciary	Primary User	Secondary User
Do you have a designated fiduciary?	Yes or No	Yes or No

If yes: Is your fiduciary an organization or an individual?   _____   _____

1. **Name/Company:** _____
   Address _____
   Telephone _____ Email _____
   Responsibilities: _____
   _____

2. **Name/Company:** _____
   Address _____
   Telephone _____ Email _____
   Responsibilities: _____
   _____

5

Real Estate Agent/Broker	Primary User	Secondary User
Do you have a real estate agent or broker?	Yes or No	Yes or No

1. **Real Estate Agent/Broker Name:**_____
   Address_____
   Telephone_____Email_____

2. **Real Estate Agent/Broker Name:**_____
   Address_____
   Telephone_____Email_____

Additional details:

Appraiser, Appraisal Company	Primary User	Secondary User
Do you have an Appraiser or use an appraisal company?	Yes or No	Yes or No

1. **Appraiser Name/Company:**_____
   Address_____
   Telephone_____Email_____

2. **Appraiser Name/Company:**_____
   Address_____
   Telephone_____Email_____

Additional details:

Other Professionals

Provide the name and details of any other specialists you may have a relationship with.

1. **Hairdresser/Hairstylist, Barber:**_____
   Address_____
   Telephone_____Email_____
   Responsibilities: _____

2. **Cleaners:**_____
   Address_____
   Telephone_____Email_____
   Responsibilities: _____

3. **Other Professional:**_____
   Address_____
   Telephone_____Email_____
   Responsibilities: _____

4. **Other Professional:**_____
   Address_____
   Telephone_____Email_____
   Responsibilities: _____

5

Health Care Proxy, Advance and/or Personal Directives, Living Will, and Do Not Resuscitate	Primary User	Secondary User

Do you have a health care proxy?
(Allows you to appoint someone - healthcare agent - to make medical decisions for you. Also known as a durable POA for health care; medical agent, surrogate or representative.)

	Primary User	Secondary User
	Yes or No	Yes or No

If yes:

	Primary User	Secondary User
Date signed	_____	_____
Name you listed	_____	_____
Telephone	_____	_____
Alternate name you listed	_____	_____
Telephone	_____	_____
Where is this document located?	_____	_____

Does the health care proxy include a **HIPPA Release / Authorization?**   Yes or No   Yes or No

Do you have a written advance and/or personal directive?
(Informs your doctor/hospital what kind of care/treatment you would like to or not like to have If you become unable to make medical decisions for yourself.)

	Primary User	Secondary User
	Yes or No	Yes or No

If yes:

	Primary User	Secondary User
Date signed	_____	_____
Where is this document located?	_____	_____

Do you have a living will?
(A living will is one type of advance directive that describes the medical care/treatment you would like if you were to become seriously or terminally ill.)

	Primary User	Secondary User
	Yes or No	Yes or No

If yes:

	Primary User	Secondary User
Date signed	_____	_____
Where is this document located?	_____	_____

Do you have a codicil to your living will?   Yes or No   Yes or No

(An addition/supplement that modifies or revokes your living will or part of it)

If yes:

	Primary User	Secondary User
Date signed	_____	_____
Where is this document located?	_____	_____

Do you have a signed Do Not Resuscitate (DNR) order?   Yes or No   Yes or No
(DNR is written instructions telling health care providers not to perform CPR. If you do not have a DNR order, health care providers will begin CPR in an emergency. DNRs need to be signed and dated. Some DNRs may expire, and will need to be resigned and dated.)

If yes:

	Primary User	Secondary User
Date signed	_____	_____
Where is this document located?	_____	_____

Additional details: *(Regarding health care proxy, advance directive, living will, or DNR)*

NOTE: Your loved ones need to be aware of whether you possess or lack certain documents. The location of document storage varies per person. Some people may store their original documents in a safe-deposit box or a lawyer's office, while others might keep them in a file cabinet, a box on the top of a closet, or a personal safe. Ensure that your loved ones are aware of where your documents are and how to access them.

Just In Case: A professional may suggest keeping all important original documents and items in a fireproof, waterproof location to ensure contents are not damaged during a catastrophic incident.

5

Power of Attorney	Primary User	Secondary User
Do you have a power of attorney (POA)?	Yes or No	Yes or No

If yes:

	Primary User	Secondary User
Date signed	_____	_____
POA Name *(Who is listed)*	_____	_____
Telephone	_____	_____
Alternative POA Name you listed	_____	_____
Telephone	_____	_____
Where is this document located?	_____	_____
Type of POA? *(Durable, financial, etc.)*	_____	_____

	Primary User	Secondary User
Does the POA include instructions on who has the authority and how to make cash/investment gifts on your behalf?	Yes or No	Yes or No

If yes: Does POA address and/or provide instructions on how you want to administer gifts(cash/investments) on your behalf if you are unable to perform these duties without assistance?

	Primary User	Secondary User
	Yes or No	Yes or No

If no: Please contact an attorney with questions!

Last Will and Testament	Primary User	Secondary User
Do you have a will?	Yes or No	Yes or No

If yes:

	Primary User	Secondary User
Date signed	_____	_____
Where is this document located?	_____	_____
Does will reference a trust or standard will to individual(s)?	_____	_____
Does will include any bequests?	Yes or No	Yes or No
Does will include any special directives or last wishes?	Yes or No	Yes or No
Do you have a codicil to your will?	Yes or No	Yes or No

(An addition/supplement that modifies or revokes your will or part of it)

If yes:

	Primary User	Secondary User
Date of the codicil	_____	_____
Where is this document located?	_____	_____

	Primary User	Secondary User
Was your will filed in court?	Yes or No	Yes or No

If yes:

	Primary User	Secondary User
Court name	_____	_____
City and state	_____	_____
County	_____	_____

	Primary User	Secondary User
Do you have a person(s) or an Institute as your executor?	Person or Institute	Person or Institute
Do you have ONLY ONE executor/executrix?	Yes or No	Yes or No
If no: How many executors/executrixes do you have?	#_____	#_____

Primary User: List name(s) of your executor/executrix

1. Name_____Telephone _____
2. Name_____Telephone _____
3. Name_____Telephone _____

Who is your Digital executor/executrix? Name _____

Secondary User: List name(s) of your executor/executrix

1. Name_____Telephone _____
2. Name_____Telephone _____
3. Name_____Telephone _____

Who is your Digital executor/executrix? Name _____

Additional details: *(Regarding your power of attorney or will)* _____

5

Trust(s) (Declaration of Trust/Deed of Trust)	Primary User	Secondary User

Do you have a trust document?　　　　　　　　　Yes or No　　　　　Yes or No

　　If yes: How many?　　　　　　　　　　　　#_____　　　#_____

---

1. Trust Agreement Name:_____

　　What type of trust?_____Trust dated: _____
　　(Revocable, living, irrevocable, children's, charitable, QPRT, QTIP, land, etc.)

　　Grantor Name: _____ EIN/Tax ID #: _____

　　How many trustees listed on this trust?　　# _____

　　　　Trustee name_____Telephone_____
　　　　Trustee name_____Telephone_____
　　　　Trustee name_____Telephone_____
　　　　Trustee name_____Telephone _____

　　How many successor trustees are on this trust? # _____

　　　　Successor trustee name_____Telephone_____
　　　　Successor trustee name_____Telephone_____

　　Does this trust have an amendment?　　Yes or No　How many amendments? # _____
　　　　If yes: What is the amendment date: _____

　　Where is this trust document and all amendments located? _____

　　Has this trust been funded? Yes or No　If yes: How? *(Real estate, assets, etc.)* _____

　　Additional details:

---

2. Trust Agreement Name:_____

　　What type of trust?_____Trust dated: _____
　　(Revocable, living, irrevocable, children's, charitable, QPRT, QTIP, land, etc.)

　　Grantor Name: _____ EIN/Tax ID #: _____

　　How many trustees listed on this trust?　　# _____

　　　　Trustee name_____Telephone_____
　　　　Trustee name_____Telephone_____
　　　　Trustee name_____Telephone_____
　　　　Trustee name_____Telephone _____

　　How many successor trustees are on this trust? # _____

　　　　Successor trustee name_____Telephone_____
　　　　Successor trustee name_____Telephone_____

　　Does this trust have an amendment?　Yes or No　How many amendments? # _____
　　　　If yes: What is the amendment date: _____

　　Where is this trust document and all amendments located? _____

　　Has this trust been funded? Yes or No　If yes: How? *(Real estate, assets, etc.)* _____

　　Additional details:

5

3. Trust Agreement Name:_____

What type of trust?_____Trust dated: _____

(Revocable, living, irrevocable, children's, charitable, QPRT, QTIP, land, etc.)

Grantor Name: _____ EIN/Tax ID #: _____

How many trustees listed on this trust?   # _____

Trustee name_____Telephone_____

Trustee name_____Telephone_____

Trustee name_____Telephone_____

Trustee name_____Telephone _____

How many successor trustees are on this trust? # _____

Successor trustee name_____Telephone_____

Successor trustee name_____Telephone_____

Does this trust have an amendment?   Yes or No   How many amendments? # _____

If yes: What is the amendment date: _____

Where is this trust document and all amendments located? _____

Has this trust been funded? Yes or No   If yes: How? *(Real estate, assets, etc.)* _____

Additional details:

---

4. Trust Agreement Name:_____

What type of trust?_____Trust dated: _____

(Revocable, living, irrevocable, children's, charitable, QPRT, QTIP, land, etc.)

Grantor Name: _____ EIN/Tax ID #: _____

How many trustees listed on this trust?   # _____

Trustee name_____Telephone_____

Trustee name_____Telephone_____

Trustee name_____Telephone_____

Trustee name_____Telephone _____

How many successor trustees are on this trust? # _____

Successor trustee name_____Telephone_____

Successor trustee name_____Telephone_____

Does this trust have an amendment?   Yes or No   How many amendments? # _____

If yes: What is the amendment date: _____

Where is this trust document and all amendments located? _____

Has this trust been funded? Yes or No   If yes: How? *(Real estate, assets, etc.)* _____

Additional details:

5

Document Storage and Storage Location	Primary User	Secondary User

Do you have a safe-deposit box?　　　　Yes or No　　　Yes or No

　If yes: How many?　　　　　　　　　　　# _____　　　# _____

　1.　Safe-deposit box location: _____
　　　Who has access to the safe-deposit box? Listed name(s): _____
　　　_____
　　　Do you have an inventory of what is inside?　　　Yes or No
　　　　If yes: Where is the inventory list located? _____
　　　　Does this safe-deposit box have keys or combination?　　Keys or Combination
　　　Where are the keys kept or what's the combination? _____

　2.　Safe-deposit box location: _____
　　　Who has access to the safe-deposit box? Listed name(s): _____
　　　_____
　　　Do you have an inventory of what is inside?　　　Yes or No
　　　　If yes: Where is the inventory list located? _____
　　　　Does this safe-deposit box have keys or combination?　　Keys or Combination
　　　Where are the keys kept or what's the combination? _____

Do you have a home safe/personal safe?　　　Yes or No　　　Yes or No

　If yes: How many?　　　　　　　　　　　# _____　　　# _____

　1.　Home safe location: _____
　　　Does the home safe have keys or combination?　　Keys or Combination
　　　Where are the keys kept? What's the combination? _____
　　　Who else has access to the keys or combinations? _____

　2.　Home safe location: _____
　　　Does the home safe have keys or combination?　　Keys or Combination
　　　Where are the keys kept? What's the combination? _____
　　　Who else has access to the keys or combinations? _____

Do you have a file cabinet?　　　　　　　Yes or No　　　Yes or No

　If yes: Where is the file cabinet located?　　　_____　_____
　　　Additional details:

Do you have a document repository?　　　　Yes or No　　　Yes or No

　If yes: Name: _____　Location: _____
　How to access it? _____
　Who else has access? _____
　Additional details: _____

Storage Location Other Items: Where do you store other items that require a key, combination, or code?

Write item details and how to access each one. *(Tool chest that locks, combination list, padlock with a key, etc.)* _____

_____
_____
_____

5

You want to ensure that your loved ones are aware of any valuable possessions you have, such as collectibles or personal belongings that hold financial value or personal importance. Examples include a stamp or coin collection, an antique car, paintings, or expensive jewelry. Some items might be a family heirloom, such as an antique vase, your grandmother's silver bracelet, or other items that have other sentimental significance.

Take pictures, obtain appraisals, and consult a professional for advice!

Personal Possessions / Valuable Items	Primary User	Secondary User
Do you have an inventory list for personal belongings?	Yes or No	Yes or No

If yes: Where is this list located? _____ _____

(Safe-deposit box, file cabinet, box in closet, here in this workbook, etc.)

Inventory List / Personal Possessions

Today's Date: _____

#	What's the Item? Personal belonging	What's the Value? Original cost, current value or is it Sentimental	Description of the Item Details	Where is the Item Located?	Do you have a specific person you want to have this item? Name or reference trust or will
1. Do you have an appraisal for this item? Yes or No Where is the appraisal located? _____ Additional Details:					
2. Do you have an appraisal for this item? Yes or No Where is the appraisal located? _____ Additional Details:					
3. Do you have an appraisal for this item? Yes or No Where is the appraisal located? _____ Additional Details:					
4. Do you have an appraisal for this item? Yes or No Where is the appraisal located? _____ Additional Details:					
5. Do you have an appraisal for this item? Yes or No Where is the appraisal located? _____ Additional Details:					

5

IMPORTANT NOTE: Additional <u>Inventory Lists for Personal Possessions</u> are provided in the **EXTRAS** section at the back of this workbook.

Legal Responsibility for Someone Else, Organization, Charity or Foundation	Primary User	Secondary User

Do you have any **legal responsibilities for someone else**?　　Yes or No　　　Yes or No

If yes: What legal responsibility do you have? Who do you have this responsibility for?
(Wife's POA, health care proxy for dad, trustee for nephew's trust, legal guardian for child, executor of mother's estate, etc.)
Write all tasks. You may have more than one **guardianship or legal responsibility**.

Primary User: _____
_____
_____
_____
_____

If you become unable to perform these legal responsibilities, who needs to be contacted?
Name _____ Telephone _____
Name _____ Telephone _____

Secondary User: _____
_____
_____
_____
_____

If you become unable to perform these legal responsibilities, who needs to be contacted?
Name _____ Telephone _____
Name _____ Telephone _____

Do you have any **legal responsibilities for an organization, charity, or foundation**?　　Yes or No　　　Yes or No

If yes: What legal responsibility do you have? Who do you have this responsibility for?
(Treasurer, trustee of condominium trust, board of directors, meeting minutes, etc.)
Write all tasks. You may have more than one legal responsibility.

Primary User: _____
_____
_____
_____

If you become unable to perform these legal responsibilities, who needs to be contacted?
Name _____ Telephone _____
Name _____ Telephone _____

Secondary User: _____
_____
_____
_____

If you become unable to perform these legal responsibilities, who needs to be contacted?
Name _____ Telephone _____
Name _____ Telephone _____

5

Just In Case SOLUTIONS

Step 5: Legal Documents and Professionals

Date Completed: _____

Fun Memory

Way to go! You have completed Step 5!

Did a fun or interesting fact from your past come to mind while you were working on this Step?

Use the space below to share a memory with your loved ones. It could be a funny story about yourself, a loving memory, or a fascinating fact about a moment in your past. This will bring joy and a smile during challenging times. Instead of writing, share your favorite song, poem, or insert a picture!

Need ideas? Here are some suggestions to write about for Step 5:
Share your most cherished possession and why it holds such significance, a special act of kindness received from a professional, a story about a family heirloom, the emotions you felt when you purchased your first home or specialty item, etc.

_____
_____
_____
_____
_____
_____
_____
_____
_____
_____
_____
_____
_____
_____
_____
_____
_____
_____
_____
_____
_____

5

Step 6

Financial and Insurance

All Steps have their importance and help your loved ones. However, there are items within this Step that are extremely important for all Just In Case scenarios.

In Step 6, you will be gathering and recording details about your financials and insurance. This Step does not ask how much money you have. Whether you have $1,000 or $1 million, your loved ones may need to know an account or policy exists and where the funds are invested. Once they know the location of the account or policy, they will be able to act accordingly.

Write the details of what you have and cross out the ones that you do not have. That way, your loved ones will know you didn't forget anything. For example, if you are receiving Social Security benefits, provide the details. If you do not have disability insurance, cross it out.

Recording these details in an organized manner will help your loved ones take one Step at a time.

Here are some ways Step 6 can be helpful:

- If you have life insurance, providing details will make it easy for your loved ones to take quick action. If you do not have life insurance, maybe it's time to talk with a professional about the best way to protect your loved ones from financial loss.

- Document the specifics for any banks or credit unions you use and if you have money market or brokerage/investment accounts, certificates of deposit, bonds, stock certificates, a college fund, or an annuity.

- Provide what type and how many retirement accounts you have. This is where you will write down if you have any lingering accounts from a past employer.

- If you use a digital wallet or a money transfer service; own digital assets with value (for example, cryptocurrencies); use a digital assets management software; or own any of the many types of digital assets (for example, blog content, online betting account or digital rights to music or videos), make sure to record the details. In addition, please consult with an estate planning attorney to ensure electronic fiduciary powers and digital assets are specified in your estate planning legal documents.

Ask Yourself, when was the last time you reviewed how your accounts are registered and confirmed that you have a primary and secondary beneficiary listed on each one?

- Have a discussion with a professional regarding how your accounts are owned (account registrations), how to avoid probate, and if you need to make any adjustments.

- If you have had a life-changing event, you may need to designate a new beneficiary.

- It's a good idea to review *all* your accounts and policies to ensure that your beneficiaries are accurately listed.

Everyone's situation is different, so please seek advice from a qualified professional if you have any questions.

STEP 6: FINANCIAL AND INSURANCE
- Social Security
  - Account, Card, Payments, Survivor Benefits, Supplemental Security Income
- Life Insurance
- Accidental Death and Dismemberment, Income Protection Insurance
- Mortgage Protection Insurance
- Disability Insurance
- Banks, Credit Unions
  - Checking, Savings
- Money Market Account, Money Market Deposit Account
- Certificate of Deposit, Bonds
- College Fund, Account for a Minor
- Brokerage (Investment) Accounts, Stocks, Annuities
- Retirement Accounts
  - IRA(s), 401(k), 403(b), Pension Plan, Profit-Sharing Plan, SEP or SARSEP Plan, Defined Benefits Plan, Government Pension, 457 Plan, Other
    - Retirement Account Details
- Financial Interest, Promissory Note, Commodities
- Money Transfer Service, Digital Wallet
- Unclaimed Property, Missing Money
- Digital Assets
- Step 6 Completion Date and Fun Memory!

Step 6: NOTE TO LOVED ONES

In Step 6, your loved one has prepared you with a detailed list of financial accounts, insurance-related products, and more.

Try not to get too overwhelmed, as these details have been provided so you can simply deal with one policy, one account, or one company at a time.

In the case of death or severe illness, you may need legal documents that are explained and listed in Step 5, such as a power of attorney or original death certificate.

Here are a few ways in which this Step can help:

- You may need to request funds to pay for medical expenses or to pay off debt.

- You may need to request forms to transfer an account, close an account, or cancel a policy. Be prepared to complete forms and submit the necessary documents to provide proof you can act on behalf of your loved one.

- If your loved one has passed away, you need to notify the Social Security Administration of the death. Timely notification is beneficial! If a deceased person receives funds from Social Security, you will have to return the funds. Avoid the hassle of needing to send money back by informing the administration to stop payments.

- If your loved one had a digital wallet and confirmed they typically keep a balance in the account, consider transferring the balance back to the linked account before closing the account or card that is attached to the money transfer service. Be prepared to provide proof that you are legally able to act on digital assets and accounts.

You got this! Be grateful that your loved one has taken the time to provide this crucial information to you.

Social Security	Primary User	Secondary User
Do you have Social Security or another government program with benefits?	Yes or No	Yes or No
If yes: Social Security Number (SSN) *(Also listed in Step 1)*	_____	_____

Account

	Primary User	Secondary User
Do you have an online account with Social Security?	Yes or No	Yes or No
If yes: How do you log in? Website:	_____	_____
Username:	_____	_____
Password:	_____	_____
Email Used:	_____	_____

Card

	Primary User	Secondary User
Do you know where your Social Security card is?	Yes or No	Yes or No
If yes: Where is it located?	_____	_____
If no: Would you say it's lost?	Yes or No	Yes or No

Payments

	Primary User	Secondary User
Are you receiving Social Security payments?	Yes or No	Yes or No
If yes: Payments received by check or direct deposit:	Check or Direct Deposit	Check or Direct Deposit
Amount:	$ _____	$ _____
If check: Where is it mailed? Address:	_____	_____
	_____	_____
If direct deposit: Bank name:	_____	_____
Account number:	_____	_____

Survivor Benefits

	Primary User	Secondary User
Do you have any survival benefits available?	Yes or No	Yes or No
If yes: Who are they for?	_____	_____
What are the survival benefits?	_____	_____
	_____	_____

Supplemental Security Income (SSI)

	Primary User	Secondary User
Are you receiving Social Security Disability Income?	Yes or No	Yes or No
If yes: Payments received by check or direct deposit?	Check or Direct Deposit	Check or Direct Deposit
Amount:	$ _____	$ _____
If check: Where is it mailed? Address:	_____	_____
	_____	_____
If direct deposit: Bank name:	_____	_____
Account number:	_____	_____

Additional details: _____

_____

_____

Note: Please contact the Social Security Administration with any questions.

Life Insurance	Primary User	Secondary User

Do you have a life insurance policy?
    If yes: How many?   Yes or No   Yes or No
                                                # _____   # _____

Circle: Primary User   or   Secondary User

1. Life Insurance Company: _____

    Website:_____   Telephone: _____

    Contract/Policy number: _____   Issue Date: _____

    Type of life insurance: *(Term, whole, universal, variable, etc.)*_____

    Name(s) on policy: _____   Expiration Date: _____

    Primary beneficiary and % *(% totals 100%)*

    _____ % _____   _____ % _____

    _____ % _____   _____ % _____

    _____ % _____   _____ % _____

    Contingent beneficiary and % *(% totals 100%)*

    _____ % _____   _____ % _____

    _____ % _____   _____ % _____

    _____ % _____   _____ % _____

    Where is the policy located? _____

    How do you receive the bill to pay premium? *(Paper via mail or paperless via electronic delivery)* _____

       If electronic delivery: Where? *(Email, online banking, etc.)* _____

    How do you make payment? *(Check, online banking manual, automatic recurring payment, etc.)* _____

    Payment amount is $_____Due date is _____

Additional details: _____

Circle: Primary User   or   Secondary User

2. Life Insurance Company: _____

    Website:_____   Telephone: _____

    Contract/Policy number: _____   Issue Date: _____

    Type of life insurance: *(Term, whole, universal, variable, etc.)*_____

    Name(s) on policy: _____   Expiration Date: _____

    Primary beneficiary and % *(% totals 100%)*

    _____ % _____   _____ % _____

    _____ % _____   _____ % _____

    _____ % _____   _____ % _____

    Contingent beneficiary and % *(% totals 100%)*

    _____ % _____   _____ % _____

    _____ % _____   _____ % _____

    _____ % _____   _____ % _____

    Where is the policy located? _____

    How do you receive the bill to pay premium? *(Paper via mail or paperless via electronic delivery)* _____

       If electronic delivery: Where? *(Email, online banking, etc.)* _____

    How do you make payment? *(Check, online banking manual, automatic recurring payment, etc.)* _____

    Payment amount is $_____Due date is _____

Additional details: _____

6

Life Insurance

Circle: Primary User or Secondary User

3. **Life Insurance Company:** _____
   Website:_____ Telephone: _____
   Contract/Policy number: _____ Issue Date: _____
   Type of life insurance: *(Term, whole, universal, variable, etc.)*_____
   Name(s) on policy: _____ Expiration Date: _____
   Primary beneficiary and % *(% totals 100%)*

   _____ % _____ _____ % _____
   _____ % _____ _____ % _____
   _____ % _____ _____ % _____

   Contingent beneficiary and % *(% totals 100%)*

   _____ % _____ _____ % _____
   _____ % _____ _____ % _____
   _____ % _____ _____ % _____

   Where is the policy located? _____
   How do you receive the bill to pay premium? *(Paper via mail or paperless via electronic delivery)* _____
      If electronic delivery: Where? *(Email, online banking, etc.)* _____
   How do you make payment? *(Check, online banking manual, automatic recurring payment, etc.)* _____
   Payment amount is $_____Due date is _____
Additional details: _____

Circle: Primary User or Secondary User

4. **Life Insurance Company:** _____
   Website:_____ Telephone: _____
   Contract/Policy number: _____ Issue Date: _____
   Type of life insurance: *(Term, whole, universal, variable, etc.)*_____
   Name(s) on policy: _____ Expiration Date: _____
   Primary beneficiary and % *(% totals 100%)*

   _____ % _____ _____ % _____
   _____ % _____ _____ % _____
   _____ % _____ _____ % _____

   Contingent beneficiary and % *(% totals 100%)*

   _____ % _____ _____ % _____
   _____ % _____ _____ % _____
   _____ % _____ _____ % _____

   Where is the policy located? _____
   How do you receive the bill to pay premium? *(Paper via mail or paperless via electronic delivery)* _____
      If electronic delivery: Where? *(Email, online banking, etc.)* _____
   How do you make payment? *(Check, online banking manual, automatic recurring payment, etc.)* _____
   Payment amount is $_____Due date is _____
Additional details: _____

Circle: Primary User   or   Secondary User

5.   **Life Insurance Company:** _____

Website:_____ Telephone: _____

Contract/Policy number: _____ Issue Date: _____

Type of life insurance: *(Term, whole, universal, variable, etc.)*_____

Name(s) on policy: _____ Expiration Date: _____

Primary beneficiary and % *(% totals 100%)*

_____ % _____   _____ % _____

_____ % _____   _____ % _____

_____ % _____   _____ % _____

Contingent beneficiary and % *(% totals 100%)*

_____ % _____   _____ % _____

_____ % _____   _____ % _____

_____ % _____   _____ % _____

Where is the policy located? _____

How do you receive the bill to pay premium? *(Paper via mail or paperless via electronic delivery)* _____

   If electronic delivery: Where? *(Email, online banking, etc.)* _____

How do you make payment? *(Check, online banking manual, automatic recurring payment, etc.)* _____

Payment amount is $_____Due date is _____

Additional details: _____

Circle: Primary User   or   Secondary User

6

6.   **Life Insurance Company:** _____

Website:_____ Telephone: _____

Contract/Policy number: _____ Issue Date: _____

Type of life insurance: *(Term, whole, universal, variable, etc.)*_____

Name(s) on policy: _____ Expiration Date: _____

Primary beneficiary and % *(% totals 100%)*

_____ % _____   _____ % _____

_____ % _____   _____ % _____

_____ % _____   _____ % _____

Contingent beneficiary and % *(% totals 100%)*

_____ % _____   _____ % _____

_____ % _____   _____ % _____

_____ % _____   _____ % _____

Where is the policy located? _____

How do you receive the bill to pay premium? *(Paper via mail or paperless via electronic delivery)* _____

   If electronic delivery: Where? *(Email, online banking, etc.)* _____

How do you make payment? *(Check, online banking manual, automatic recurring payment, etc.)* _____

Payment amount is $_____Due date is _____

Additional details: _____

Accidental Death and Dismemberment (AD&D)	Primary User	Secondary User

Do you have an AD&D policy?   Yes or No   Yes or No
If yes: How many?   # _____   # _____

Circle: Primary User or Secondary User

1. **AD&D Company:** _____
      Website:_____ Telephone: _____
      Contract/Policy number: _____
      Name(s) on policy: _____
      Primary beneficiary and % *(% totals 100%)*

      _____ % _____   _____ % _____
      _____ % _____   _____ % _____
      _____ % _____   _____ % _____

      Contingent beneficiary and % *(% totals 100%)*

      _____ % _____   _____ % _____
      _____ % _____   _____ % _____
      _____ % _____   _____ % _____

      Where is the policy located? _____
      How do you receive the bill to pay premium? *(Paper via mail or paperless via electronic delivery)* _____
         If electronic delivery: Where? *(Email, online banking, etc.)* _____
      How do you make payment? *(Check, online banking manual, automatic recurring payment, etc.)* _____
      Payment amount is $_____Due date is _____
Additional details: _____

Circle: Primary User   or   Secondary User

2. **AD&D Company:** _____
      Website:_____ Telephone: _____
      Contract/Policy number: _____
      Name(s) on policy: _____
      Primary beneficiary and % *(% totals 100%)*

      _____ % _____   _____ % _____
      _____ % _____   _____ % _____
      _____ % _____   _____ % _____

      Contingent beneficiary and % *(% totals 100%)*

      _____ % _____   _____ % _____
      _____ % _____   _____ % _____
      _____ % _____   _____ % _____

      Where is the policy located? _____
      How do you receive the bill to pay premium? *(Paper via mail or paperless via electronic delivery)* _____
         If electronic delivery: Where? *(Email, online banking, etc.)* _____
      How do you make payment? *(Check, online banking manual, automatic recurring payment, etc.)* _____
      Payment amount is $_____Due date is _____
Additional details: _____

6

Income Protection Insurance	Primary User	Secondary User

Do you have income protection insurance?   Yes or No   Yes or No
   If yes: How many policies?   # _____   # _____

Circle: Primary User   or   Secondary User

1. Income Protection Insurance Company: _____
    Website:_____ Telephone: _____
    Contract/Policy number: _____
    Name(s) on policy: _____
    Primary beneficiary and % *(% totals 100%)*
      _____ % _____   _____ % _____
      _____ % _____   _____ % _____
    Contingent beneficiary and % *(% totals 100%)*
      _____ % _____   _____ % _____
      _____ % _____   _____ % _____
    Where is the policy located? _____
    How do you receive the bill to pay premium? *(Paper via mail or paperless via electronic delivery)* _____
      If electronic delivery: Where? *(Email, online banking, etc.)* _____
    How do you make payment? *(Check, online banking manual, automatic recurring payment, etc.)* _____
    Payment amount is $_____Due date is _____
Additional details: _____

Circle: Primary User   or   Secondary User

2. Income Protection Insurance Company: _____
    Website:_____ Telephone: _____
    Contract/Policy number: _____
    Name(s) on policy: _____
    Primary beneficiary and % *(% totals 100%)*
      _____ % _____   _____ % _____
      _____ % _____   _____ % _____
    Contingent beneficiary and % *(% totals 100%)*
      _____ % _____   _____ % _____
      _____ % _____   _____ % _____
    Where is the policy located? _____
    How do you receive the bill to pay premium? *(Paper via mail or paperless via electronic delivery)* _____
      If electronic delivery: Where? *(Email, online banking, etc.)* _____
    How do you make payment? *(Check, online banking manual, automatic recurring payment, etc.)* _____
    Payment amount is $_____Due date is _____
Additional details: _____

6

Mortgage Protection Insurance ("MPI")	Primary User	Secondary User

Do you have Mortgage Protection Insurance?   Yes or No   Yes or No

> This insurance varies per person. Please contact an insurance specialist with any questions.
> **This is NOT PMI**. Private Mortgage Insurance will be covered in Step 7.

Circle: Primary User   or   Secondary User

1. **Mortgage Protection Insurance Company:** _____
   Website:_____ Telephone: _____
   Contract/Policy number: _____
   Name(s) on policy: _____
   Primary beneficiary and % (% totals 100%)
   _____ % _____ _____ % _____
   Is there a death benefit? Yes or No
   Where is the policy located? _____
   How do you receive the bill to pay premium? *(Paper via mail or paperless via electronic delivery)* _____
      If electronic delivery: Where? *(Email, online banking, etc.)* _____
   How do you make payment? *(Check, online banking manual, automatic recurring payment, etc.)* _____
   Payment amount is $_____Due date is _____
Additional details: _____
_____

Circle: Primary User   or   Secondary User

2. **Mortgage Protection Insurance Company:** _____
   Website:_____ Telephone: _____
   Contract/Policy number: _____
   Name(s) on policy: _____
   Primary beneficiary and % (% totals 100%)
   _____ % _____ _____ % _____
   Is there a death benefit? Yes or No
   Where is the policy located? _____
   How do you receive the bill to pay premium? *(Paper via mail or paperless via electronic delivery)* _____
      If electronic delivery: Where? *(Email, online banking, etc.)* _____
   How do you make payment? *(Check, online banking manual, automatic recurring payment, etc.)* _____
   Payment amount is $_____Due date is _____
Additional details: _____
_____

6

Disability Insurance	Primary User	Secondary User
Do you have disability insurance?	Yes or No	Yes or No

Circle: Primary User   or   Secondary User

1. **Disability Insurance Company:** _____
   Website:_____ Telephone: _____
   Contract/Policy number: _____
   Name(s) on policy: _____
   Individual or family?_____If family, who else is on policy? _____
   Is this short-term or long-term? _____
   What type of plan? Provide details/benefits: _____
   _____
   Where is the policy located? _____
      How do you receive the bill to pay premium? *(Paper via mail or paperless via electronic delivery)* _____
   If electronic delivery: Where? *(Email, online banking, etc.)* _____
   How do you make payment? *(Check, online banking manual, automatic recurring payment, etc.)* _____
   Payment amount is $_____Due date is _____
Additional details: _____

Circle: Primary User   or   Secondary User

2. **Disability Insurance Company:** _____
   Website:_____ Telephone: _____
   Contract/Policy number: _____
   Name(s) on policy: _____
   Individual or family?_____If family, who else is on policy? _____
   Is this short-term or long-term? _____
   What type of plan? Provide details/benefits: _____
   _____
   Where is the policy located? _____
      How do you receive the bill to pay premium? *(Paper via mail or paperless via electronic delivery)* _____
   If electronic delivery: Where? *(Email, online banking, etc.)* _____
   How do you make payment? *(Check, online banking manual, automatic recurring payment, etc.)* _____
   Payment amount is $_____Due date is _____
Additional details: _____

6

This section is for traditional (standard/basic) checking and savings accounts.
Note: Money market accounts will be recorded in the next section.

Banks, Credit Unions		Primary User	Secondary User	Joint
Checking	Do you have a checking account?	Yes or No	Yes or No	Yes or No
	If yes: How many?	# _____	# _____	# _____
Savings	Do you have a savings account?	Yes or No	Yes or No	Yes or No
	If yes: How many?	# _____	# _____	# _____

Circle: Primary User   or   Secondary User   or   Joint

1. **Bank or Credit Union Name:** _____Telephone:_____
   Address:_____
   Account number: _____
   Name(s) on account: _____
   How is the account registered? *(Individual, joint, trust name, TOD, etc.)* _____
   Type of Account: Checking or Savings   Personal or Commercial
   Where is your checkbook located? _____
   Is there an assigned debit card?   Yes or No   If yes: What is the PIN? _____
   Do you use online banking?   Yes or No
       Website:_____
       Username:_____Password: _____
   Do you pay bills from this account?   Yes or No
       If yes: Details: _____
       _____
   Do you have any automatic withdrawals from this account?   Yes or No
   How do you receive statements? *(Paper via mail or paperless via electronic delivery)* _____
       If electronic delivery: Where? *(Email, online banking, etc.)* _____
Additional details: _____

Circle: Primary User   or   Secondary User   or   Joint

2. **Bank or Credit Union Name:**_____Telephone:_____
   Address:_____
   Account number: _____
   Name(s) on account: _____
   How is the account registered? *(Individual, joint, trust name, TOD, etc.)* _____
   Type of Account: Checking or Savings   Personal or Commercial
   Where is your checkbook located? _____
   Is there an assigned debit card?   Yes or No   If yes: What is the PIN? _____
   Do you use online banking?   Yes or No
       Website:_____
       Username:_____Password: _____
   Do you pay bills from this account?   Yes or No
       If yes: Details: _____
       _____
   Do you have any automatic withdrawals from this account?   Yes or No
   How do you receive statements? *(Paper via mail or paperless via electronic delivery)* _____
       If electronic delivery: Where? *(Email, online banking, etc.)* _____
Additional details: _____

6

Circle: Primary User   or   Secondary User   or   Joint

3. **Bank or Credit Union Name:**_____Telephone:_____
   Address:_____
   Account number: _____
   Name(s) on account: _____
   How is the account registered? *(Individual, joint, trust name, TOD, etc.)* _____
   Type of Account: Checking or Savings   Personal or Commercial
   Where is your checkbook located? _____
   Is there an assigned debit card?   Yes or No   If yes: What is the PIN? _____
   Do you use online banking?   Yes or No
        Website:_____
        Username:_____Password: _____
   Do you pay bills from this account?   Yes or No
        If yes: Details: _____
        _____
   Do you have any automatic withdrawals from this account?   Yes or No
   How do you receive statements? *(Paper via mail or paperless via electronic delivery)* _____
        If electronic delivery: Where? *(Email, online banking, etc.)* _____
Additional details: _____

Circle: Primary User   or   Secondary User   or   Joint

4. **Bank or Credit Union Name:**_____Telephone:_____
   Address:_____
   Account number: _____
   Name(s) on account: _____
   How is the account registered? *(Individual, joint, trust name, TOD, etc.)* _____
   Type of Account: Checking or Savings   Personal or Commercial
   Where is your checkbook located? _____
   Is there an assigned debit card?   Yes or No   If yes: What is the PIN? _____
   Do you use online banking?   Yes or No
        Website:_____
        Username:_____Password: _____
   Do you pay bills from this account?   Yes or No
        If yes: Details: _____
        _____
   Do you have any automatic withdrawals from this account?   Yes or No
   How do you receive statements? *(Paper via mail or paperless via electronic delivery)* _____
        If electronic delivery: Where? *(Email, online banking, etc.)* _____
Additional details: _____

6

Money Market Account (MMA) / Money Market Deposit Account (MMDA)	Primary User	Secondary User	Joint
Do you have a Money Market Account?	Yes or No	Yes or No	Yes or No
If yes: How many?	# _____	# _____	# _____

Name/Telephone of the person(s) or financial company that helps you with your Money Market Account(s):

_____

MMA / MMDA Name(s) listed on the account	How is the Account Registered? Individual, Trust, Joint WROS, Tenants in Common, etc.	Financial Company or Bank Name	Account Number	How do you Receive Statements? Paper via mail or paperless via electronic delivery	Additional Details
1.					
2.					
3.					
4.					
5.					
6.					
7.					
8.					

6

Certificate of Deposit (CDs)	Primary User	Secondary User	Joint
Do you have a CD? If yes: How many?	Yes or No # _____	Yes or No # _____	Yes or No # _____

Name/Telephone of the person(s) or bank that helps you with your CDs: _____

_____

CD Name(s) listed on the account	How is the Account Registered? Individual, Trust, Joint WROS, Tenants in Common, etc.	Financial Company or Bank Name	Account Number or Deposit Number	Purchase Date - and - Maturity Date	How do you Receive Statements? Paper via mail or paperless via electronic delivery	Where is the CD Located? Held at the bank, you physically have it/where is it kept, safe-deposit box, file cabinet, etc.
1.						
Maturity Date / Details: _____						
2.						
Maturity Date / Details: _____						
3.						
Maturity Date / Details: _____						
4.						
Maturity Date / Details: _____						
5.						
Maturity Date / Details: _____						
6.						
Maturity Date / Details: _____						

6

CD Name(s) listed on the account	How is the Account Registered? Individual, Trust, Joint WROS, Tenants in Common, etc.	Financial Company or Bank Name	Account Number or Deposit Number	Purchase Date - and - Maturity Date	How do you Receive Statements? Paper via mail or paperless via electronic delivery	Where is the CD Located? Held at the bank, you physically have it/where is it kept, safe-deposit box, file cabinet, etc.
7.						
Maturity Date / Details: _____						
8.						
Maturity Date / Details: _____						
9.						
Maturity Date / Details: _____						
10.						
Maturity Date / Details: _____						
11.						
Maturity Date / Details: _____						
12.						
Maturity Date / Details: _____						

Note: If you own more than 12, assemble and insert a detailed list.

If your additional list of CDs is electronic, where is it located? _____

Bond(s)		Primary User	Secondary User	Joint

Do you have/own any bonds? Yes or No   Yes or No   Yes or No

If yes: How many? # _____   # _____   # _____

Name/Telephone of person(s) or financial company that helps you with your bonds: _____

_____

Bond Name(s) listed on bond	How is the Account Registered? Individual, Trust, Joint WROS, Tenants in Common, etc.	Financial Company or Bank Name	Account Number	Type of Bond Treasury, Series EE, H U.S. Government, Corporate Bond, Foreign Bank, Savings Bond, etc.	How do you Receive Statements? Paper via mail or paperless via electronic delivery	Where is the Bond Located? Held at the bank, you physically have it, where is it kept, safe-deposit box, filecabinet, etc.
1.						
Maturity Date / Details: _____						
2.						
Maturity Date / Details: _____						
3.						
Maturity Date / Details: _____						
4.						
Maturity Date / Details: _____						
5.						
Maturity Date / Details: _____						
6.						
Maturity Date / Details: _____						

6

Bond Name(s) listed on bond	How is the Account Registered? Individual, Trust, Joint WROS, Tenants in Common, etc.	Financial Company or Bank Name	Account Number	Type of Bond Treasury, Series EE, H U.S. Government, Corporate Bond, Foreign Bank, Savings Bond, etc.	How do you Receive Statements? Paper via mail or paperless via electronic delivery	Where is the Bond Located? Held at the bank, you physically have it, where is it kept, safe-deposit box, filecabinet, etc.
7.						
Maturity Date / Details: _____						
8.						
Maturity Date / Details: _____						
9.						
Maturity Date / Details: _____						
10.						
Maturity Date / Details: _____						
11.						
Maturity Date / Details: _____						
12.						
Maturity Date / Details: _____						

Note: If you own more than 12, assemble and insert a detailed list.

If your additional list of bonds is electronic, where is it located? _____

College Fund - OR – Account for a Minor	Primary User	Secondary User
Do you have an account for a minor or a college fund?	Yes or No	Yes or No
If yes: How many?	# _____	# _____

Name/Telephone of person(s) or Financial Company who helps you with the College Fund or Minor Account:

_____

College Fund or Account for Minor Custodian name(s) listed on the account	What Type of Account? UTMA/UGMA, 529 Plan, College Savings Plan, etc.	Financial Company or Bank Name	Account Number	Beneficiary (Child) Name	Beneficiary Relationship to You	How do you Receive Statements? Paper via mail or paperless via electronic delivery
1. Additional details:						
2. Additional details:						
3. Additional details:						
4. Additional details:						
5. Additional details:						
6. Additional details:						

6

Brokerage (Investment) Accounts	Primary User	Secondary User	Joint
Do you have a brokerage (investment) account?	Yes or No	Yes or No	Yes or No
If yes: How many?	# _____	# _____	# _____

Circle: Primary User or Secondary User or Joint

1. **Financial Institution Name:** _____
   Who manages this account? *(Professional/name, yourself, etc.)* _____
   Type of account: _____
   Name(s) listed on account (Registration/Ownership)? *(First/middle/last, sole ownership, trust name, joint tenants in common, joint tenants with rights of survivorship, transfer on death, etc.)* _____
   _____
   Account number: _____
   Website:_____Telephone:_____
   How do you receive statements? *(Paper via mail or paperless via electronic delivery)* _____
   Do you currently make deposits?   Yes or No
       If yes: How/When: *(Annual check, monthly electronic deposit, employee payroll, etc.)*_____
       _____
       Are you currently receiving a distribution?   Yes or No
       If yes: How/Where: *(Check in the mail, direct deposit into checking, etc.)* _____
   Additional details:

Circle: Primary User or Secondary User or Joint

2. **Financial Institution Name:** _____
   Who manages this account? *(Professional/name, yourself, etc.)* _____
   Type of account: _____
   Name(s) listed on account (Registration/Ownership)? *(First/middle/last, sole ownership, trust name, joint tenants in common, joint tenants with rights of survivorship, transfer on death, etc.)* _____
   _____
   Account number: _____
   Website:_____Telephone:_____
   How do you receive statements? *(Paper via mail or paperless via electronic delivery)* _____
   Do you currently make deposits?   Yes or No
       If yes: How/When: *(Annual check, monthly electronic deposit, employee payroll, etc.)*_____
       _____
       Are you currently receiving a distribution?   Yes or No
       If yes: How/Where: *(Check in the mail, direct deposit into checking, etc.)* _____
   Additional details:

6

Brokerage (Investment) Accounts

Circle: Primary User or Secondary User or Joint

3. **Financial Institution Name:** _____
   Who manages this account? *(Professional/name, yourself, etc.)* _____
   Type of account: _____
   Name(s) listed on account (Registration/Ownership)? *(First/middle/last, sole ownership, trust name, joint tenants in common, joint tenants with rights of survivorship, transfer on death, etc.)* _____
   _____
   Account number: _____
   Website:_____Telephone:_____
   How do you receive statements? *(Paper via mail or paperless via electronic delivery)* _____
   Do you currently make deposits?   Yes or No
       If yes: How/When: *(Annual check, monthly electronic deposit, employee payroll, etc.)*_____
       _____
       Are you currently receiving a distribution?   Yes or No
       If yes: How/Where: *(Check in the mail, direct deposit into checking, etc.)* _____
Additional details:

Circle: Primary User or Secondary User or Joint

4. **Financial Institution Name:** _____
   Who manages this account? *(Professional/name, yourself, etc.)* _____
   Type of account: _____
   Name(s) listed on account (Registration/Ownership)? *(First/middle/last, sole ownership, trust name, joint tenants in common, joint tenants with rights of survivorship, transfer on death, etc.)* _____
   _____
   Account number: _____
   Website:_____Telephone:_____
   How do you receive statements? *(Paper via mail or paperless via electronic delivery)* _____
   Do you currently make deposits?   Yes or No
       If yes: How/When: *(Annual check, monthly electronic deposit, employee payroll, etc.)*_____
       _____
       Are you currently receiving a distribution?   Yes or No
       If yes: How/Where: *(Check in the mail, direct deposit into checking, etc.)* _____
Additional details:

6

Brokerage (Investment) Accounts

Circle: Primary User   or   Secondary User   or   Joint

5. Financial Institution Name: _____

Who manages this account? *(Professional/name, yourself, etc.)* _____

Type of account: _____

Name(s) listed on account (Registration/Ownership)? *(First/middle/last, sole ownership, trust name, joint tenants in common, joint tenants with rights of survivorship, transfer on death, etc.)* _____
_____

Account number: _____

Website:_____Telephone:_____

How do you receive statements? *(Paper via mail or paperless via electronic delivery)* _____

Do you currently make deposits?   Yes or No

   If yes: How/When: *(Annual check, monthly electronic deposit, employee payroll, etc.)*_____
_____

   Are you currently receiving a distribution?   Yes or No

      If yes: How/Where: *(Check in the mail, direct deposit into checking, etc.)* _____

Additional details:

Circle: Primary User   or   Secondary User   or   Joint

6. Financial Institution Name: _____

Who manages this account? *(Professional/name, yourself, etc.)* _____

Type of account: _____

Name(s) listed on account (Registration/Ownership)? *(First/middle/last, sole ownership, trust name, joint tenants in common, joint tenants with rights of survivorship, transfer on death, etc.)* _____
_____

Account number: _____

Website:_____Telephone:_____

How do you receive statements? *(Paper via mail or paperless via electronic delivery)* _____

Do you currently make deposits?   Yes or No

   If yes: How/When: *(Annual check, monthly electronic deposit, employee payroll, etc.)*_____
_____

   Are you currently receiving a distribution?   Yes or No

      If yes: How/Where: *(Check in the mail, direct deposit into checking, etc.)* _____

Additional details:

6

Just In Case, consult a professional to ensure your accounts are titled/registered appropriately for your desired disbursement or continuation.

Stocks	Primary User	Secondary User	Joint
Do you own any stocks? *(Outside of your brokerage acct)*	Yes or No	Yes or No	Yes or No
If yes: How many?	# _____	# _____	# _____

If yes: What type of stock(s) do you own:

	Primary User	Secondary User	Joint
Common Stock	Yes or No	Yes or No	Yes or No
Employee Stock Option Plan	Yes or No	Yes or No	Yes or No
Restricted Stock	Yes or No	Yes or No	Yes or No
Preferred Stock	Yes or No	Yes or No	Yes or No

> **Note:** If you have any questions regarding cost basis tracking of your shares, please contact a financial or tax professional.

Circle: Primary User   or   Secondary User   or   Joint

1. **Name of Stock:** _____
   Name of stock transfer company: _____
   Name(s) listed on account (Registration/Ownership)? *(First/middle/last, sole ownership, trust name, joint tenants in common, joint tenants with rights of survivorship, transfer on death, etc.)* _____
   _____
   Account number: _____
   Website:_____Telephone:_____
   How do you receive statements? *(Paper via mail or paperless via electronic delivery)*
   Do you have any physical certificate(s)?   Yes or No
      If yes: Where are the original certificates located? _____
      Are any of the shares you own Restricted?   Yes or No
   Additional details:

Circle: Primary User   or   Secondary User   or   Joint

2. **Name of Stock:** _____
   Name of stock transfer company: _____
   Name(s) listed on account (Registration/Ownership)? *(First/middle/last, sole ownership, trust name, joint tenants in common, joint tenants with rights of survivorship, transfer on death, etc.)* _____
   _____
   Account number: _____
   Website:_____Telephone:_____
   How do you receive statements? *(Paper via mail or paperless via electronic delivery)*
   Do you have any physical certificate(s)?   Yes or No
      If yes: Where are the original certificates located? _____
      Are any of the shares you own Restricted?   Yes or No
   Additional details:

6

Stock Details

Circle: Primary User or Secondary User or Joint

3. Name of Stock: _____
Name of stock transfer company: _____
Name(s) listed on account (Registration/Ownership)? *(First/middle/last, sole ownership, trust name, joint tenants in common, joint tenants with rights of survivorship, transfer on death, etc.)* _____
_____
Account number: _____
Website:_____Telephone:_____
How do you receive statements? *(Paper via mail or paperless via electronic delivery)*
Do you have any physical certificate(s)?   Yes or No
    If yes: Where are the original certificates located? _____
  Are any of the shares you own Restricted?   Yes or No
Additional details:

Circle: Primary User or Secondary User or Joint

4. Name of Stock: _____
Name of stock transfer company: _____
Name(s) listed on account (Registration/Ownership)? *(First/middle/last, sole ownership, trust name, joint tenants in common, joint tenants with rights of survivorship, transfer on death, etc.)* _____
_____
Account number: _____
Website:_____Telephone:_____
How do you receive statements? *(Paper via mail or paperless via electronic delivery)*
Do you have any physical certificate(s)?   Yes or No
    If yes: Where are the original certificates located? _____
  Are any of the shares you own Restricted?   Yes or No
Additional details:

IMPORTANT NOTE: Physical Stock Certificates: It's essential to locate all your physical stock certificates and keep them safe. If a certificate is lost, stolen, or destroyed, a specific document needs to be completed, and sometimes a fee is associated with replacing a missing certificate. Take care of replacing lost certificates for your loved ones before a Just In Case scenario occurs. When obtaining assistance, inquire if it's possible to have the shares held in book-entry (held electronically).

If you have multiple certificates, create a detailed list so your loved ones know what certificates you have and where they are located.

Annuities	Primary User	Secondary User
Do you have an annuity?	Yes or No	Yes or No
If yes: How many?	# _____	# _____

Circle: Primary User or Secondary User

1. Annuity Insurance Company: _____

    Website:_____ Telephone: _____

    Contract number: _____

    Name(s) on contract *(Owner)*: _____

    Where is the contract located? _____Type of annuity: _____

    Primary beneficiary and % *(% totals 100%)*

        _____ % _____ _____ % _____

        _____ % _____ _____ % _____

    Contingent beneficiary and % *(% totals 100%)*

        _____ % _____ _____ % _____

        _____ % _____ _____ % _____

    How do you receive statements? _____

Payout/Income: Do you receive funds from this annuity? Yes or No

    If yes: When do you receive funds? *(Monthly, quarterly, annually, etc.)* _____

    Where/How do you receive funds? *(via check, direct deposit/checking, etc.)* _____

        Does payment continue for someone else? Yes or No If yes: Who? _____

    Payout details: _____

Deposit: Do you add money into this annuity? Yes or No

    If yes: When? *(Annually/March, bi-annually, monthly)* _____

    Deposit details: _____

Any riders or spousal benefits? _____

Circle: Primary User or Secondary User

2. Annuity Insurance Company: _____

    Website:_____ Telephone: _____

    Contract number: _____

    Name(s) on contract *(Owner)*: _____

    Where is the contract located? _____Type of annuity: _____

    Primary beneficiary and % *(% totals 100%)*

        _____ % _____ _____ % _____

        _____ % _____ _____ % _____

    Contingent beneficiary and % *(% totals 100%)*

        _____ % _____ _____ % _____

        _____ % _____ _____ % _____

    How do you receive statements? _____

Payout/Income: Do you receive funds from this annuity? Yes or No

    If yes: When do you receive funds? *(Monthly, quarterly, annually, etc.)* _____

    Where/How do you receive funds? *(via check, direct deposit/checking, etc.)* _____

    Does payment continue for someone else? Yes or No If yes: Who? _____

    Payout details: _____

Deposit: Do you add money into this annuity? Yes or No

    If yes: When? *(Annually/March, bi-annually, monthly)* _____

    Deposit details: _____

Any riders or spousal benefits? _____

6

Circle: Primary User   or   Secondary User

3. Annuity Insurance Company: _____

      Website:_____ Telephone: _____

      Contract number: _____

      Name(s) on contract *(Owner)*: _____

      Where is the contract located? _____Type of annuity: _____

      Primary beneficiary and % *(% totals 100%)*

        _____ % _____ _____ % _____

        _____ % _____ _____ % _____

      Contingent beneficiary and % *(% totals 100%)*

        _____ % _____ _____ % _____

        _____ % _____ _____ % _____

      How do you receive statements? _____

Payout/Income: Do you receive funds from this annuity?　　　Yes or No

   If yes: When do you receive funds? *(Monthly, quarterly, annually, etc.)* _____

   Where/How do you receive funds? *(via check, direct deposit/checking, etc.)* _____

     Does payment continue for someone else? Yes or No　　If yes: Who? _____

   Payout details: _____

Deposit: Do you add money into this annuity?　　　　　Yes or No

   If yes: When? *(Annually/March, bi-annually, monthly)* _____

   Deposit details: _____

Any riders or spousal benefits? _____

Circle: Primary User   or   Secondary User

4. Annuity Insurance Company: _____

      Website:_____ Telephone: _____

      Contract number: _____

      Name(s) on contract *(Owner)*: _____

      Where is the contract located? _____Type of annuity: _____

      Primary beneficiary and % *(% totals 100%)*

        _____ % _____ _____ % _____

        _____ % _____ _____ % _____

      Contingent beneficiary and % *(% totals 100%)*

        _____ % _____ _____ % _____

        _____ % _____ _____ % _____

      How do you receive statements? _____

Payout/Income: Do you receive funds from this annuity?　　　Yes or No

   If yes: When do you receive funds? *(Monthly, quarterly, annually, etc.)* _____

   Where/How do you receive funds? *(via check, direct deposit/checking, etc.)* _____

     Does payment continue for someone else? Yes or No　　If yes: Who? _____

   Payout details: _____

Deposit: Do you add money into this annuity?　　　　　Yes or No

   If yes: When? *(Annually/March, bi-annually, monthly)* _____

   Deposit details: _____

Any riders or spousal benefits? _____

6

Retirement Accounts	Primary User	Secondary User
Do you have an IRA? If yes: How many?	Yes or No # _____	Yes or No # _____
If yes: Do you have a Traditional IRA? Joint IRA SEP IRA? ROTH IRA? SIMPLE IRA? Other _____	 Yes or No Yes or No Yes or No Yes or No Yes or No Yes or No	 Yes or No Yes or No Yes or No Yes or No Yes or No Yes or No
Do you have a 401(k)? If yes: How many?	Yes or No # _____	Yes or No # _____
Do you have a 403(b)? If yes: How many?	Yes or No # _____	Yes or No # _____
Do you have a pension plan? If yes: How many?	Yes or No # _____	Yes or No # _____
Do you have a profit-sharing plan? If yes: How many?	Yes or No # _____	Yes or No # _____
Do you have a SEP or SARSEP plan? (Simplified Employee Pension or Salary Reduction Simplified Employee Pension) If yes: How many?	Yes or No # _____	Yes or No # _____
Do you have a defined benefits plan? If yes: How many?	Yes or No # _____	Yes or No # _____
Do you have a government pension? If yes: How many?	Yes or No # _____	Yes or No # _____
Do you have a 457 plan? If yes: How many?	Yes or No # _____	Yes or No # _____
OTHER Retirement plan: _____ If yes: How many?	Yes or No # _____	Yes or No # _____
OTHER Retirement plan: _____ If yes: How many?	Yes or No # _____	Yes or No # _____

6

Note: If any of your retirement accounts will continue for your spouse after your passing, ensure they are set up correctly and spousal continuation documents are prepared.

In addition, make sure your accounts have accurate primary and secondary beneficiaries listed.

Retirement Account Details

Circle: Primary User   or   Secondary User

1. **Company Name:** _____
    Retirement Plan Name / Type: _____
    Account number: _____ Employer sponsored?   Yes or No
    Website: _____ Telephone: _____
    How do you receive statements? _____
    Do you make contributions?   Yes or No
       If yes: How/When: *(Annual check, monthly electronic deposit, employee payroll, etc.)* _____
    Are you receiving a required minimum distribution (RMD)?   Yes or No
       If yes: How/Where: *(Check in the mail, direct deposit into checking, etc.)* _____
       If receiving funds/payout: Month/Year started:_____End date: _____
    Primary beneficiary and % *(% totals 100%)*
       _____ % _____ _____ % _____
       _____ % _____ _____ % _____
       _____ % _____ _____ %_____
    Contingent beneficiary and % *(% totals 100%)*
       _____ % _____ _____ % _____
       _____ % _____ _____ % _____
       _____ % _____ _____ %_____
       Will this account continue for your spouse?   Yes or No
Additional details:

Circle: Primary User   or   Secondary User

2. **Company Name:** _____
    Retirement Plan Name / Type: _____
    Account number: _____ Employer sponsored?   Yes or No
    Website: _____ Telephone: _____
    How do you receive statements? _____
    Do you make contributions?   Yes or No
       If yes: How/When: *(Annual check, monthly electronic deposit, employee payroll, etc.)* _____
    Are you receiving a required minimum distribution (RMD)?   Yes or No
       If yes: How/Where: *(Check in the mail, direct deposit into checking, etc.)* _____
       If receiving funds/payout: Month/Year started:_____End date: _____
    Primary beneficiary and % *(% totals 100%)*
       _____ % _____ _____ % _____
       _____ % _____ _____ % _____
       _____ % _____ _____ %_____
    Contingent beneficiary and % *(% totals 100%)*
       _____ % _____ _____ % _____
       _____ % _____ _____ % _____
       _____ % _____ _____ %_____
       Will this account continue for your spouse?   Yes or No
Additional details:

6

Retirement Account Details

3. **Company Name:** _____

    Retirement Plan Name / Type: _____

    Account number: _____ Website: _____

    Employer sponsored? Yes or No Telephone: _____

    How do you receive statements? _____

    Do you make contributions?   Yes or No

        If yes: How/When: *(Annual check, monthly electronic deposit, employee payroll, etc.)* _____

      Are you receiving a required minimum distribution (RMD)?   Yes or No

        If yes: How/Where: *(Check in the mail, direct deposit into checking, etc.)* _____

        If receiving funds/payout: Month/Year started:_____End date: _____

      Primary beneficiary and % *(% totals 100%)*

        _____ % _____   _____ % _____

        _____ % _____   _____ % _____

        _____ % _____   _____ % _____

      Contingent beneficiary and % *(% totals 100%)*

        _____ % _____   _____ % _____

        _____ % _____   _____ % _____

        _____ % _____   _____ % _____

      Will this account continue for your spouse?   Yes or No

Additional details:

---

4. **Company Name:** _____

    Retirement Plan Name / Type: _____

    Account number: _____ Website: _____

    Employer sponsored? Yes or No Telephone: _____

    How do you receive statements? _____

    Do you make contributions?   Yes or No

        If yes: How/When: *(Annual check, monthly electronic deposit, employee payroll, etc.)* _____

      Are you receiving a required minimum distribution (RMD)?   Yes or No

        If yes: How/Where: *(Check in the mail, direct deposit into checking, etc.)* _____

        If receiving funds/payout: Month/Year started:_____End date: _____

      Primary beneficiary and % *(% totals 100%)*

        _____ % _____   _____ % _____

        _____ % _____   _____ % _____

        _____ % _____   _____ % _____

      Contingent beneficiary and % *(% totals 100%)*

        _____ % _____   _____ % _____

        _____ % _____   _____ % _____

        _____ % _____   _____ % _____

      Will this account continue for your spouse?   Yes or No

Additional details:

6

Retirement Account Details

Circle: **Primary User   or   Secondary User**

5. **Company Name:** _____
    Retirement Plan Name / Type: _____
    Account number: _____ Website: _____
    Employer sponsored?   Yes or No Telephone: _____
    How do you receive statements? _____
    Do you make contributions?   Yes or No
        If yes: How/When: *(Annual check, monthly electronic deposit, employee payroll, etc.)* _____
    Are you receiving a required minimum distribution (RMD)?   Yes or No
        If yes: How/Where: *(Check in the mail, direct deposit into checking, etc.)* _____
        If receiving funds/payout: Month/Year started:_____End date: _____
    Primary beneficiary and % *(% totals 100%)*

_____ % _____	_____ % _____
_____ % _____	_____ % _____
_____ % _____	_____ % _____

    Contingent beneficiary and % *(% totals 100%)*

_____ % _____	_____ % _____
_____ % _____	_____ % _____
_____ % _____	_____ % _____

        Will this account continue for your spouse?   Yes or No
Additional details:

Circle: **Primary User   or   Secondary User**

6. **Company Name:** _____
    Retirement Plan Name / Type: _____
    Account number: _____ Website: _____
    Employer sponsored?   Yes or No Telephone: _____
    How do you receive statements? _____
    Do you make contributions?   Yes or No
        If yes: How/When: *(Annual check, monthly electronic deposit, employee payroll, etc.)* _____
    Are you receiving a required minimum distribution (RMD)?   Yes or No
        If yes: How/Where: *(Check in the mail, direct deposit into checking, etc.)* _____
        If receiving funds/payout: Month/Year started:_____End date: _____
    Primary beneficiary and % *(% totals 100%)*

_____ % _____	_____ % _____
_____ % _____	_____ % _____
_____ % _____	_____ % _____

    Contingent beneficiary and % *(% totals 100%)*

_____ % _____	_____ % _____
_____ % _____	_____ % _____
_____ % _____	_____ % _____

        Will this account continue for your spouse?   Yes or No
Additional details:

6

Retirement Account Details

Circle: Primary User   or   Secondary User

7. **Company Name:** _____

    Retirement Plan Name / Type: _____

    Account number: _____ Employer sponsored? Yes or No

    Website: _____ Telephone: _____

    How do you receive statements? _____

    Do you make contributions?   Yes or No

       If yes: How/When: *(Annual check, monthly electronic deposit, employee payroll, etc.)* _____

    Are you receiving a required minimum distribution (RMD)?   Yes or No

       If yes: How/Where: *(Check in the mail, direct deposit into checking, etc.)* _____

       If receiving funds/payout: Month/Year started:_____End date: _____

    Primary beneficiary and % *(% totals 100%)*

      _____ % _____   _____ % _____

      _____ % _____   _____ % _____

      _____ % _____   _____ % _____

    Contingent beneficiary and % *(% totals 100%)*

      _____ % _____   _____ % _____

      _____ % _____   _____ % _____

      _____ % _____   _____ % _____

    Will this account continue for your spouse?   Yes or No

Additional details:

Circle: Primary User   or   Secondary User

8. **Company Name:** _____

    Retirement Plan Name / Type: _____

    Account number: _____ Employer sponsored? Yes or No

    Website: _____ Telephone: _____

    How do you receive statements? _____

    Do you make contributions?   Yes or No

       If yes: How/When: *(Annual check, monthly electronic deposit, employee payroll, etc.)* _____

    Are you receiving a required minimum distribution (RMD)?   Yes or No

       If yes: How/Where: *(Check in the mail, direct deposit into checking, etc.)* _____

       If receiving funds/payout: Month/Year started:_____End date: _____

    Primary beneficiary and % *(% totals 100%)*

      _____ % _____   _____ % _____

      _____ % _____   _____ % _____

      _____ % _____   _____ % _____

    Contingent beneficiary and % *(% totals 100%)*

      _____ % _____   _____ % _____

      _____ % _____   _____ % _____

      _____ % _____   _____ % _____

    Will this account continue for your spouse?   Yes or No

Additional details:

6

Retirement Account Details

Circle: Primary User   or   Secondary User

9. **Company Name:** _____

    Retirement Plan Name / Type: _____

    Account number: _____ Employer sponsored? Yes or No

    Website: _____ Telephone: _____

    How do you receive statements? _____

    Do you make contributions?   Yes or No

       If yes: How/When: *(Annual check, monthly electronic deposit, employee payroll, etc.)* _____

    Are you receiving a required minimum distribution (RMD)?   Yes or No

       If yes: How/Where: *(Check in the mail, direct deposit into checking, etc.)* _____

       If receiving funds/payout: Month/Year started:_____End date: _____

    Primary beneficiary and % *(% totals 100%)*

_____	% _____	_____	% _____
_____	% _____	_____	% _____
_____	% _____	_____	% _____

    Contingent beneficiary and % *(% totals 100%)*

_____	% _____	_____	% _____
_____	% _____	_____	% _____
_____	% _____	_____	% _____

       Will this account continue for your spouse?   Yes or No

Additional details:

Circle: Primary User   or   Secondary User

10. **Company Name:** _____

    Retirement Plan Name / Type: _____

    Account number: _____ Employer sponsored? Yes or No

    Website: _____ Telephone: _____

    How do you receive statements? _____

    Do you make contributions?   Yes or No

       If yes: How/When: *(Annual check, monthly electronic deposit, employee payroll, etc.)* _____

    Are you receiving a required minimum distribution (RMD)?   Yes or No

       If yes: How/Where: *(Check in the mail, direct deposit into checking, etc.)* _____

       If receiving funds/payout: Month/Year started:_____End date: _____

    Primary beneficiary and % *(% totals 100%)*

_____	% _____	_____	% _____
_____	% _____	_____	% _____
_____	% _____	_____	% _____

    Contingent beneficiary and % *(% totals 100%)*

_____	% _____	_____	% _____
_____	% _____	_____	% _____
_____	% _____	_____	% _____

       Will this account continue for your spouse?   Yes or No

Additional details:

6

Financial Interest	Primary User	Secondary User
Do you have a financial interest in a business?	Yes or No	Yes or No

If yes: Where is this document located?

      Provide details   Name

                             Telephone

                             Address

                             Type of business

                             What is the % of interest

Additional details:

Promissory Note	Primary User	Secondary User
Do you have a promissory note? If yes: How many?	Yes or No	Yes or No

If yes: Where is this document located?

      Provide details   Name *(with whom)*

                             Telephone

Additional details:

6

Commodities	Primary User	Secondary User
Do you own any or part of a commodity?	Yes or No	Yes or No

If yes: Where is this document located?

      Provide details   Name

                             Telephone

                             Address

                             Type of business

                             What is the % of interest

Additional details:

Money Transfer Service, Digital Wallet	Primary User	Secondary User

Do you use a money transfer service, digital wallet?
(Apple Pay, Android Pay, Venmo, Zelle, PayPal, Google Wallet, etc.)

Yes or No   Yes or No

If yes: How many?   #_____   #_____

Do you typically keep a balance?   Yes   No   Sometimes   Yes   No   Sometimes

---

Service Name:_____

App or Website:_____

Login credentials
    Username:_____
    Password:_____
    Email: _____
What account or credit card is linked: _____
_____

Service Name:_____

App or Website:_____

Login credentials
    Username:_____
    Password:_____
    Email: _____
What account or credit card is linked: _____
_____

Service Name:_____

App or Website:_____

Login credentials
    Username:_____
    Password:_____
    Email: _____
What account or credit card is linked: _____
_____

Service Name:_____

App or Website:_____

Login credentials
    Username:_____
    Password:_____
    Email: _____
What account or credit card is linked: _____
_____

Additional details: _____
_____
_____
_____

6

Unclaimed Property, Missing Money	Primary User	Secondary User

Have you checked if there is any unclaimed property or missing money under your name?

Yes   or   No   Yes   or   No

If yes: When was the last time you inquired/searched?   Date: _____   Date: _____

Additional details: _____
_____

> **Note:** When searching for missing funds, looking at all unclaimed property sites in the states you've been affiliated with is a good idea. If you have questions, consult with a professional.

Digital Assets	Primary User	Secondary User

Do you have any digital assets? Yes or No   Yes or No

This workbook has already covered a lot of digital assets, such as your computer, tablet, cell phone, device backup, file storage, emails, social media accounts, etc. Below, **list all other digital assets that hold value**.
(Cryptocurrencies; NTF's; digital assets trading platform; online betting account; blog content; digital rights to literature, music, or videos, etc.)

Do you use a digital assets management software? Yes or No   Yes or No
    If yes: How many? # _____   # _____
    Software name and details: _____
_____
_____

Type of Digital Asset: _____

Name: _____
Location/How to access: *(Website, app)* _____
_____
Name(s) on account: *(Account registration)* _____
_____
Login credentials
    Username: _____
    Password: _____
    PIN and/or Private Key: _____
    Email: _____
Additional details: _____
_____
_____

Type of Digital Asset: _____

Name: _____
Location/How to access: *(Website, app)* _____
_____
Name(s) on account: *(Account registration)* _____
_____
Login credentials
    Username: _____
    Password: _____
    PIN and/or Private Key: _____
    Email: _____
Additional details: _____
_____
_____

Type of Digital Asset: _____

Name: _____
Location/How to access: *(Website, app)* _____
_____
Name(s) on account: *(Account registration)* _____
_____
Login credentials
    Username: _____
    Password: _____
    PIN and/or Private Key: _____
    Email: _____
Additional details: _____
_____
_____

Type of Digital Asset: _____

Name: _____
Location/How to access: *(Website, app)* _____
_____
Name(s) on account: *(Account registration)* _____
_____
Login credentials
    Username: _____
    Password: _____
    PIN and/or Private Key: _____
    Email: _____
Additional details: _____
_____
_____

6

Digital Assets

Type of Digital Asset: _____

Name: _____
Location/How to access: *(Website, app)* _____

_____

Name(s) on account: *(Account registration)* _____

_____

Login credentials
    Username: _____
    Password: _____
    PIN and/or Private Key: _____
    Email: _____
Additional details: _____

_____

_____

Type of Digital Asset: _____

Name: _____
Location/How to access: *(Website, app)* _____

_____

Name(s) on account: *(Account registration)* _____

_____

Login credentials
    Username: _____
    Password: _____
    PIN and/or Private Key: _____
    Email: _____
Additional details: _____

_____

_____

Type of Digital Asset: _____

Name: _____
Location/How to access: *(Website, app)* _____

_____

Name(s) on account: *(Account registration)* _____

_____

Login credentials
    Username: _____
    Password: _____
    PIN and/or Private Key: _____
    Email: _____
Additional details: _____

_____

_____

Type of Digital Asset: _____

Name: _____
Location/How to access: *(Website, app)* _____

_____

Name(s) on account: *(Account registration)* _____

_____

Login credentials
    Username: _____
    Password: _____
    PIN and/or Private Key: _____
    Email: _____
Additional details: _____

_____

_____

6

Important Note for Digital Assets

Please contact a professional with any questions you may have regarding digital assets.

Have a discussion with an estate planning attorney to ensure your estate plan references digital assets (including beneficiaries) and documents allowing for resetting passwords. Consider asking how often you should relook at your estate plan regarding digital assets.

These types of assets may not have a physical branch to walk into for assistance. Passwords, crypto wallet access, private keys, etc., are essential to keep track of. Loved ones will need access to smartphones, cloud accounts, apps, online betting accounts, virtual currencies, and passcodes to access your digital assets.

Help prepare your loved ones and always remember to protect your privacy!

Step 6: Financial and Insurance

Date Completed: _____

Fun Memory

Way to go! You have completed Step 6!

Did a fun or interesting fact from your past come to mind while you were working on this Step?

Use the space below to share a memory with your loved ones. It could be a funny story about yourself, a loving memory, or a fascinating fact about a moment in your past. This will bring joy and a smile during challenging times. Instead of writing, share your favorite song, poem, or insert a picture!

Need ideas? Here are some suggestions to write about for Step 6:
Share a memorable college experience, the most expensive or regrettable purchase you've ever made; the first or best concert you attended; your favorite song and music group; or, if you could go back in time, what advice you would give your 20-year-old self, etc.

_____
_____
_____
_____
_____
_____
_____
_____
_____
_____
_____
_____
_____
_____
_____
_____
_____
_____
_____
_____
_____
_____

6

Step 7

Residence, Bills, and Loans

In Step 7, you will complete details that will be extremely helpful if someone needs to step in and take care of your home life, such as paying your bills or caring for your property.

Please **DO NOT WAIT** to complete this Step! Whether it's an accident, illness, or death, locating essential documents or paying bills during a difficult time can be emotional, confusing, and overwhelming. Your loved ones need to be able to address each item in an organized manner rather than trying to figure out what needs to be changed, stopped, paid, or sold.

Step 7 will help you record details relating to the expenses for your home - whether you own, rent or live in a facility - and for any other real estate that you own, lease, or rent. (May differ depending on the state/country.)

Ask Yourself, what can you do now to help make things easier for your loved ones later? You can help shift their overwhelming feelings of anxiety, worry, or grief to more positive emotions like feeling gratitude and appreciation! Recording this information will also simplify the process, helping your loved ones make efficient use of their time.

Here's how Step 7 can be helpful:

- Loved ones will need to know where to find your original documents, such as the property title.

- List details such as whose name is on the deed or how you pay the mortgage, or if you have a reverse mortgage. Provide contact information for any property owner associations, homeowners association fees, and how and when you pay any real estate taxes.

- If you rent, list the contact for your landlord, as well as lease details and even the number of your parking space.

- If you live in a facility such as a long-term care center, include the name of your social worker or advocate.

- Be sure to include insurance policy details. Often loved ones know they need to cancel homeowners' or renters' insurance policies but have no idea what company to contact.

- If you have a security system, video surveillance, or a doorbell camera, list all the necessary details.

- If you have a timeshare, provide the property name, ownership details, expenses, and where the paperwork is located.

- If your spouse does not pay the bills, write down instructions for them or tell someone else who can assist or take over regular payments.

- Describe daily household chores and home maintenance basics, such as where to turn off the water or how to maintain the swimming pool or take care of the garden.

Ask Yourself, during a crisis, is there a loved one or friend who might do tasks such as watering plants or taking out the trash? This is a good time to have a conversation with someone about what might need to be done.

Please take a moment to review what's included in this Step:

STEP 7: RESIDENCE, BILLS, AND LOANS
- Residence, Property - Where You Live
  - Facility Living, Social Worker/Advocate
- 1. Rent/Lease (Number 1)
  - Landlord Contact Info, Rental/Lease Agreement, Parking, Rent Payment, Rental Insurance
- 2. Rent/Lease (Number 2) *(Details same as Number 1)*
- 1. Homeowner/Property Owner (Number 1)
  - Property Address, Details, Mortgage, Real Estate Tax (Property Tax), Title, Title Insurance, Deed, Declaration of Homestead, Community Property, Association/Dues, Insurance
- 2. Homeowner/Property Owner (Number 2) *(Details same as Number 1)*
- Umbrella Insurance Policy
- Home Equity Line of Credit, Home Equity Loan
- Loans (Personal, Private, Student), Details
- Section 1: Set of Bills (Property Number 1)
  - Security System, Alarm, Smart Home Device, Cameras, Video Surveillance
  - Oil, Electric, Gas, Propane, Water, Sewer, Septic System
  - Boiler/Furnace, Pellet/Wood-Burning Stove, Central Air Conditioning, Thermostat, Other
  - Cable Television, Internet, Telephone Landline, Mobile/Cell Phone(s)
  - House Cleaning, Disposal/Trash Removal and Recycling, Pest Control, Landscaper, Lawn Treatments, Snow Removal, Irrigation
  - Swimming Pool
  - Credit Card(s), Credit Service/Monitoring
  - Other
- Section 2: Set of Bills (Property Number 2) *(Details same as Number 1)*
- Home Improvements, Projects, Warranties
- Storage Unit, Storage Facility
- Step 7 Completion Date and Fun Memory!

Step 7: NOTE TO LOVED ONES

In Step 7, your loved one has listed details regarding their residence, property, bills, and loans that will help should you need to take over caring for their home.

This Step provides you with a comprehensive list so you can easily address each item and what may need to be stopped, paid, changed, transferred, or sold. Take a moment and review the entire Step to get an understanding of what you are dealing with.

How can this Step be helpful?

- If your loved one has passed away, this list will help if you need to change the name, ownership, and/or contact details associated with home accounts and policies. Or, maybe you need to cancel bills or services that are no longer needed.

- Keeping bills up-to-date during an accident or illness will keep your loved one's credit score from plummeting and prevent bills from going to collection.

- If your situation requires you to sell or transfer the ownership of the real estate, please make sure to reach out to the appropriate legal and real estate professionals for assistance.

- If your situation requires an estate sale, gather any appraisals, and decide what will be sold, kept, or gifted. Review the inventory lists specified in Step 5 and in EXTRAS.

- Decide what to do with any outstanding home improvement projects, and don't forget about cleaning out any storage units or items stored in another location.

This is an emotional time for you. Remember, everything does not need to be done in one day. Allow yourself to take your time and feel gratitude that this is all organized for you to handle one item at a time.

7

Residence, Property Where You Live	Primary User	Secondary User	Joint
Are you a **homeowner or renter**?	Homeowner or Renter	Homeowner or Renter	Homeowner or Renter
How many properties do you **own**? *(Include: residence, secondary residence, land, condo, co-op, income property, etc.)*	# _____	# _____	# _____
How many properties do you **rent/lease**? *(Include: residence, land, condo, investment property, barn, etc.)*	# _____	# _____	# _____
Facility Living: Do you live in a facility? If yes: What type of facility? *(Assisted living, adult home, nursing home, independent living apartment, LTC center, etc.).*	Yes or No _____	Yes or No _____	Yes or No _____

If none of these options apply to you, please specify your primary living situation:

_____

_____

_____

If you live in a facility:

Facility Living	Primary User	Secondary User
Facility Name: Address:	_____ _____ _____	_____ _____ _____
Contact person's name: Telephone:	_____ _____	_____ _____

Social Worker/Advocate:

	Primary User	Secondary User
Do you have a social worker?	Yes or No	Yes or No
Do you have an advocate?	Yes or No	Yes or No
If yes: Name: Telephone:	_____ _____	_____ _____

Additional details: _____

_____

_____

_____

_____

_____

_____

_____

7

Rent/Lease　　(Number 1)　　(If you do not have Rent/Lease, skip this section)

Circle:　Primary User　or　Secondary User　or　Joint

1. Rent/Lease

Street_____Apartment/Suite_____

City_____State_____Zip_____

What do you rent or lease? *(Apartment, house, barn, etc.)* _____

Do you sublet?　Yes　or　No　　If yes: Details: _____

_____

Landlord's Contact Information

Name_____

Address_____

Telephone_____Email_____

Rental/Lease Agreement

Name(s) listed on the document _____

Where is the document located? _____

Lease term_____Lease end date _____

Additional lease terms:_____

Parking

Do you have a designated parking area?　　Yes　or　No　Details:_____

If yes: Do you pay for the parking spot?　　Yes　or　No

　　　　Cost for parking: $_____How do you pay? _____

Rent Payment

When is the rent due? *(Monthly on the 1st, etc.)* _____

How do you pay? _____
(Handwritten check, automatic from checking, auto-renewal on VISA credit card, etc.)

If automatic recurring payment, provide name of the bank, account type, or credit card:

_____

Rental Insurance

Do you have renter's insurance?　Yes　or　No

　　If yes: Company name _____

　　　　　Address_____

　　　　　Contact person's name_____Telephone _____

Policy number_____Policy expiration date _____

How do you pay your premium/Frequency of payment? _____
(Monthly/automatic from checking, annual/handwritten check, quarterly/deducted from money market, etc.)

If automatic recurring payment, provide name of the bank, account type, or credit card:

_____

Rent/Lease additional details: _____

_____

_____

_____

_____

_____

_____

7

Circle: Primary User   or   Secondary User   or   Joint

2. Rent/Lease

Street_____Apartment/Suite_____

City_____State_____Zip_____

What do you rent or lease? *(Apartment, house, barn, etc.)* _____

Do you sublet?   Yes or No   If yes: Details: _____

_____

Landlord's Contact Information

Name_____

Address_____

Telephone_____Email_____

Rental/Lease Agreement

Name(s) listed on the document _____

Where is the document located? _____

Lease term_____Lease end date _____

Additional lease terms:_____

Parking

Do you have a designated parking area?   Yes or No   Details:_____

If yes: Do you pay for the parking spot?   Yes or No

Cost for parking: $_____How do you pay? _____

Rent Payment

When is the rent due? *(Monthly on the 1st, etc.)* _____

How do you pay? _____

(Handwritten check, automatic from checking, auto-renewal on VISA credit card, etc.)

If automatic recurring payment, provide name of the bank, account type, or credit card:

_____

Rental Insurance

Do you have renter's insurance?   Yes or No

If yes: Company name _____

Address_____

Contact person's name_____Telephone _____

Policy number_____Policy expiration date _____

How do you pay your premium/Frequency of payment? _____

(Monthly/automatic from checking, annual/handwritten check, quarterly/deducted from money market, etc.)

If automatic recurring payment, provide name of the bank, account type, or credit card:

_____

Rent/Lease additional details: _____

_____

_____

_____

_____

_____

_____

_____

7

Homeowner/Property Owner (Number 1)   (If you are not a property owner, skip section)

Circle: Primary User   or   Secondary User   or   Joint

1. Property Address

Street_____Apartment/Suite _____

City_____State_____Zip_____

County _____

Is this your primary residence?   Yes or No

Is this your secondary residence?   Yes or No

Did you inherit this property?   Yes or No

Type of property: *(Single-family house, condo, apartment, townhouse, land, etc.)* _____

If land: Lot information: _____

Any structures on land, or is it vacant?_____

Is this land community property?   Yes or No

Is this a farm?   Yes or No   If yes: Farm details: _____

_____

If not primary residence: What is the purpose of this property? _____

(Vacation home, rental income, providing a home for a child, land, investment, etc.)

If property is used for rental income: Who do you rent to? How does the renter pay you?

Where do you keep the rental contract/agreement(s) for this property? Details: _____

_____

_____

Mortgage

Do you have a mortgage for this property?   Yes or No

If yes: Mortgage Company's Name: _____

Website:_____Telephone:_____

Account number: _____

Name(s) listed on the mortgage: _____

(First/ middle/ last, sole owner, trust name, joint tenants in common, joint with rights of survivorship, etc.)

Type of mortgage: *(Fixed, adjustable, reverse, etc.)* _____

Mortgage documents are located where? _____

Does this **mortgage have an escrow account**?   Yes or No

If yes: What is paid from escrow? *(Insurance and/or taxes)* _____

_____

When is the mortgage **payment due**? *(Monthly on 1ˢᵗ, etc.)* _____

_____

How do you pay? _____

(Handwritten check, automatic from checking, auto-renewal from money market, etc.)

If automatic recurring payment, provide name of the bank, account type, or credit card:

_____

How do you receive bill/statement? *(Paper via mail or paperless via electronic delivery)* _____

If electronic: How? Email: _____

Do you **have/pay private mortgage insurance (PMI)**?   Yes or No

If yes: PMI details: _____

Is this a **reverse mortgage**?   Yes or No   If yes: Details: _____

_____

Do you have a **2ⁿᵈ Mortgage**?   Yes or No   If yes: Details: _____

_____

If no: When was the **mortgage paid in full**? (Month/Year) _____

Where is the pay-off paperwork located? _____

7

Real Estate Tax (Property Tax)

Town/City and State: _____

Is real estate tax paid by your mortgage company via escrow, or do you direct pay? _____

    If escrow: See Mortgage section above.

    If direct pay: How do you receive the bill/statement? *(Paper bill in the mail, electronically/email address, etc.)*

_____

When are taxes due? *(Quarterly on 15th, monthly on 1st, etc.)*_____

How do you make the payment/Frequency of payment? _____

(Monthly/automatic from checking, annual/handwritten check, quarterly/deducted from money market, etc.)

    If automatic recurring payment, provide name of the bank, account type, or credit card:

_____

Additional details: _____

_____

_____

Title, Title Insurance, Deed, Declaration of Homestead, Community Property

Title: Do you have the original title?   Yes or No

        If yes: Where is the title located? _____

Name(s) listed on the title: _____

(First/middle/last, sole owner, trust name, joint tenants in common, joint with rights of survivorship, etc.)

Title Insurance: Do you have title insurance?   Yes or No

    If yes: Name of the title insurance company:_____

        Where is the title insurance paperwork located? _____

        Details: _____

Deed: Do you have the original deed?   Yes or No

        If yes: Where is the deed located? _____

What type of deed? *(QuickClaim, general warranty, etc.)* _____

Name(s) listed on deed: _____

(First/middle/last, sole owner, trust name, joint tenants in common, joint with rights of survivorship, etc.)

Declaration of Homestead: Do you have a Declaration of Homestead? Yes or No

        If yes: Where is the paperwork located? _____

           What state?_____Details: _____

Community Property: Is this community property?   Yes or No

        If yes: How is the property owned? _____

        Details: _____

Additional details: (Title, Deed, Title Insurance, Declaration of Homestead, Community Property)

_____

_____

_____

7

Association (Homeowners Association (HOA)/ **Property Owners Association** (POA)**)**

Do you have an association with this property?   Yes or No

    If yes: Name of association: _____

              Contact information: _____

              _____

Association Dues: Do you have association dues? *(Condo fee)*   Yes or No

          How do you receive the bill/statement? *(Paper bill in the mail, electronically/email address, etc.)*

          _____

          When is payment due? *(Quarterly/15th, monthly/1st, annually/December, etc.)* _____

          How do you make the payment/Frequency of payment? _____

          (Monthly/automatic from checking, annual/handwritten check, quarterly/deducted from money market, etc.)

          If automatic recurring payment, provide name of the bank, account type, or credit card:

          _____

Additional details: _____

_____

_____

Insurance

Do you have insurance on this property?   Yes or No

    If yes: Type of insurance? _____

              (Homeowners' insurance, vacant property insurance, liability, land insurance, etc.)

              Insurance company name: _____

              Website:_____Telephone:_____

              Contact person's name _____

              Policy number_____Policy expiration date:_____

Is this policy paid by your mortgage company via escrow, or do you direct pay? _____

    If Escrow: See Mortgage section above.

    If Direct Pay: How do you receive the bill/statement? *(Paper bill in the mail, electronically/email address, etc.)*

    _____

    How do you pay your premium/Frequency of payment? _____

    (Monthly/automatic from checking, annual/handwritten check, quarterly/deducted from money market, etc.)

    If automatic recurring payment, provide name of the bank, account type, or credit card: _____

    _____

Do you have an insurance rider(s)?   Yes or No

    If yes: List the specific items on the insurance rider(s) *(Jewelry, antiques, oriental rug, etc.)*

    _____

    _____

    _____

    _____

    _____

    Where are your appraisals located? _____

    Note: Providing the appropriate appraisals and photos to your insurance company will ensure that your valuable personal items are properly insured.

Additional details: _____

_____

_____

Homeowner/Property Owner (Number 2) (If you do not have a 2nd property, skip section)

Circle: Primary User   or   Secondary User   or   Joint
2. Property Address

Street_____Apartment/Suite_____

City_____State_____Zip_____

Is this your primary residence?   Yes or No   County _____

Is this your secondary residence?   Yes or No

Did you inherit this property?   Yes or No

Type of property: *(Single-family house, condo, apartment, townhouse, land, etc.)* _____

If land: Lot information: _____

_____

Any structures on land, or is it vacant?_____

Is this land community property?   Yes or No

Is this a farm?   Yes or No   If yes: Farm details: _____

_____

If not primary residence: What is the purpose of this property? _____

(Vacation home, rental income, provide a home for a child, land, investment, etc.)

If property is used for rental income: Who do you rent to? How does renter pay you?

Where do you keep the rental contract/agreement(s) for this property? Details: _____

_____

Mortgage

Do you have a mortgage for this property?   Yes or No

If yes: Mortgage Company's Name: _____

Website:_____Telephone:_____

Account number: _____

Name(s) listed on the mortgage: _____

(First/middle/last, sole owner, trust name, joint tenants in common, joint with rights of survivorship, etc.)

Type of mortgage: *(Fixed, adjustable, reverse, etc.)* _____

Mortgage documents are located where? _____

Does this **mortgage have an escrow account**?   Yes or No

If yes: What is paid from escrow? *(Insurance and/or taxes)* _____

When is mortgage **payment due**? *(Monthly on 1st, etc.)* _____

_____

How do you pay? _____

(Handwritten check, automatic from checking, auto-renewal from money market, etc.)

If automatic recurring payment, provide name of the bank, account type, or credit card:

_____

How do you receive bill/statement? *(Paper via mail or paperless via electronic delivery)* _____

If electronic: How? Email: _____

Do you **have/pay private mortgage insurance (PMI)?** Yes or No

If yes: PMI details: _____

Is this a **reverse mortgage**? Yes or No   If yes: Details: _____

_____

Do you have a **2nd mortgage**?   Yes or No   If yes: Details: _____

_____

If no: When was the **mortgage paid in full**? (Month/Year) _____

Where is the pay-off paperwork located? _____

Real Estate Tax (Property Tax)

Town/City and State: _____

Is real estate tax paid by your mortgage company via escrow, or do you direct pay? _____

    If escrow: See Mortgage section above.

    If direct pay: How do you receive the bill/statement? *(Paper bill in the mail, electronically/email address, etc.)*

_____

When are taxes due? *(Quarterly on 15th, monthly on 1st, etc.)* _____

How do you make the payment/Frequency of payment? _____

(Monthly/automatic from checking, annual/handwritten check, quarterly/deducted from money market, etc.)

    If automatic recurring payment, provide name of the bank, account type, or credit card:

_____

Additional details: _____

_____

_____

Title, Title Insurance, Deed, Declaration of Homestead, Community Property

Title: Do you have the original title?   Yes or No

        If yes: Where is the title located? _____

Name(s) listed on the title: _____

(First/middle/last, sole owner, trust name, joint tenants in common, joint with rights of survivorship, etc.)

Title Insurance: Do you have title Insurance?   Yes or No

    If yes: Name of title insurance company: _____

        Where is the title insurance paperwork located? _____

        Details: _____

Deed: Do you have the original deed?   Yes or No

        If yes: Where is the deed located? _____

What type of deed? *(QuickClaim, general warranty, etc.)* _____

Name(s) listed on deed: _____

(First/middle/last, sole owner, trust name, joint tenants in common, joint with rights of survivorship, etc.)

Declaration of Homestead: Do you have a Declaration of Homestead? Yes or No

        If yes: Where is the paperwork located? _____

          What state?_____Details: _____

Community Property: Is this community property?   Yes or No

        If yes: How is the property owned? _____

        Details: _____

Additional details: (Title, Deed, Title Insurance, Declaration of Homestead, Community Property) _____

_____

_____

_____

7

Association (Homeowners Association (HOA)/ Property Owners Association (POA))

Do you have an association with this property?   Yes or No

    If yes: Name of association: _____

            Contact information: _____

            _____

Association Dues: Do you have association dues? *(Condo fee)*   Yes or No

        How do you receive the bill/statement? *(Paper bill in the mail, electronically/email address, etc.)*

_____

        When is the payment due? *(Quarterly/15th, monthly/1st, annually/December, etc.)* _____

        How do you make the payment/Frequency of payment? _____
        (Monthly/automatic from checking, annual/handwritten check, quarterly/deducted from money market, etc.)
        If automatic recurring payment, provide name of the bank, account type, or credit card:

_____

Additional details: _____

_____
_____

Insurance

Do you have insurance on this property?   Yes or No

    If yes: Type of insurance? _____
          (Homeowners' insurance, vacant property insurance, liability, land insurance, etc.)
          Insurance company name: _____
          Website:_____Telephone:_____
          Contact person's name _____
          Policy number_____Policy expiration date:_____

Is this policy paid by your mortgage company via escrow, or do you direct pay? _____

    If escrow: See Mortgage section above.

    If direct pay: How do you receive the bill/statement? *(Paper bill in the mail, electronically/email address, etc.)*

_____

        How do you pay your premium/Frequency of payment? _____
        (Monthly/automatic from checking, annual/handwritten check, quarterly/deducted from money market, etc.)
        If automatic recurring payment, provide name of the bank, account type, or credit card: _____

_____

Do you have an insurance rider(s)?   Yes or No

    If yes: List the specific items on the insurance rider(s) *(Jewelry, antiques, oriental rug, etc.)*

_____
_____
_____
_____
_____

    Where are your appraisals located: _____

Note: Providing the appropriate appraisals and photos to your insurance company will ensure that your valuable personal items are properly insured.

Additional details: _____

_____

7

Umbrella Insurance Policy

Do you have an umbrella policy?   Yes or No

    If yes: Company Name: _____

        Website:_____Telephone:_____

        Contact person's name: _____

        Policy number:_____Policy expiration date:: _____

        Where is the policy located? _____

        How do you receive the bill/statement? *(Paper bill in the mail, electronically/email address, etc.)*

        _____

        How do you pay/Frequency of payment? _____
        (Monthly/automatic from checking, annual/handwritten check, quarterly/deducted from money market, etc.)

        If automatic recurring payment, provide name of the bank, account type, or credit card:

        _____

Additional details: _____

_____

_____

_____

_____

Home Equity Line of Credit, Home Equity Loan

Do you have a Home Equity Line of Credit (HELOC) or a Home Equity Loan (HEL)?   Yes or No

    If yes: What do you have, a HELOC or HEL or both? _____

        Property address: _____

        Company: (Lender name) _____

        Website:_____Telephone:_____

        _____

        Account number: _____

        Name(s) on account: _____

        Where is the paperwork located? _____

        How do you receive the bill/statement? *(Paper bill in the mail, electronically/email address, etc.)*

        _____

        How do you pay/Frequency of payment? _____
        (Monthly/automatic from checking, annual/handwritten check, quarterly/deducted from money market, etc.)

        If automatic recurring payment, provide name of the bank, account type, or credit card:

        _____

Additional details: _____

_____

_____

_____

_____

7

Loans (Personal, Private, Student)	Primary User	Secondary User	Joint
Do you have any personal/private loans? If yes: How many?	Yes or No # _____	Yes or No # _____	Yes or No # _____
Do you have any student loans? If yes: How many private student loans?	Yes or No # _____	Yes or No # _____	Yes or No # _____
How many federal student loans?	# _____	# _____	# _____
Just In Case scenario of death: Will any of your loans be completely discharged?	Yes or No	Yes or No	Yes or No

Loan Details

Circle: Primary User or Secondary User or Joint

1. **Loan   Type of Loan:** _____
    Company: (Lender name) _____
    Account number: _____
    Website:_____Telephone:_____
    Do you have a co-signer on the loan?   Yes or No
    Name(s) listed on loan: _____
    How do you receive the bill/statement? *(Paper bill in the mail, electronically/email address, etc.)*

    _____
    How do you pay/Frequency of payment? _____
    (Monthly/automatic from checking, annual/handwritten check, quarterly/deducted from money market, etc.)

    Loan term:_____Date of last payment: _____
    Additional details: _____

2. **Loan   Type of Loan:** _____
    Company: (Lender name) _____
    Account number: _____
    Website:_____Telephone:_____
    Do you have a co-signer on the loan?   Yes or No
    Name(s) listed on loan: _____
    How do you receive the bill/statement? *(Paper bill in the mail, electronically/email address, etc.)*

    _____
    How do you pay/Frequency of payment? _____
    (Monthly/automatic from checking, annual/handwritten check, quarterly/deducted from money market, etc.)

    Loan term:_____Date of last payment: _____
    Additional details: _____

7

Loan Details

Circle: Primary User   or   Secondary User   or   Joint

3. **Loan   Type of Loan:** _____
    Company: (Lender name) _____
    Account number: _____
    Website:_____Telephone:_____
    Do you have a co-signer on the loan?   Yes or No
    Name(s) listed on loan: _____
    How do you receive the bill/statement? *(Paper bill in the mail, electronically/email address, etc.)*

    _____
    How do you pay/Frequency of payment? _____
    (Monthly/automatic from checking, annual/handwritten check, quarterly/deducted from money market, etc.)

    Loan term:_____Date of last payment: _____

    Additional details: _____

4. **Loan   Type of Loan:** _____
    Company: (Lender name) _____
    Account number: _____
    Website:_____Telephone:_____
    Do you have a co-signer on the loan?   Yes or No
    Name(s) listed on loan: _____
    How do you receive the bill/statement? *(Paper bill in the mail, electronically/email address, etc.)*

    _____
    How do you pay/Frequency of payment? _____
    (Monthly/automatic from checking, annual/handwritten check, quarterly/deducted from money market, etc.)

    Loan term:_____Date of last payment: _____

    Additional details: _____

5. **Loan   Type of Loan:** _____
    Company: (Lender name) _____
    Account number: _____
    Website:_____Telephone:_____
    Do you have a co-signer on the loan?   Yes or No
    Name(s) listed on loan: _____
    How do you receive the bill/statement? *(Paper bill in the mail, electronically/email address, etc.)*

    _____
    How do you pay/Frequency of payment? _____
    (Monthly/automatic from checking, annual/handwritten check, quarterly/deducted from money market, etc.)

    Loan term:_____Date of last payment: _____

    Additional details: _____

7

Type of Bill	Do you have this bill? Yes or No	Company Name	Account Number	Telephone Website	Whose name is on the bill?	How do you receive this bill? Paper via mail or paperless via electronic delivery	If electronic delivery: Where? Email, online banking, etc.	How do you make payment? Check, online banking manual, automatic recurring payment	Notes
Security System									
Smart Home Device									

Section 1: Set of Bills   (Property Number 1)

In a Just In Case scenario of an accident, illness, or death, your loved ones or designated personal representative will need to know your bills. Include whose name(s) are listed on the bill, how you pay it (via check or online banking), and whether statements are received physically or electronically. Be specific about what you have and where to find it. This will help them to easily take over paying bills or act on cancellations if needed.

The following pages will provide details for all the bills located at this address: _____

Security System, Alarm, Smart Home Device, Cameras, Video Surveillance

Do you have a security system/alarm?   Yes or No   Do you have a doorbell camera?   Yes or No

Do you have a home automation system?   Yes or No   Do you have cameras?   Yes or No

Do you have video surveillance?   Yes or No

If yes: What kind of system do you have? (Include make and model)

What is the password or code? _____

Company name/Telephone that performs service/Maintenance:

_____

Location of panel/alarm(s)/camera(s):

_____

Provide step-by-step instructions or necessary details: *(How to access doorbell camera, do cameras have batteries or need charging, name of the app and username/password, etc.)*

Type of Bill	Do you have this bill? Yes or No	Company Name	Account Number	Telephone Website	Whose name is on the bill?	How do you receive this bill? Paper via mail or paperless via electronic delivery	If electronic delivery: Where? Email, online banking, etc.	How do you make payment? Check, online banking manual, automatic recurring payment	Notes
Oil									
Electric									
Gas									
Propane									
Water									
Sewer									
Septic System									

Additional details: _____

_____

<u>NOTE:</u> More details regarding the above bills on the next page.

7

Water

Do you have city/town water or a well? _____

Company name/Telephone that performs maintenance: _____

Do you have a hot water tank?   Yes or No

If yes: Where is the tank located? _____

When was tank installed? _____

Where/How to turn off water: _____

_____

Sewer/Septic System

Do you have a sewer or septic system? _____

Company name/Telephone that performs maintenance: _____

If sewer: Is sewer included in your water bill?   Yes or No

When was the system last pumped? _____

When was the last time the system was inspected? _____

Where is the paperwork located? _____

Additional details: _____

Septic System: What inspections, certifications, or compliance regulations do you have or need in order to help sell your property?

(Inspection/compliance certificate, a state might require a full inspection and needs pass Title V certification, or passing inspection within a certain time period, etc.)

Boiler/Furnace

Do you have a furnace or a boiler? _____

Company name/Telephone that performs maintenance: _____

Additional details: _____

Pellet Stove

Do you have a pellet stove?   Yes or No

Company name/Telephone that performs maintenance: _____

Additional details: _____

Wood-Burning Stove

Do you have a wood-burning stove?   Yes or No

Company name/Telephone that performs maintenance: _____

Additional details: _____

Central Air/Air Conditioning

Do you have central air or air conditioning?   Yes or No

Company name/Telephone that performs maintenance: _____

Additional details: _____

Other:

Company name/Telephone that performs maintenance: _____

Additional details: _____

Other:

Company name/Telephone that performs maintenance: _____

Additional details: _____

Thermostats:

Location/Details: _____

Is your thermostat digital?   Yes or No   Instructions: _____

If yes: Username/Password: _____

7

Type of Bill	Do you have this bill? Yes or No	Company Name	Account Number	Telephone Website	Whose name is on the bill?	How do you receive this bill? Paper via mail or paperless via electronic delivery	If electronic delivery: Where? Email, online banking, etc.	How do you make payment? Check, online banking manual, automatic recurring payment	Notes
Cable Television									
Internet									
Telephone Landline									

Do you have consolidated billing?   Yes or No
If yes: What services are on the combined bill? _____

1. Mobile Cell Phone									
2. Mobile Cell Phone									
3. Mobile Cell Phone									

Mobile/Cell phone(s)

How many mobile/cell phones are on your bill/plan?   # _____

Name(s) of the individuals who are on your bill/plan? _____

7

Type of Bill	Do you have this bill? Yes or No	Company Name	Account Number	Telephone Website	Whose name is on the bill?	How do you receive this bill? Paper via mail or paperless via electronic delivery	If electronic delivery: Where? Email, online banking, etc.	How do you make payment? Check, online banking manual, automatic recurring payment	Notes
House Cleaning									
Disposal Trash Removal									
Pest Control									
Landscaper									
Lawn Treatments									
Snow Removal									
Irrigation									

NOTE: More details regarding the above bills on the next page.

House Cleaning

When does house cleaning occur? *(Weekly/Tuesdays, bi-weekly, monthly/15th, etc.)* _____

Additional details: _____
_____

Pest Control

When does pest control occur? *(Monthly/15th, quarterly, etc.)* _____

Additional details: _____
_____

Snow Removal

What type of snow removal do they perform? *(Driveway, walkway, stairs, etc.)* _____

Additional details: _____
_____

Disposal/Trash Removal and Recycling

When does trash removal occur? *(Weekly/Tuesdays, bi-weekly, etc.)* _____

Additional details: *(Weekly curbside recycling pickup, manual drop-off, etc.)* _____

Landscaper/Lawn Treatments

What yard service(s) do they perform? *(Mow lawn only, spring and/or fall clean up(s), full yard services, etc.)* _____

Additional details: _____

Irrigation

Does someone open and close your irrigation system?   Yes   or   No

If yes: Who and when: _____

Additional details: _____

Swimming Pool

Do you have a swimming pool?   Yes   or   No

Do you have help maintaining your pool?   Yes   or   No   Details: _____

Company name/Telephone that performs service/maintenance: _____

Chemical(s) used and schedule: _____

Filter: (make and model) _____   How often do you clean your pool? _____

Provide step-by-step instructions or necessary details: _____
_____

Type of Bill	Do you have this bill? Yes or No	Company Name	Account Number	Telephone Website	Whose name is on the bill?	How do you receive this bill? Paper via mail or paperless via electronic delivery	If electronic delivery: Where? Email, online banking, etc.	How do you make payment? Check, online banking manual, automatic recurring payment	Notes: Type of credit card VISA, AMEX, MC, Discover, etc.
1. Credit Card									
2. Credit Card									
3. Credit Card									
4. Credit Card									
5. Credit Card									
6. Credit Card									

Credit card additional details: _____

_____

_____

_____

_____

_____

7

Type of Bill	Do you have this bill? Yes or No	Company Name	Account Number	Telephone Website	Whose name is on the bill?	How do you receive this bill? Paper via mail or paperless via electronic delivery	If electronic delivery: Where? Email, online banking, etc.	How do you make payment? Check, online banking manual, automatic recurring payment	Notes: Type of credit card VISA, AMEX, MC, Discover, etc.
7. Credit Card									
8. Credit Card									
9. Credit Card									
10. Credit Card									
11. Credit Card									
12. Credit Card									

Do you have an account with a credit service, card processing, reporting agency, credit monitoring or fraud resolution company?   Yes or No

Do you use a company or app that monitors your credit?   Yes or No

If yes: Company name: _____ Account number: _____

         Website: _____ Username: _____ Password: _____

If yes: Company name: _____ Account number: _____

         Website: _____ Username: _____ Password: _____

Have you recently pulled your credit report?   Yes or No   If yes: Where is it located? _____

Do you have a copy of your credit report?   Yes or No

7

Other: Use the space below for any additional bills you may have.

Type of Bill	Do you have this bill? Yes or No	Company Name	Account Number	Telephone Website	Whose name is on the bill?	How do you receive this bill? Paper via mail or paperless via electronic delivery	If electronic delivery: Where? Email, online banking, etc.	How do you make payment? Check, online banking manual, automatic recurring payment	Notes

Additional details: _____

_____

_____

_____

Note: Streaming services and App subscriptions are referenced in Step 1.

Section 2: Set of Bills (Property Number 2)

(If you do not have another property with a second set of bills skip section)

In a Just In Case scenario of an accident, illness, or death, your loved ones or designated personal representative will need to know your bills. Include whose name(s) are listed on the bill, how you pay it (via check or online banking), and whether statements are received physically or electronically. Be specific about what you have and where to find it. This will help them to easily take over paying bills or act on cancellations if needed.

The following pages will provide details for all the bills located at this address: _____

Security System, Alarm, Smart Home Device, Cameras, Video Surveillance

Do you have a security system/alarm?   Yes or No   Do you have a doorbell camera?   Yes or No

Do you have a home automation system?   Yes or No   Do you have cameras?   Yes or No

Do you have video surveillance?   Yes or No

If yes: What kind of system do you have? (Include make and model): _____

What is the password or code? _____

Company name/Telephone that performs service/Maintenance: _____

Location of panel/alarm(s)/camera(s): _____

Provide step-by-step instructions or necessary details: *(How to access doorbell camera, do cameras have batteries or need charging, name of the app and username/password, etc.)*

Type of Bill	Do you have this bill? Yes or No	Company Name	Account Number	Telephone Website	Whose name is on the bill?	How do you receive this bill? Paper via mail or paperless via electronic delivery	If electronic delivery: Where? Email, online banking, etc.	How do you make payment? Check, online banking manual, automatic recurring payment	Notes
Security System									
Smart Home Device									

7

161

Type of Bill	Do you have this bill? Yes or No	Company Name	Account Number	Telephone Website	Whose name is on the bill?	How do you receive this bill? Paper via mail or paperless via electronic delivery	If electronic delivery: Where? Email, online banking, etc.	How do you make payment? Check, online banking manual, automatic recurring payment	Notes
Oil									
Electric									
Gas									
Propane									
Water									
Sewer									
Septic System									

Additional details: _____

NOTE: More details regarding above bills on next page.

7

Water

Do you have city/town water or a well? _____

Company name/Telephone that performs maintenance: _____

Do you have a hot water tank?   Yes or No
    If yes: Where is the tank located? _____
    When was tank installed? _____
    Where/How to turn off water: _____
_____

Septic System: What inspections, certifications, or compliance regulations do you have or need in order to help sell your property?
(Inspection/compliance certificate, a state might require a full inspection and needs pass Title V certification, or passing inspection within a certain time period, etc.)

Sewer/Septic System

Do you have a sewer or septic system? _____

Company name/Telephone that performs maintenance: _____

If sewer: Is sewer included in your water bill?   Yes or No
When was the system last pumped? _____
When was the last time the system was inspected? _____
Where is the paperwork located? _____
Additional details: _____

Boiler/Furnace

Do you have a furnace or a boiler? _____

Company name/Telephone that performs maintenance: _____

Additional details: _____

Wood-Burning Stove

Do you have a wood-burning stove?   Yes or No

Company name/Telephone that performs maintenance: _____

Additional details: _____

Other:

Company name/Telephone that performs maintenance: _____

Additional details: _____

Pellet Stove

Do you have a pellet stove? Yes or No

Company name/Telephone that performs maintenance: _____

Additional details: _____

Central Air/Air Conditioning

Do you have central air or air conditioning?   Yes or No

Company name/Telephone that performs maintenance: _____

Additional details: _____

Other:

Company name/Telephone that performs maintenance: _____

Additional details: _____

Thermostats:

Location/Details: _____

Is your thermostat digital?   Yes or No   Instructions: _____

    If yes: Username/Password: _____

7

7

Type of Bill	Do you have this bill? Yes or No	Company Name	Account Number	Telephone Website	Whose name is on the bill?	How do you receive this bill? Paper via mail or paperless via electronic delivery	If electronic delivery: Where? Email, online banking, etc.	How do you make payment? Check, online banking manual, automatic recurring payment	Notes
Cable Television									
Internet									
Telephone Landline									

Cable TV/Internet/Telephone

Do you have consolidated billing?   Yes or No

If yes: What services are on the combined bill? _____

1. Mobile Cell Phone									
2. Mobile Cell Phone									
3. Mobile Cell Phone									

Mobile/Cell Phone(s)

How many mobile/cell phones are on your bill/plan?   # _____

Name(s) of the individuals who are on your bill/plan? _____

Type of Bill	Do you have this bill? Yes or No	Company Name	Account Number	Telephone Website	Whose name is on the bill?	How do you receive this bill? Paper via mail or paperless via electronic delivery	If electronic delivery: Where? Email, online banking, etc.	How do you make payment? Check, online banking manual, automatic recurring payment	Notes
House Cleaning									
Disposal Trash Removal									
Pest Control									
Landscaper									
Lawn Treatments									
Snow Removal									
Irrigation									

NOTE: More details regarding the above bills on the next page.

7

House Cleaning

When does house cleaning occur? *(Weekly/Tuesdays, bi-weekly, monthly/15th, etc.)*
_____

Additional details: _____

Pest Control

When does pest control occur? *(Monthly/15th, quarterly, etc.)* _____

Additional details: _____
_____

Snow Removal

What type of snow removal do they perform? *(Driveway, walkway, stairs, etc.)*
_____

Additional details: _____
_____

Disposal/Trash Removal and Recycling

When does trash removal occur? *(Weekly/Tuesdays, bi-weekly, etc.)*
_____

Additional details: *(Weekly curbside recycling pickup, manual drop-off, etc.)*
_____

Landscaper/Lawn Treatments

What yard service(s) do they perform? *(Mow lawn only, spring and/or fall clean up(s), full yard services, etc.)* _____

Additional details: _____

Irrigation

Does someone open and close your irrigation system?   Yes   or   No

If yes: Who and when: _____

Additional details: _____

Swimming Pool

Do you have a swimming pool?   Yes   or   No

Do you have help maintaining your pool?   Yes   or   No   Details: _____

Company Name/Telephone that performs service/maintenance: _____

Chemical(s) used and schedule: _____

Filter: (make and model) _____   How often do you clean your pool? _____

Provide step-by-step instructions or necessary details:
_____
_____

Type of Bill	Do you have this bill? Yes or No	Company Name	Account Number	Telephone Website	Whose name is on the bill?	How do you receive this bill? Paper via mail or paperless via electronic delivery	If electronic delivery: Where? Email, online banking, etc.	How do you make payment? Check, online banking manual, automatic recurring payment	Notes: Type of credit card VISA, AMEX, MC, Discover, etc.
1. Credit Card									
2. Credit Card									
3. Credit Card									
4. Credit Card									
5. Credit Card									
6. Credit Card									

Credit card additional details: _____

7

Type of Bill	Do you have this bill? Yes or No	Company Name	Account Number	Telephone Website	Whose name is on the bill?	How do you receive this bill? Paper via mail or paperless via electronic delivery	If electronic delivery: Where? Email, online banking, etc.	How do you make payment? Check, online banking manual, automatic recurring payment	Notes: Type of credit card VISA, AMEX, MC, Discover, etc.
7. Credit Card									
8. Credit Card									
9. Credit Card									
10. Credit Card									
11. Credit Card									
12. Credit Card									

Do you have an account with a credit service, card processing, reporting agency, credit monitoring or fraud resolution company?　Yes or No

Do you use a company or app that monitors your credit?　Yes or No

If yes:　Company name: _____　Account number: _____

　　　　Website: _____　Username: _____　Password: _____

I f yes:　Company name: _____　Account number: _____

　　　　Website: _____　Username: _____　Password: _____

Have you recently pulled your credit report?　Yes or No

Do you have a copy of your credit report?　Yes or No　If yes: Where is it located? _____

7

Other: Use the space below for any additional bills you may have.

Type of Bill	Do you have this bill? Yes or No	Company Name	Account Number	Telephone Website	Whose name is on the bill?	How do you receive this bill? Paper via mail or paperless via electronic delivery	If electronic delivery: Where? Email, online banking, etc.	How do you make payment? Check, online banking manual, automatic recurring payment	Notes

Additional details: _____

Note: Streaming services and App subscriptions are referenced in Step 1.

7

Home Improvements, Projects, Warranties

Do you have a home improvement list?   Yes or No

     If yes: Where is it located? _____

If your property needs to be sold, list any home improvements, projects, or issues that someone should be aware of.

Property Address	Home Improvement, Project, or Issue

Do you have any warranties that are still in effect?   Yes or No

     If yes: Provide details below.

Warranty for What	Warranty Location

Storage Unit, Storage Facility	Primary User	Secondary User

Do you have a storage unit or storage facility?   Yes or No   Yes or No

    If yes: How many?   # _____   # _____

1. Facility name: _____ Address: _____

    Unit # _____ Location of Unit: _____ Details: _____

       Keys or Combination   Location of Keys: _____ Combination: _____

2. Facility name: _____ Address: _____

    Unit # _____ Location of Unit: _____ Details: _____

       Keys or Combination   Location of Keys: _____ Combination: _____

3. Facility name: _____ Address: _____

    Unit # _____ Location of Unit: _____ Details: _____

       Keys or Combination   Location of Keys: _____ Combination: _____

Do you have any items stored at someone else's house?   Yes or No   Yes or No

    If yes: Details: _____

7

Step 7: Residence, Bills, and Loans

 **Date Completed:** _____

Fun Memory

Way to go! You have completed Step 7!

Did a fun or interesting fact from your past come to mind while you were working on this Step?

Use the space below to share a memory with your loved ones. It could be a funny story about yourself, a loving memory, or a fascinating fact about a moment in your past. This will bring joy and a smile during challenging times. Instead of writing, share your favorite song, poem, or insert a picture!

Need ideas? Here are some suggestions to write about for Step 7:

Share a personal story, a home improvement project, your experience with wallpaper, a funny encounter with a rodent in your home, a memorable snow-shoveling experience, the time it took to pay off your student loans, your favorite movie or TV show, etc.

_____
_____
_____
_____
_____
_____
_____
_____
_____
_____
_____
_____
_____
_____
_____
_____
_____
_____
_____
_____
_____

7

Step 8

Vehicles and Transportation

In Step 8, you will complete details about any vehicles you may own or lease. This includes all vehicles, not just your car. Please make sure to indicate if you own a motorcycle, boat, trailer, airplane, camper, RV, tractor, or any commercial vehicles.

Take the time now to locate all the documents associated with all your vehicles so your loved ones do not have to carry the burden of dealing with lost or misplaced titles, registrations, proof of insurance, or tax bills.

Ask Yourself, where are *all* the vehicle keys stored? Do you have any special tools that are needed for tires or trailers? Are there any combinations or locks needed for a truck toolbox? Are there any parts that you've stored in a garage or barn that might need to be re-installed before a vehicle is sold?

Here are some ways in which Step 8 can be helpful:

- Recording details regarding the loan or lease of your vehicles is imperative to make it easier when it comes time to transfer ownership, sell, or return the vehicle.

- Details pertaining to any memberships, such as satellite radio, AAA/CAA, or other automobile clubs and assistance programs, will be helpful if someone needs to cancel subscriptions or update them.

- Someone may need to return or cancel toll tags or stop payments on toll accounts. Make sure to record the information – including passwords and the appropriate credit card or bank information – needed to accomplish these tasks.

- Step 8 will allow someone to renew or cancel any parking passes, permits, or stickers you use for designated lots or access to places such as the beach, state park, or transfer station.

- Describe where you keep vehicle maintenance records and who usually does the work.

Whether you have one automobile or you are a collector with multiple vehicles, providing your loved ones with information ahead of time will help make the process easier for them in a Just In Case scenario of an accident, illness, or death.

8

STEP 8: VEHICLES AND TRANSPORTATION
- Vehicle Inventory
  - Automobile/Car, Motorcycle, Trailer, Snowmobile, RV, Camper, Aircraft, Bus, Commercial Vehicle, Other
- Vehicle Details (Number 1-8)
  - Year, Make, Model, Keys, Tax, Ownership, Loan/Lease, Title, Stickers, Insurance, Maintenance
- Passes
  - Electronic Toll Collection
  - Parking Pass; Disabled Permit; Bus, Subway, Train, Ferry Pass; Ride Sharing
- Automobile Club, Roadside Assistance, Group Association
- Sirius XM, Satellite Radio
- Step 8 Completion Date and Fun Memory!

Step 8: NOTE TO LOVED ONES

In Step 8, your loved one has prepared details relevant to any vehicles they own or lease, the transportation they use, any passes or permits they have, or any automobile clubs or emergency services they subscribe to.

How can this Step be helpful?

- You may need to continue making loan, lease, or insurance payments while your loved one is healing from an accident or illness. Making important payments while they recover helps keep things on track and avoids credit issues.

- This Step also lists the information you may need to obtain a disability parking permit or placard for your loved one while they recover from surgery or illness.

- You might need to locate the original title if you need to sell a vehicle and transfer the ownership to someone else. You may need to cancel insurance policies, as well as any permits, memberships, or roadside assistance programs associated with that vehicle.

- You may need to take over the responsibility of paying for or canceling a bus, train, or ferry pass, or shutting down a rideshare account.

- Perhaps you have to return or cancel a toll tag and stop any automatic payments associated with the account.

- This information will help you to sell a specialty vehicle such as a camper or boat if, for example, the money is needed for medical expenses.

Everyone's situation is different, so please take a moment to review this entire Step to learn where you need to focus.

8

Provide an inventory of all the vehicles you have.

Vehicle Inventory	Primary User	Secondary User
Do you have an automobile/car? If yes: How many?	Yes or No # _____	Yes or No # _____
Do you have a motorcycle? If yes: How many?	Yes or No # _____	Yes or No # _____
Do you have a trailer? If yes: How many?	Yes or No # _____	Yes or No # _____
Does the trailer have a hitch lock? If yes: Where is the storage location for the key/PIN?	Yes or No _____ _____	Yes or No _____ _____
Do you have a snowmobile? If yes: How many?	Yes or No # _____	Yes or No # _____
Do you have a recreational vehicle (RV)? If yes: How many?	Yes or No # _____	Yes or No # _____
Do you have a camper? If yes: How many?	Yes or No # _____	Yes or No # _____
Do you have an airplane or helicopter? If yes: How many?	Yes or No # _____	Yes or No # _____
Do you have a bus? If yes: How many?	Yes or No # _____	Yes or No # _____
Do you have a commercial vehicle? If yes: How many?	Yes or No # _____	Yes or No # _____
(Tractor, passenger vehicle, etc.) Other:_____ If yes: How many?	Yes or No # _____	Yes or No # _____
Other:_____ If yes: How many?	Yes or No # _____	Yes or No # _____
Other:_____ If yes: How many?	Yes or No # _____	Yes or No # _____
Other:_____ If yes: How many?	Yes or No # _____	Yes or No # _____

On the following pages, provide details for each of your vehicles.

8

Vehicle Details (Number 1)   (If you do not have a vehicle, skip section)

Circle: Primary User   or   Secondary User

1. Year_____Make_____Model_____

Plate number: _____State/Country issued: _____

Name(s) on registration: _____

Where is the registration kept?_____Registration renewal month: _____

Keys: Where are the keys located? _____

Door combination code: _____

Tax: Do you pay annual tax on this vehicle?   Yes or No

If yes: How/Where is the tax paid? _____
(Check mailed, paid in person at town hall, automatic deduction from account, etc.)

Ownership: Do you have a **loan** on this vehicle?   Yes or No

Do you **lease** this vehicle?   Yes or No

If yes: Loan or Lease, Company name:_____Telephone: _____

Account number: _____

How do you receive statements?   Mail or Electronic   Pay-off date:_____

If electronic, where/email: _____

How do you pay/Frequency of payment? _____

_____
(Annually via handwritten check, quarterly, monthly automatic from checking, auto-renewal on VISA credit card, etc.)

If no: You **own** this vehicle. Name(s) on the title: _____

Where is the **original title** located? _____

Stickers: Are there any stickers on this vehicle that would need attention?   Yes or No

If yes: What kind of sticker:*(Dump, beach, parking, etc.)*_____

Details: (How/When you pay, Where/How to cancel) _____

_____

_____

Insurance: Do you have insurance on this vehicle?   Yes or No

If yes: Insurance Company name:_____

Policy number:_____Telephone:_____

How do you receive statements?   Mail or Electronic

If electronic, where/email: _____

How do you pay/Frequency of payment? _____

_____
(Annually via handwritten check, quarterly, monthly automatic from checking, auto-renewal on VISA credit card, etc.)

Maintenance Records: Where do you keep the records? _____

Mechanic: *(Auto Technician)* Who does the maintenance/repairs? _____

_____

Important additional details: Include websites with login credentials, toolbox locks or combinations, the location of special tools required for tires or trailers, and detailed instructions, etc.

_____

_____

_____

8

Circle: Primary User   or   Secondary User

2.   Year_____Make_____Model_____

   Plate number: _____State/Country issued: _____

Name(s) on registration: _____

   Where is the registration kept?_____Registration renewal month: _____

Keys: Where are the keys located? _____

   Door combination code: _____

Tax: Do you pay annual tax on this vehicle?   Yes or No

   If yes: How/Where is the tax paid? _____
                             (Check mailed, paid in person at town hall, automatic deduction from account, etc.)

Ownership: Do you have a **loan** on this vehicle?   Yes or No

              Do you **lease** this vehicle?   Yes or No

   If yes: Loan or Lease, Company name:_____Telephone: _____

      Account number: _____

      How do you receive statements?   Mail or Electronic   Pay-off date:_____

      If electronic, where/email: _____

      How do you pay/Frequency of payment? _____

      _____
      (Annually via handwritten check, quarterly, monthly automatic from checking, auto-renewal on VISA credit card, etc.)

   If no: You **own** this vehicle. Name(s) on the title: _____

         Where is the **original title** located? _____

Stickers: Are there any stickers on this vehicle that would need attention?   Yes or No

   If yes: What kind of sticker:*(Dump, beach, parking, etc.)*_____

      Details: (How/When you pay, Where/How to cancel) _____

      _____

      _____

Insurance: Do you have insurance on this vehicle?   Yes or No

   If yes: Insurance Company name:_____

      Policy number:_____Telephone:_____

      How do you receive statements?   Mail or Electronic

      If electronic, where/email: _____

      How do you pay/Frequency of payment? _____

      _____
      (Annually via handwritten check, quarterly, monthly automatic from checking, auto-renewal on VISA credit card, etc.)

Maintenance Records: Where do you keep the records? _____

Mechanic: *(Auto Technician)* Who does the maintenance/repairs? _____

_____

Important additional details: Include websites with login credentials, toolbox locks or combinations, the location of special tools required for tires or trailers, and detailed instructions, etc.

_____

_____

_____

Vehicle Details (Number 3)

Circle: Primary User   or   Secondary User

3. Year_____Make_____Model_____

Plate number: _____State/Country issued: _____

Name(s) on registration: _____

Where is the registration kept?_____Registration renewal month: _____

Keys: Where are the keys located? _____

Door combination code: _____

Tax: Do you pay annual tax on this vehicle?   Yes or No

If yes: How/Where is the tax paid? _____
(Check mailed, paid in person at town hall, automatic deduction from account, etc.)

Ownership: Do you have a **loan** on this vehicle?   Yes or No

Do you **lease** this vehicle?   Yes or No

If yes: Loan or Lease, Company name:_____Telephone: _____

Account number: _____

How do you receive statements?   Mail or Electronic   Pay-off date:_____

If electronic, where/email: _____

How do you pay/Frequency of payment? _____

_____

(Annually via handwritten check, quarterly, monthly automatic from checking, auto-renewal on VISA credit card, etc.)

If no: You **own** this vehicle. Name(s) on the title: _____

Where is the **original title** located? _____

Stickers: Are there any stickers on this vehicle that would need attention?   Yes or No

If yes: What kind of sticker:*(Dump, beach, parking, etc.)*_____

Details: (How/When you pay, Where/How to cancel) _____

_____

_____

Insurance: Do you have insurance on this vehicle?   Yes or No

If yes: Insurance Company name:_____

Policy number:_____Telephone:_____

How do you receive statements?   Mail or Electronic

If electronic, where/email: _____

How do you pay/Frequency of payment? _____

_____

(Annually via handwritten check, quarterly, monthly automatic from checking, auto-renewal on VISA credit card, etc.)

Maintenance Records: Where do you keep the records? _____

Mechanic: *(Auto Technician)* Who does the maintenance/repairs? _____

_____

Important additional details: Include websites with login credentials, toolbox locks or combinations, the location of special tools required for tires or trailers, and detailed instructions, etc.

_____

_____

_____

8

Vehicle Details   (Number 4)

Circle: Primary User   or   Secondary User

4.   Year_____Make_____Model_____

Plate number: _____State/Country issued: _____

Name(s) on registration: _____

Where is the registration kept?_____Registration renewal month: _____

Keys: Where are the keys located? _____

Door combination code: _____

Tax: Do you pay annual tax on this vehicle?   Yes or No

If yes: How/Where is the tax paid? _____

(Check mailed, paid in person at town hall, automatic deduction from account, etc.)

Ownership: Do you have a **loan** on this vehicle?   Yes or No

Do you **lease** this vehicle?   Yes or No

If yes: Loan or Lease, Company name:_____Telephone: _____

Account number: _____

How do you receive statements?   Mail or Electronic   Pay-off date:_____

If electronic, where/email: _____

How do you pay/Frequency of payment? _____

_____

(Annually via handwritten check, quarterly, monthly automatic from checking, auto-renewal on VISA credit card, etc.)

If no: You **own** this vehicle. Name(s) on the title: _____

Where is the **original title** located? _____

Stickers: Are there any stickers on this vehicle that would need attention?   Yes or No

If yes: What kind of sticker:*(Dump, beach, parking, etc.)*_____

Details: (How/When you pay, Where/How to cancel) _____

_____

_____

Insurance: Do you have insurance on this vehicle?   Yes or No

If yes: Insurance Company name:_____

Policy number:_____Telephone:_____

How do you receive statements?   Mail or Electronic

If electronic, where/email: _____

How do you pay/Frequency of payment? _____

_____

(Annually via handwritten check, quarterly, monthly automatic from checking, auto-renewal on VISA credit card, etc.)

Maintenance Records: Where do you keep the records? _____

Mechanic: *(Auto Technician)* Who does the maintenance/repairs? _____

_____

Important additional details: Include websites with login credentials, toolbox locks or combinations, the location of special tools required for tires or trailers, and detailed instructions, etc.

_____

_____

_____

8

Vehicle Details (Number 5)

Circle: Primary User   or   Secondary User

5. Year_____Make_____Model_____

Plate number: _____State/Country issued: _____

Name(s) on registration: _____

Where is the registration kept?_____Registration renewal month: _____

Keys: Where are the keys located? _____

Door combination code: _____

Tax: Do you pay annual tax on this vehicle?   Yes or No

If yes: How/Where is the tax paid? _____
_____*(Check mailed, paid in person at town hall, automatic deduction from account, etc.)*

Ownership: Do you have a **loan** on this vehicle?   Yes or No

Do you **lease** this vehicle?   Yes or No

If yes: Loan or Lease, Company name:_____Telephone: _____

Account number: _____

How do you receive statements?   Mail or Electronic   Pay-off date:_____

If electronic, where/email: _____

How do you pay/Frequency of payment? _____
_____

(Annually via handwritten check, quarterly, monthly automatic from checking, auto-renewal on VISA credit card, etc.)

If no: You **own** this vehicle. Name(s) on the title: _____

Where is the **original title** located? _____

Stickers: Are there any stickers on this vehicle that would need attention?   Yes or No

If yes: What kind of sticker:*(Dump, beach, parking, etc.)*_____

Details: (How/When you pay, Where/How to cancel) _____
_____
_____

Insurance: Do you have insurance on this vehicle?   Yes or No

If yes: Insurance Company name:_____

Policy number:_____Telephone:_____

How do you receive statements?   Mail or Electronic

If electronic, where/email: _____

How do you pay/Frequency of payment? _____
_____

(Annually via handwritten check, quarterly, monthly automatic from checking, auto-renewal on VISA credit card, etc.)

Maintenance Records: Where do you keep the records? _____

Mechanic: *(Auto Technician)* Who does the maintenance/repairs? _____
_____

Important additional details: Include websites with login credentials, toolbox locks or combinations, the location of special tools required for tires or trailers, and detailed instructions, etc.
_____
_____
_____

8

Vehicle Details   (Number 6)

Circle: Primary User   or   Secondary User

6. Year_____Make_____Model_____
Plate number: _____State/Country issued: _____
Name(s) on registration: _____
Where is the registration kept?_____Registration renewal month: _____

Keys: Where are the keys located? _____
Door combination code: _____

Tax: Do you pay annual tax on this vehicle?   Yes or No
If yes: How/Where is the tax paid? _____
(Check mailed, paid in person at town hall, automatic deduction from account, etc.)

Ownership: Do you have a **loan** on this vehicle?   Yes or No
Do you **lease** this vehicle?   Yes or No
If yes: Loan or Lease, Company name:_____Telephone: _____
Account number: _____
How do you receive statements?   Mail or Electronic   Pay-off date:_____
If electronic, where/email: _____
How do you pay/Frequency of payment? _____

_____
(Annually via handwritten check, quarterly, monthly automatic from checking, auto-renewal on VISA credit card, etc.)
If no: You **own** this vehicle. Name(s) on the title: _____
Where is the **original title** located? _____

Stickers: Are there any stickers on this vehicle that would need attention?   Yes or No
If yes: What kind of sticker:*(Dump, beach, parking, etc.)*_____
Details: (How/When you pay, Where/How to cancel) _____

_____
_____

Insurance: Do you have insurance on this vehicle?   Yes or No
If yes: Insurance Company name:_____
Policy number:_____Telephone:_____
How do you receive statements?   Mail or Electronic
If electronic, where/email: _____
How do you pay/Frequency of payment? _____

_____
(Annually via handwritten check, quarterly, monthly automatic from checking, auto-renewal on VISA credit card, etc.)
Maintenance Records: Where do you keep the records? _____
Mechanic: *(Auto Technician)* Who does the maintenance/repairs? _____

_____

Important additional details: Include websites with login credentials, toolbox locks or combinations, the location of special tools required for tires or trailers, and detailed instructions, etc.

_____
_____
_____

8

Circle: Primary User   or   Secondary User

7. Year_____Make_____Model_____

   Plate number: _____State/Country issued: _____

Name(s) on registration: _____

   Where is the registration kept?_____Registration renewal month: _____

Keys: Where are the keys located? _____

   Door combination code: _____

Tax: Do you pay annual tax on this vehicle?   Yes or No

   If yes: How/Where is the tax paid? _____
   (Check mailed, paid in person at town hall, automatic deduction from account, etc.)

Ownership: Do you have a **loan** on this vehicle?   Yes or No

           Do you **lease** this vehicle?   Yes or No

   If yes: Loan or Lease, Company name:_____Telephone: _____

   Account number: _____

   How do you receive statements?   Mail or Electronic   Pay-off date:_____

   If electronic, where/email: _____

   How do you pay/Frequency of payment? _____

   _____

   (Annually via handwritten check, quarterly, monthly automatic from checking, auto-renewal on VISA credit card, etc.)

   If no: You **own** this vehicle. Name(s) on the title: _____

       Where is the **original title** located? _____

Stickers: Are there any stickers on this vehicle that would need attention?   Yes or No

   If yes: What kind of sticker:*(Dump, beach, parking, etc.)*_____

   Details: (How/When you pay, Where/How to cancel) _____

   _____

   _____

Insurance: Do you have insurance on this vehicle?   Yes or No

   If yes: Insurance Company name:_____

   Policy number:_____Telephone:_____

   How do you receive statements?   Mail or Electronic

   If electronic, where/email: _____

   How do you pay/Frequency of payment? _____

   _____

   (Annually via handwritten check, quarterly, monthly automatic from checking, auto-renewal on VISA credit card, etc.)

Maintenance Records: Where do you keep the records? _____

Mechanic: *(Auto Technician)* Who does the maintenance/repairs? _____

_____

Important additional details: Include websites with login credentials, toolbox locks or combinations, the location of special tools required for tires or trailers, and detailed instructions, etc.

_____

_____

_____

8

Vehicle Details   (Number 8)

Circle: Primary User   or   Secondary User

8. Year_____Make_____Model_____

Plate number: _____State/Country issued: _____

Name(s) on registration: _____

Where is the registration kept?_____Registration renewal month: _____

Keys: Where are the keys located? _____

Door combination code: _____

Tax: Do you pay annual tax on this vehicle?   Yes or No

If yes: How/Where is the tax paid? _____
(Check mailed, paid in person at town hall, automatic deduction from account, etc.)

Ownership: Do you have a **loan** on this vehicle?   Yes or No

Do you **lease** this vehicle?   Yes or No

If yes: Loan or Lease, Company name:_____Telephone: _____

Account number: _____

How do you receive statements?   Mail or Electronic   Pay-off date:_____

If electronic, where/email: _____

How do you pay/Frequency of payment? _____

_____
(Annually via handwritten check, quarterly, monthly automatic from checking, auto-renewal on VISA credit card, etc.)

If no: You **own** this vehicle. Name(s) on the title: _____

Where is the **original title** located? _____

Stickers: Are there any stickers on this vehicle that would need attention?   Yes or No

If yes: What kind of sticker:*(Dump, beach, parking, etc.)*_____

Details: (How/When you pay, Where/How to cancel) _____

_____

_____

Insurance: Do you have insurance on this vehicle?   Yes or No

If yes: Insurance Company name:_____

Policy number:_____Telephone:_____

How do you receive statements?   Mail or Electronic

If electronic, where/email: _____

How do you pay/Frequency of payment? _____

_____
(Annually via handwritten check, quarterly, monthly automatic from checking, auto-renewal on VISA credit card, etc.)

Maintenance Records: Where do you keep the records? _____

Mechanic: *(Auto Technician)* Who does the maintenance/repairs? _____

_____

Important additional details: Include websites with login credentials, toolbox locks or combinations, the location of special tools required for tires or trailers, and detailed instructions, etc.

_____

_____

_____

8

Passes	Primary User	Secondary User

Electronic Toll Collection
(EZ Pass/Toll Tag/Sun Pass, etc.)

	Primary User	Secondary User
Do you have an electronic toll collector?	Yes or No	Yes or No
If yes: How many?	# _____	# _____
What kind do you have?	_____	_____
What state issued your pass/tag?	_____	_____
Where is the pass/tag kept?	_____	_____
How do you pay?	_____	_____
If automatic: What credit card or bank account is linked for payment?	_____	_____

Parking Pass, Disabled Permit

	Primary User	Secondary User
Do you have a parking pass?	Yes or No	Yes or No
If yes: Details of parking pass: _____	_____	_____
_____	_____	_____
Do you have a placard/disabled parking permit?	Yes or No	Yes or No
If yes: Where was the pass/permit issued?	_____	_____
Expiration date of the pass/permit:	_____	_____
Where is this pass/permit kept?	_____	_____
Name of doctor who certified your disability:	_____	_____

Bus, Subway, Train, or Ferry Pass

	Primary User	Secondary User
Do you have a bus, subway, train, or ferry pass? If yes: What kind?	Yes or No	Yes or No
	_____	_____
Where was the pass issued?	_____	_____
Expiration date of pass:	_____	_____
Where is this pass kept?	Yes or No	Yes or No
How do you pay?	_____	_____
If automatic: What credit card or bank account is linked for payment?	_____	_____
	_____	_____

Ride Sharing

	Primary User	Secondary User
Do you have a ride share account?	Yes or No	Yes or No
If yes: Name?	_____	_____
How do you pay? What credit card or bank account is linked for payment?	_____	_____
	_____	_____
Do you typically have a cash balance?	Yes or No	Yes or No

Details: _____

Additional details: _____

_____

_____

Automobile Club, Roadside Assistance, Group Association	Primary User	Secondary User
Do you have a AAA membership/policy? **American Automobile Association**	Yes or No	Yes or No
Do you have a CAA membership/policy? **Canadian Automobile Association**	Yes or No	Yes or No
Any other roadside assistance, safety plan or security service?	Yes or No	Yes or No
A member of an automobile group association? *(Motor club)*	Yes or No	Yes or No

Primary User	Membership number: _____
	 Telephone:_____
	 Is this an individual or family membership? Individual or Family
	 Primary account holder's name: _____
	     Name(s) of members: _____
	     Annual renewal month:_____Expiration date: _____
	 Where do you keep your card? _____
	 How do you receive statements? Mail or Electronic
	     If electronic, where? Email: _____
	 How do you pay/Frequency of payment? _____
	 _____
	 (Annually via handwritten check, quarterly, monthly automatic from checking, auto-renewal on VISA credit card, etc.)

Secondary User	Membership number: _____
	 Telephone:_____
	 Is this an individual or family membership? Individual or Family
	 Primary account holder's name: _____
	     Name(s) of members: _____
	     Annual renewal month:_____Expiration date: _____
	 Where do you keep your card? _____
	 How do you receive statements? Mail or Electronic
	     If electronic, where? Email: _____
	 How do you pay/Frequency of payment? _____
	 _____
	 (Annually via handwritten check, quarterly, monthly automatic from checking, auto-renewal on VISA credit card, etc.)

_____	Membership number: _____
	 Telephone:_____
	 Is this an individual or family membership? Individual or Family
	 Primary account holder's name: _____
	     Name(s) of members: _____
	     Annual renewal month:_____Expiration date: _____
	 Where do you keep your card? _____
	 How do you receive statements? Mail or Electronic
	     If electronic, where? Email: _____
	 How do you pay/Frequency of payment? _____
	 _____
	 (Annually via handwritten check, quarterly, monthly automatic from checking, auto-renewal on VISA credit card, etc.)

Additional details: _____

_____

Sirius XM, Satellite Radio	Primary User	Secondary User

Do you have Sirius XM or a satellite radio in any vehicle?　　　Yes　or　No　　　Yes　or　No

Primary User	Name:_____Website:_____ Account number:_____Telephone: _____ Primary account holder's name(s): _____ Vehicle(s) that are on this subscription: _____ _____ What does your account include? *(Just music, music, and navigation, etc.)*_____ How do you receive statements?　Mail　or　Electronic 　　If electronic, where? Email: _____ How do you pay/Frequency of payment? _____ _____ *(Annually via handwritten check, quarterly, monthly automatic from checking, auto-renewal on VISA credit card, etc.)*
Secondary User	Name:_____Website:_____ Account number:_____Telephone: _____ Primary account holder's name(s): _____ Vehicle(s) that are on this subscription: _____ _____ What does your account include? *(Just music, music, and navigation, etc.)*_____ How do you receive statements?　Mail　or　Electronic 　　If electronic, where? Email: _____ How do you pay/Frequency of payment? _____ _____ *(Annually via handwritten check, quarterly, monthly automatic from checking, auto-renewal on VISA credit card, etc.)*

Additional details:_____

_____

_____

_____

_____

_____

_____

_____

_____

_____

_____

_____

_____

8

Just In Case
SOLUTIONS

Step 8: Vehicles and Transportation

Date Completed: _____

Fun Memory

Way to go! You have completed Step 8!

Did a fun or interesting fact from your past come to mind while you were working on this Step?

Use the space below to share a memory with your loved ones. It could be a funny story about yourself, a loving memory, or a fascinating fact about a moment in your past. This will bring joy and a smile during challenging times. Instead of writing, share your favorite song, poem, or insert a picture!

Need ideas? Here are some suggestions to write about for Step 8:
Share a memorable experience you had behind the wheel, your favorite car that you've owned, the price of gas when you first started driving, afunny moment on the subway, did your car break down in an unusual location, was your vacation canceled due to a pandemic, favorite song to listen to while driving on the highway, etc.

_____

_____

_____

_____

_____

_____

_____

_____

_____

_____

_____

_____

_____

_____

_____

_____

_____

_____

_____

_____

8

Step 9

Religion, Activities, Volunteer, Clubs, Subscriptions, and Memberships

Step 9 is all about what you do in your spare time. These are activities or hobbies that you enjoy, organizations that you are involved with, and any subscriptions or memberships you have.

Some folks might feel that this Step is not important, but it is. Your loved ones may need to take action such as canceling subscriptions or notifying your house of worship. Compiling a list will make things easier and save them time. And, you want to avoid unwanted automatic payments that may occur if your accounts and cards are not closed or canceled.

Here's how Step 9 can be helpful:

- If you can't fulfill your commitment to an organization, timely notification will help them find a replacement for you. If you are an active volunteer, provide the details of how to contact the organization and/or your supervisor. This will help your loved ones to efficiently notify everyone who might miss you.

- If you belong to a religious organization, make sure your loved ones have their name and contact information.

- Share the location of important religious documents, such as your baptism certificate or proof of membership. Some religious-associated cemeteries may require them.

- Don't forget to list all your activities, whether it's a book club with good friends, a yacht club, an artist's group, a gym, or a travel club.

- In the case of your death, this section provides a way for your loved ones to share the news with people who care about you but whom they may not personally know.

- List all your subscriptions and memberships. Be sure to include news or magazines, meal delivery programs, online learning, senior center, or even wine club memberships.

- Keep an updated list of any trips you have planned and any travel deposits or fares you've paid. Your loved ones will have to contact organizers and travel companies, including airlines, to reschedule, cancel or ask for refunds.

- There's also room to list information about your frequent flyer miles and other travel reward programs. They might be transferable, although policies vary according to the airline, hotel, or loyalty program. Please contact the airline and a legal professional for advice.

Ask Yourself, are you enjoying all the subscriptions you have? Perhaps this is a good time to make sure you are only paying for the ones that you actually use.

9

STEP 9: RELIGION, ACTIVITIES, VOLUNTEER, CLUBS, SUBSCRIPTIONS, AND MEMBERSHIPS
- Religion, House of Worship, Details
- Gym, Fitness Facility, Studio
- Clubs
- Senior Center
- Volunteer
- Travel Agent, Agency
    - Future Travel, Frequent Flyer, Travel Reward Program, Air Miles/Points after Death
- Timeshare, Vacation Club
    - Details, Expenses/Dues, Ownership
- Other Memberships and Subscriptions
- Other Activities, Hobbies
- Step 9 Completion Date and Fun Memory!

Step 9: NOTE TO LOVED ONES

In Step 9, your loved ones have prepared you with details about their activities, clubs, subscriptions, memberships, and religious affiliations.

Here are a few ways in which this Step can help:

- If your loved one is an active volunteer, this association may be extremely important to them. Please make sure to handle even their volunteer commitments with care – they have been making a difference in the lives of others! The organization or charity that's depending on their commitment will greatly appreciate being notified in a timely manner.

- Look carefully for anything that may have an automatic payment associated with it. You may need to decide if the ownership of the club, membership, or subscription needs to be changed or canceled.

- In the Just In Case scenario of death, be proactive with any cancellations to avoid unnecessary charges after the date of death.

Primary User	Secondary User

Religion

What is your religion? _____
Do you belong to house of worship?   Yes or No
    If yes: Church   Mosque   Synagogue
        Temple   Other: _____

House of Worship: _____
Telephone:_____
Address: _____
    _____

Do you offer an automatic recurring donation?
                      Yes or No
Details of offering: *(How do you pay and frequency)* _____
_____
_____

Significant religious life events:
(Baptism date, confirmation date, church membership date,bar/bat mitzvah, pilgrimage to Mecca, etc.)
_____
_____
_____
_____
_____
_____

Do you have a certificate of baptism?   Yes or No
Where are your documents located to confirm your religious life events? _____
_____
(Note: Some cemeteries may require your religious documentation).
Do you have an ongoing responsibility at this house of worship?   Yes or No
(Board member, vocalist, treasurer, deacon, cantor, etc.)

Your responsibility: _____
_____

Just In Case scenario: Who should be notified?
Name:_____
Telephone: _____

Religion

What is your religion? _____
Do you belong to house of worship?   Yes or No
    If yes: Church   Mosque   Synagogue
        Temple   Other: _____

House of Worship: _____
Telephone:_____
Address: _____
    _____

Do you offer an automatic recurring donation?
                      Yes or No
Details of offering: *(How do you pay and frequency)* _____
_____
_____

Significant religious life events:
(Baptism date, confirmation date, church membership date,bar/bat mitzvah, pilgrimage to Mecca, etc.)
_____
_____
_____
_____
_____
_____

Do you have a certificate of baptism?   Yes or No
Where are your documents located to confirm your religious life events? _____
_____
(Note: Some cemeteries may require your religious documentation).
Do you have an ongoing responsibility at this house of worship?   Yes or No
(Board member, vocalist, treasurer, deacon, cantor, etc.)

Your responsibility: _____
_____

Just In Case scenario: Who should be notified?
Name:_____
Telephone: _____

Additional details: _____
_____
_____
_____
_____
_____

9

Clubs, Memberships and Subscriptions

Gym, Fitness Facility, Studio

Primary User

Do you have a membership to a gym, yoga studio, tennis club, or any other fitness facility?

Yes or No

If yes: How many # _____

1. Name: _____
Telephone: _____
Address: _____
_____

What type of membership?   Individual or Family

Payment/Frequency: _____
(Credit card annually, automatic monthly from checking, etc.)

_____
Additional details:

2. Name: _____
Telephone: _____
Address: _____
_____

What type of membership?   Individual or Family

Payment/Frequency: _____
(Credit card annually, automatic monthly from checking, etc.)

_____
Additional details:

3. Name: _____
Telephone: _____
Address: _____
_____

What type of membership?   Individual or Family

Payment/Frequency: _____
(Credit card annually, automatic monthly from checking, etc.)

_____
Additional details:

Secondary User

Do you have a membership to a gym, yoga studio, tennis club, or any other fitness facility?

Yes or No

If yes: How many # _____

1. Name: _____
Telephone: _____
Address: _____
_____

What type of membership?   Individual or Family

Payment/Frequency: _____
(Credit card annually, automatic monthly from checking, etc.)

_____
Additional details:

2. Name: _____
Telephone: _____
Address: _____
_____

What type of membership?   Individual or Family

Payment/Frequency: _____
(Credit card annually, automatic monthly from checking, etc.)

_____
Additional details:

3. Name: _____
Telephone: _____
Address: _____
_____

What type of membership?   Individual or Family

Payment/Frequency: _____
(Credit card annually, automatic monthly from checking, etc.)

_____
Additional details:

9

Primary User	Secondary User

Clubs

Are you involved in any clubs?   Yes or No

1. Club Name:_____

Do you have an ongoing responsibility? Yes or No
(Board member, treasurer, secretary, etc.)
Your responsibility:_____
_____

Is there a membership fee?   Yes or No
Details: _____
Just In Case scenario: Who should be notified?
Name: _____
Telephone:_____

2. Club Name:_____

Do you have an ongoing responsibility? Yes or No
(Board member, treasurer, secretary, etc.)
Your responsibility:_____
Is there a membership fee?   Yes or No
Details: _____
Just In Case scenario: Who should be notified?
Name: _____
Telephone:_____

Clubs

Are you involved in any clubs?   Yes or No

1. Club Name: _____

Do you have an ongoing responsibility? Yes or No
(Board member, treasurer, secretary, etc.)
Your responsibility: _____
_____

Is there a membership fee?   Yes or No
Details: _____
Just In Case scenario: Who should be notified?
Name:_____
Telephone: _____

2. Club Name: _____

Do you have an ongoing responsibility? Yes or No
(Board member, treasurer, secretary, etc.)
Your responsibility: _____
Is there a membership fee?   Yes or No
Details: _____
Just In Case scenario: Who should be notified?
Name:_____
Telephone: _____

Additional details: _____
_____
_____

Senior Center

Do you go to a senior center?   Yes or No

Center Name: _____

Do you have an ongoing responsibility?   Yes or No
(Activity organizer, secretary, musician, etc.)
Your responsibility: _____
_____

Is there a membership fee?   Yes or No
Details:
Just In Case scenario: Who should be notified?
Name: _____
Telephone: _____

Senior Center

Do you go to a senior center?   Yes or No

Center Name: _____

Do you have an ongoing responsibility?   Yes or No
(Activity organizer, secretary, musician, etc.)
Your responsibility: _____
_____

Is there a membership fee?   Yes or No
Details:
Just In Case scenario: Who should be notified?
Name: _____
Telephone: _____

Additional details: _____
_____
_____

9

191

Primary User	Secondary User

Volunteer

Do you volunteer?　　Yes　or　No

1. Volunteer Place:

_____

_____

Do you have an ongoing responsibility?　Yes　or　No
(Board member, treasurer, secretary, etc.)
Your responsibility:

_____

Just In Case scenario: Who should be notified?
Name:_____
Telephone: _____

2. Volunteer Place:

_____

_____

Do you have an ongoing responsibility?　Yes　or　No
(Board member, treasurer, secretary, etc.)
Your responsibility:

_____

Just In Case scenario: Who should be notified?
Name:_____
Telephone: _____

3. Volunteer Place:

_____

_____

Do you have an ongoing responsibility?　Yes　or　No
(Board member, treasurer, secretary, etc.)
Your responsibility:

_____

Just In Case scenario: Who should be notified?
Name:_____
Telephone: _____

4. Volunteer Place:

_____

_____

Do you have an ongoing responsibility?　Yes　or　No
(Board member, treasurer, secretary, etc.)
Your responsibility:

_____

Just In Case scenario: Who should be notified?
Name:_____
Telephone: _____

Volunteer

Do you volunteer?　　Yes　or　No

1. Volunteer Place:

_____

_____

Do you have an ongoing responsibility?　Yes　or　No
(Board member, treasurer, secretary, etc.)
Your responsibility:

_____

Just In Case scenario: Who should be notified?
Name:_____
Telephone: _____

2. Volunteer Place:

_____

_____

Do you have an ongoing responsibility?　Yes　or　No
(Board member, treasurer, secretary, etc.)
Your responsibility:

_____

Just In Case scenario: Who should be notified?
Name:_____
Telephone: _____

3. Volunteer Place:

_____

_____

Do you have an ongoing responsibility?　Yes　or　No
(Board member, treasurer, secretary, etc.)
Your responsibility:

_____

Just In Case scenario: Who should be notified?
Name:_____
Telephone: _____

4. Volunteer Place:

_____

_____

Do you have an ongoing responsibility?　Yes　or　No
(Board member, treasurer, secretary, etc.)
Your responsibility:

_____

Just In Case scenario: Who should be notified?
Name:_____
Telephone: _____

9

Additional details: _____

_____

Travel Agent, Agency	Primary User	Secondary User

Do you have a travel agent or use a travel agency? Yes or No   Yes or No

1. **Travel Agency/Agent Name:**_____
   Address_____
   Telephone_____Email _____
2. **Travel Agency/Agent Name:**_____
   Address_____
   Telephone_____Email _____

Future Travel	Primary User	Secondary User

Do you have any future travel plans?   Yes or No   Yes or No

Any back-and-forth travel already booked?   Yes or No   Yes or No

Date	Travel Details: *(Do you spend 3 months a year someplace else?)*

Frequent Flyer (Air Miles), Travel Reward Program (Points)

Primary User

Do you have an airline frequent flyer   Yes or No
Travel rewards program? *(Airline, hotel, etc.)* Yes or No

    If yes: How many? # _____

1. **Airline**: _____
   Frequent Flyer number: _____

2. **Travel Loyalty**: _____
   Number: _____

3. Name: _____
   Number: _____

4. Name: _____
   Number: _____

5. Name: _____
   Number: _____

Secondary User

Do you have an airline frequent flyer   Yes or No
Travel rewards program? *(Airline, hotel, etc.)* Yes or No

    If yes: How many? # _____

1. **Airline**: _____
   Frequent Flyer number: _____

2. **Travel Loyalty**: _____
   Number: _____

3. Name: _____
   Number: _____

4. Name: _____
   Number: _____

5. Name: _____
   Number: _____

Airline Miles/Points after Death:

Are you leaving your airline miles or points to a specific person?   Yes or No
    If yes: Who? Name: _____

Are you leaving your airline miles or points to a specific person?   Yes or No
    If yes: Who? Name: _____

Please contact the airline and a legal professional for advice; miles may or may not be transferrable.

9

Timeshare, Vacation Club	Primary User	Secondary User

Do you own or have a financial interest in a
timeshare or vacation club?   Yes or No   Yes or No

     If yes: What do you have? *(Timeshare, vacation club)* _____ _____

             How many?   # _____   # _____

Circle: Primary User   or   Secondary User

1. **Property Name:** _____

Address:_____

Website:_____Telephone:_____

    Contact Name/Email: _____

Expenses and Payments: Dues/Interest: _____

                      Annual maintenance fees: _____

                      When do you pay? *(Annually/January)* _____

                      How do you pay and frequency? _____

                         (Credit card monthly, annual check, automatic recurring from checking, etc.)

Ownership: Name(s) listed: _____

Do you own more than one week?   Yes or No

Date of week(s):   _____   _____   _____

Where is the paperwork located? _____

Is this a buy-in membership?   Yes or No

Do you have a deed?   Yes or No   If yes: Where is deed located? _____

Note: Has this timeshare/vacation club been addressed in your estate plan?   Yes or No

Just In Case scenario of your death: What will happen to this timeshare/vacation club?
(Automatic transfer to spouse or kids, dues/interest still need to be paid, if no one wants the timeshare what needs to be done, etc.)

_____

_____

Circle: Primary User   or   Secondary User

2. **Property Name:** _____

Address:_____

Website:_____Telephone:_____

    Contact Name/Email: _____

Expenses and Payments: Dues/Interest: _____

                      Annual maintenance fees: _____

                      When do you pay? *(Annually/January)* _____

                      How do you pay and frequency? _____

                         (Credit card monthly, annual check, automatic recurring from checking, etc.)

Ownership: Name(s) listed: _____

Do you own more than one week?   Yes or No

Date of week(s):   _____   _____   _____

Where is the paperwork located? _____

Is this a buy-in membership?   Yes or No

Do you have a deed?   Yes or No   If yes: Where is deed located? _____

Note: Has this timeshare/vacation club been addressed in your estate plan?   Yes or No

Just In Case scenario of your death: What will happen to this timeshare/vacation club?
(Automatic transfer to spouse or kids, dues/interest still need to be paid, if no one wants the timeshare what needs to be done, etc.)

_____

_____

9

Other Memberships and Subscriptions

Do you have any other memberships or subscriptions?

(Meal delivery, AARP, wine club, news, magazines, online learning, etc.)

Primary User:	Yes or No
Secondary User:	Yes or No
Primary User:	# _____
Secondary User:	# _____

If yes: How many that require payment?

Provide details:

	Name Membership or Subscription	Account Information Phone Number	Payment and Frequency? Automatic monthly payment from checking, digital wallet, VISA credit card annually, etc.	MISC Details
1				
2				
3				
4				
5				
6				
7				
8				
9				
10				

9

Other Activities, Hobbies

Provide details about any other activities or hobbies your loved ones may need or want to be aware of.

_____
_____
_____
_____
_____
_____
_____
_____
_____
_____
_____
_____
_____
_____
_____
_____
_____
_____
_____
_____
_____
_____
_____
_____
_____
_____
_____
_____
_____
_____

9

Just In Case
SOLUTIONS

Step 9: Religion, Activities, Clubs, Subscriptions, and Memberships

Date Completed: _____

Fun Memory

Way to go! You have completed Step 9!

Did a fun or interesting fact from your past come to mind while you were working on this Step?

Use the space below to share a memory with your loved ones. It could be a funny story about yourself, a loving memory, or a fascinating fact about a moment in your past. This will bring joy and a smile during challenging times. Instead of writing, share your favorite song, poem, or insert a picture!

Need ideas? Here are some suggestions to write about for Step 9:
Share your favorite hobbies as a child, a special memory from a vacation, your favorite sports team, the most exotic place you traveled to, a beloved beach location, a rewarding volunteer experience, an activity or place that brings you calm, a moment from your past that had a significant impact on your future, a memorable religious moment, etc.

_____

_____

_____

_____

_____

_____

_____

_____

_____

_____

_____

_____

_____

_____

_____

_____

_____

_____

9

Step 10
Just In Case of Death

In Step 10, you will gather and record information pertaining to your wishes when your death occurs.

This is always a hard topic, both for you and for the ones who love you. Whether it's the funeral or burial, type of service, or the obituary, these are tough topics to think about and discuss.

If you already have all your affairs in order, you will use this Step to relay to your loved ones what you have already decided and where things are located.

Or, if you have been avoiding this difficult subject and have found it too emotional to talk with your loved ones, you can use this Step to help start the conversation about plans.

Ask Yourself, if you are just starting this process, can you think about it on your own, or would it help to talk to a loved one, friend, or counselor?

Here are some ways Step 10 can be helpful:

- If you have prepaid for a funeral service, casket, plot, or headstone, your loved ones are going to need to know where you prepaid and where the paperwork is located.

- They will also need to know if you are an organ donor or plan on donating your body to a medical organization or school.

- If you prefer to be cremated, you might want to communicate where you would like your ashes to be placed or if you want them scattered in a place that's important to you.

- You might want to suggest something for the service that is important to you or share that you have already written your obituary.

- You also might want to share specifics regarding a religious service to be in line with your beliefs or military funeral honors.

- Perhaps you have a strong preference for what you do *not* want, such as an open casket. If you have a strong preference one way or another, make sure to write it down and have a discussion with your loved ones so they can respect your wishes.

- Try to decide what you prefer, and do as much preplanning and prepaying as you are able. This will assist your loved ones so they do not have the additional stress and pressure of figuring everything out. This way, they will not be left to guess what you would have wanted.

- If a topic in this section does not matter to you or you would like your loved ones to choose whatever makes them comfortable, simply note your thoughts or feelings. They will appreciate following the directions and be grateful to you for providing details.

- Remember, if you have anything embarrassing that you would rather your best friend dispose of instead of risking a family member finding it, be sure to communicate this to them. ☺

This is an emotional time for everyone. The more details you can provide, the bigger the difference it will make to your loved ones.

10

Please note that this workbook is not legally binding. Its purpose is to allow you to communicate your wishes and preparation details to your loved ones. Providing this information can help make a difficult time a little easier. If you have any questions or require advice, please seek assistance from a professional.

Please take a moment to review what's included in this Step:

STEP 10: JUST IN CASE OF DEATH
- Organ Donor, Autopsy
- Funeral, Burial & More
    - Funeral Home, Director, Funeral Service Fee/Agreement, Casket, Embalming, Green/Natural, Burial, Burial Insurance, Cemetery, Plot, Crypt/Niche, Entombment, Memorial Stone,Crematory, Memorial Society
- Service and/or Gathering
    - Gathering (Tribute Service), Ethnic Customs, Visitation (Wake/Viewing), Clothing, Personal Items, Music, Pallbearers, Flowers, Memorial Donations, Eulogy/Dedication Speech, Military Service, Religious Service, Reception, Virtual, Other
- Obituary
    - Write your Own Obituary (Primary User and Secondary User)
    - Obituary Writing Assistance
- Step 10 Advice, Guidance, Loving Thought!

Step 10: NOTE TO LOVED ONES

In Step 10, your loved one has given you details pertaining to their wishes in case of their death. This might make you feel overwhelmed or sad; however, please try to be grateful that you have been provided with this information.

Take a moment to review the entire Step 10. If they have strong preferences, consider how you might be able to honor their wishes.

How can this Step be helpful?

- Maybe your loved one has preplanned and prepaid for their funeral and burial. In this Step, they can share all the details and the location of the paperwork. This will allow you to start making phone calls to the contacts that have been provided to you.

- Maybe your loved one is not prepared but has provided you with some details. Start by contacting a local funeral home to discuss final arrangements. They will be able to assist you with either a memorial or funeral service and help with details like death certificates.

- If your loved one was a member of the military, review Step 4 if you want to honor their time in the service.

- Look to see if your loved one wrote their own obituary or provided you with details to help you write or organize it. The funeral home or whoever is assisting you with the publication of the obituary should be able to help with ensuring lifetime achievements, important relationships, and experiences are featured.

This is an emotional and overwhelming time, and as the author I express my deepest sympathy for your loss. I truly hope this Solution eases your grief and makes a difficult time a little easier.

10

Organ Donor	Primary User	Secondary User

Autopsy: Regardless of whether or not you are an organ donor, some situations or states may require an autopsy; in other cases, a doctor may suggest one. Let your loved ones know your preferences regarding autopsies, as it may be an emotionally difficult decision to make, even if not required by law.

	Primary User	Secondary User
Would you be okay with an autopsy?	Yes or No	Yes or No
Are you an **organ donor**?	Yes or No	Yes or No
If yes: A whole-body donor?	Yes or No	Yes or No
If yes: Have you already registered on your state registry?	Yes or No	Yes or No
Where is your donor card located?	_____	_____
Are you listed as an organ donor on your driver's license?	Yes or No	Yes or No
What is your blood type?		
What are the details of your commitment? (What organs?)	_____ _____ _____	_____ _____ _____
Are you planning on donating your body **to a medical school**?	Yes or No	Yes or No
If yes: Medical school name	_____	_____
If your body is NOT able to be donated, what is your Plan B?	_____ _____	_____ _____

Donor Note: When registering as an organ donor, you can choose which organs and/or tissues to donate or donate everything. Please check your state registry for details and consult an expert to answer your questions.

Funeral, Burial & More	Primary User	Secondary User

Funeral Home

	Primary User	Secondary User
Do you have a preferred funeral home?	Yes or No or Doesn't Matter	Yes or No or Doesn't Matter
Preferred: Funeral Home name Telephone Address	_____ _____ _____	_____ _____ _____
Name any funeral home you definitely DO NOT want:	Do Not Use: _____	Do Not Use: _____

Funeral Director

	Primary User	Secondary User
Do you have a specific funeral director you would like?	Yes or No	Yes or No
Funeral Director name Telephone	_____ _____	_____ _____

Funeral, Burial & More	Primary User	Secondary User

Funeral Service Fee/Agreement

Do you have a funeral
prearrangement agreement?   Yes or No   Yes or No

If yes: Where is the agreement
           listing your details located?   _____   _____

Have you prepaid for your funeral?   Yes or No   Yes or No
Is the funeral paid in full?   Yes or No   Yes or No
If no: How much do you still owe? $_____ $_____

Is the price you paid locked in and
guaranteed, or will price increase?   _____   _____

Casket

Have you selected a casket?   Yes or No   Yes or No
If yes: Where?   Name: _____   _____
                     Telephone   _____   _____
                     Address   _____   _____
Have you prepaid for a casket?   Yes or No   Yes or No
If yes: Where is the paperwork
           located?   _____   _____
Is the casket paid in full?   Yes or No   Yes or No
If no: How much do you still owe? $_____ $_____

Embalming

Do you want to be embalmed?   Yes or No   Yes or No

Green/Natural

Do you want a green burial?   Yes or No   Yes or No

Burial

Have you already made burial
arrangements?   Yes or No   Yes or No
If yes: Where is the agreement
           listing your details located?   _____   _____
                                      _____   _____

Burial Insurance

Do you have burial insurance?   Yes or No   Yes or No
If yes: Burial Insurance Company   _____   _____
           Telephone   _____   _____
           Policy number   _____   _____
           Benefits/Details   _____   _____
           Where is the policy located?   _____   _____

10

Funeral, Burial & More	Primary User	Secondary User
Cemetery		
Do you have a preferred cemetery?	Yes or No or Doesn't Matter	Yes or No or Doesn't Matter
Preferred Cemetery name	_____	_____
Telephone	_____	_____
Address	_____	_____
	_____	_____
Does cemetery offer grave liners?	Yes or No	Yes or No
Name any cemetery you definitely DO NOT want:	Do Not Use: _____	Do Not Use: _____

Plot		
Do you already have a plot at the cemetery?	Yes or No	Yes or No
If yes: Where is the paperwork located?	_____	
Are all fees addressed in paperwork? *(Gravesite opening/closing fees, etc.)* If no: Details:	Yes or No	Yes or No
Do you have a family plot/estate?	Yes or No	Yes or No
Have you prepaid for a plot?	Yes or No	Yes or No
Is the plot paid in full?	Yes or No	Yes or No
If no: How much do you still owe? If paid in full:	$ _____	$ _____
Where is the deed located?	_____	

Crypt/Entombment (Mausoleum)		
Do you want/have a crypt?	Yes or No	Yes or No
Details:	_____	_____
	_____	_____
If yes: Where is the paperwork located?	_____	_____
Niche (Columbarium)		
Do you want/have a niche?	Yes or No	Yes or No
Details:	_____	_____
If yes: Where is the paperwork located?	_____	_____
	_____	_____

Funeral, Burial & More	Primary User	Secondary User
Memorial Stone (Headstone/Marker)		
Have you selected a gravestone?	Yes or No	Yes or No
If yes: Company name	_____	_____
Telephone	_____	_____
Address	_____	_____
	_____	_____
Have you prepaid for your stone?	Yes or No	Yes or No
Is the stone paid in full?	Yes or No	Yes or No
If no: How much do you still owe?	$ _____	$ _____
If paid in full:		
Where is the paperwork located?	_____	_____
Do you have a preference for what is engraved?	Yes or No	Yes or No
If yes: What do you want engraved?	_____	_____
	_____	_____
	_____	_____
	_____	_____
Crematory		
Do you want to be cremated?	Yes or No	Yes or No
Do you have a preferred crematory?	Yes or No	Yes or No
If yes: Crematory name	_____	_____
Telephone	_____	_____
Address	_____	_____
	_____	_____
Do you have a wish for your ashes?	Yes or No	Yes or No
If yes: What are they?	_____	_____
(Columbarium, buried, scattered/where)	_____	_____
	_____	_____
Have you selected an urn?	Yes or No	Yes or No
Have you prepaid for your urn?	Yes or No	Yes or No
If paid in full:		
Where is the paperwork located?	_____	_____
Details:	_____	_____
(Where was it purchased, where is the urn stored, remaining balance, etc.)	_____	_____
Memorial Society		
Are you a memorial society member?	Yes or No	Yes or No
If yes: Name	_____	_____
Telephone	_____	_____
Address	_____	_____
Where is paperwork located?	_____	_____
Details: *(Disposition of remains/any limitations of your wishes)*	_____	_____

Service and/or Gathering	Primary User	Secondary User
Gathering (Tribute Service) Would you prefer a Celebration of Life gathering instead of visiting hours?	Yes or No	Yes or No
What type of gathering would you prefer? *(Public, private, no gathering)*	_____ _____	_____ _____
Do you want your body/ashes present or not present during the gathering? Or does it not matter?	_____ _____	_____ _____
Ethnic Customs Do you have any specific customs you wish to be carried out? If yes: Details	Yes or No _____ _____	Yes or No _____ _____
Visitation (Wake/Viewing) Do you want visiting hours? Would you prefer: Public, private or doesn't matter	Yes or No _____	Yes or No _____
Do you want an open or closed casket during visiting hours?	Open or Closed	Open or Closed
Clothing for Deceased, Personal Items, Buried With Do you have specific clothing you would like to be buried in?	Yes or No	Yes or No
If yes: Details	_____ _____	_____ _____
Do you have any personal items you wish to be in the casket with you? If yes: Details *(Photo, eyeglasses, etc.)*	Yes or No _____ _____	Yes or No _____ _____
Do you wish to be buried with a loved one, pet or something else?	Yes or No _____ _____	Yes or No _____ _____
Music Do you want music to be played? If yes: Specific music Favorite song(s)	Yes or No _____ _____	Yes or No _____ _____

Service and/or Gathering	Primary User	Secondary User

Pallbearers
Names of who you would like to
be your pallbearers:

Primary User:
1._____
2._____
3._____
4._____
5._____
6._____

Secondary User:
1._____
2._____
3._____
4._____
5._____
6._____

Flowers
Do you want flowers?

Primary User: Yes or No
Secondary User: Yes or No

What is your favorite flower?

_____   _____

Do you have a preferred florist?

Primary User: Yes or No
Secondary User: Yes or No

If yes: Name
           Address

           Telephone

_____   _____
_____   _____
_____   _____
_____   _____

Memorial Donations
Would you like donations sent to a
specific organization or charity?
If yes: Details

Primary User: Yes or No
Secondary User: Yes or No

_____   _____
_____   _____
_____   _____

Eulogy/Dedication Speech
Would you like a dedication speech
or eulogy?

Primary User: Yes or No
Secondary User: Yes or No

Name of person if you have someone
specific you would like to speak:
(Pastor, spouse, child, whoever wants to)

_____   _____
_____   _____

Specific requests:

_____   _____
_____   _____

Military Service
Would you like a military service?

Primary User: Yes or No
Secondary User: Yes or No

Are you a veteran?

Primary User: Yes or No
Secondary User: Yes or No

> **Military Details in Step 4:**
> Please refer to Step 4's military section for honoring military
> service and funeral wishes.

Service and/or Gathering	Primary User	Secondary User
Religious Service		
See Religion Section:	**Religion Details: Step 9**	**Religion Details: Step 9**
Do you want a religious service?	Yes or No	Yes or No
Do you have a specific religious leader(s) that you would like to perform your service?	Yes or No	Yes or No
If yes: Name	_____	_____
Telephone	_____	_____
Do you have favorite hymns you would like played during service?	Yes or No	Yes or No
If yes: Hymn name(s)	_____ _____ _____	_____ _____ _____
Do you want your casket/ashes present during the service?	Yes or No	Yes or No
Would you like a traditional religious service or an alternative service?	Traditional or Alternative	Traditional or Alternative
Where would you like your service to be held if not at a place of worship?	_____ _____	_____ _____

Reception Afterwards (Repast)

Have a preplanned a reception or want to suggest your favorite place?	Yes or No	Yes or No
If yes: Where/Details	_____ _____	_____ _____

Virtual Gathering or Memory Book

If you don't wish to have an in-person funeral, you can suggest a virtual gathering or create a virtual memory book for your loved ones to share. Details: _____

_____

Other/Additional Details: Funeral, Burial, Service, Gathering

(Is there a special message you would like the person giving your eulogy to say to your family and friends, do you have a favorite photograph that you would like displayed, are you allergic to a flower and you wish to not have them present, etc.)

_____
_____
_____
_____

10

Obituary - Primary User

Do you want to **write your own obituary**?   Yes or No

    If yes: Please write it below.

    If no: Answer the questions on the following pages to assist your loved ones with your obituary.

Secondary User Obituary

Obituary - Secondary User

Do you want to **write your own obituary**?   Yes or No

    If yes: Please write it below.

    If no: Answer the questions on the following pages to assist your loved ones with your obituary.

Secondary User Obituary

_____

_____

_____

_____

_____

_____

_____

_____

_____

_____

_____

_____

_____

_____

_____

_____

_____

_____

_____

_____

_____

_____

_____

The following will help your loved ones write your obituary.   Today's Date: _____

Obituary Writing Assistance	Primary User	Secondary User
Your **full legal name**	_____	_____
Nickname (if applicable)	_____	_____
Date of birth	_____	_____
City/State of your birth	_____	_____
Current residence: Town/State	_____	_____
Where you were born/raised	_____	_____
Family	Family Details: Step 1 & 2	Family Details: Step 1 & 2
Name of **Parents**	_____	_____
City/State where they currently live	_____	_____
City/State where they were born	_____	_____
Are your parents living or deceased?	_____	_____
	_____	_____
Name of **Spouse or Partner**	_____	_____
How long married/together	_____	_____
Living or deceased?	_____	_____
How many **Children**?	# _____	# _____
How many **Grandchildren**?	# _____	# _____
How many **Great-grandchildren**?	# _____	# _____
How many **Siblings**?	# _____	# _____
How many **Aunts**?	# _____	# _____
How many **Uncles**?	# _____	# _____
How many **Nieces**?	# _____	# _____
How many **Nephews**?	# _____	# _____
How many **Great-Nieces**?	# _____	# _____
How many **Great-Nephews**?	# _____	# _____
Other Relatives	_____	_____
Education		
High School	_____	_____
Year graduated	_____	_____
College/University	_____	_____
Year graduated	_____	_____
College/University	_____	_____
Year graduated	_____	_____
Additional Education	_____	_____

10

Obituary Writing Assistance	Primary User	Secondary User
Career / Occupation *(Employment Details: Step 4)*		
Career achievements *(Member of bar association, owned a business, lieutenant, 40 years of service, published work, etc.)*		
Awards		
Civic duties		
Recognitions		
Military Did you serve in the military?	Yes or No Military Details: Step 4	Yes or No Military Details: Step 4
Religious affiliation	Religion Details: Step 9	Religion Details: Step 9
Hobbies/Clubs/Activities	Step 9	Step 9
A wonderful memory *(Fun memories featured at the end of each Step)*		
Miscellaneous Do you have any specific requests to be included in your obituary or anything you want to be remembered for?		
Do Not Include Is there anything you DO NOT want to be mentioned in your obituary?	Yes or No	Yes or No
If yes: Details		

10

Obituary Writing Assistance	Primary User	Secondary User

Photograph

Would you like a particular photo of
yourself to be featured in your obituary?

Yes or No   Yes or No

If yes: Describe the photo.
        Where is it located?

_____   _____

_____   _____

_____   _____

Publication(s)

Do you want your obituary in a
publication?

Yes or No   Yes or No

If yes: Which publication(s) would you
        like your obituary to appear in?
        Newspaper, City/State

_____   _____

_____   _____

_____   _____

_____   _____

Additional details: _____

_____

_____

_____

_____

_____

_____

_____

_____

_____

_____

_____

_____

_____

_____

_____

_____

_____

10

Step 10: Just In Case of Death

Date Completed: _____

Advice, Guidance, Loving Thought

Way to go! You have completed Step 10!

Offering advice, guidance, or words of love and support to your loved ones during a difficult time would be extremely valuable and meaningful. **Please use the space below to share your thoughts:**

Need ideas? Here are some suggestions to write about for Step 10:

Some advice or tips for living life to the fullest, never forget to dance with the ones you love, do not worry about getting rid of useless things, my love for you will last forever, always have faith in yourself, or share your favorite memories with your loved ones for them to read and cherish, etc.

_____

_____

_____

_____

_____

_____

_____

_____

_____

_____

_____

_____

_____

10

Congratulations!

Congratulations on completing **Just In Case Solutions**!
This is a great accomplishment!

It's recommended that you review this entire workbook every year to ensure that your loved ones always have access to your updated information. Select a date that works best for you to review all your essential life details.

Annual Review Date: _____

> **Note:** Don't forget to add your annual review date to your calendar!

In the event of a Just In Case scenario:

Who will be responsible for this workbook? Name: _____

- Please let this responsible person know your designated storage location for this workbook.

Extras

Take a moment and look at the items included in the "Extras" section:

- Additional Comments, Notes, Cards

- **CHARTS**

  - **Inventory List for Personal Possessions**

  - **Prescription Drugs** (Primary and Secondary User)

  - **Over-the-Counter Medication / Supplements** (Primary and Secondary User)

  - **Username and Password List with Security Questions**

> **Note:** It's best practice to generate strong, unique passwords and enable 2-step verifications (two-factor authentication) for every account.

Additional Comments, Notes, Cards

Primary and/or Secondary User

Write a note to your loved ones, heirs, or particular person to communicate anything you want or need them to know. <u>If you want your loved ones to deliver a message to someone special, write it here or place a handwritten card in this workbook addressed to that person.</u>

Additional Comments, Notes, Cards

Date	Note

Inventory List / Personal Possessions

Name: _____   Today's Date: _____

#	What's the Item? Personal belonging	What's the Value? Original cost, current value or is it sentimental	Description of the Item	Where is the Item Located?	Do you have a specific person you want to give this item to? (Name of person or reference trust/will)
1.					
Do you have an appraisal for this item? Yes or No Where is the appraisal located? _____ Additional Details:					
2.					
Do you have an appraisal for this item? Yes or No Where is the appraisal located? _____ Additional Details:					
3.					
Do you have an appraisal for this item? Yes or No Where is the appraisal located? _____ Additional Details:					
4.					
Do you have an appraisal for this item? Yes or No Where is the appraisal located? _____ Additional Details:					
5.					
Do you have an appraisal for this item? Yes or No Where is the appraisal located? _____ Additional Details:					
6.					
Do you have an appraisal for this item? Yes or No Where is the appraisal located? _____ Additional Details:					
7.					
Do you have an appraisal for this item? Yes or No Where is the appraisal located? _____ Additional Details:					

Name: _____   Today's Date: _____

Inventory

#	What's the Item? Personal belonging	What's the Value? Original cost, current value or is it sentimental	Description of the Item	Where is the Item Located?	Do you have a specific person you want to give this item to? (Name of person or reference trust/will)
8.					

Do you have an appraisal for this item?   Yes or No   Where is the appraisal located? _____
Additional Details:

| 9. | | | | | |

Do you have an appraisal for this item?   Yes or No   Where is the appraisal located? _____
Additional Details:

| 10. | | | | | |

Do you have an appraisal for this item?   Yes or No   Where is the appraisal located? _____
Additional Details:

| 11. | | | | | |

Do you have an appraisal for this item?   Yes or No   Where is the appraisal located? _____
Additional Details:

| 12. | | | | | |

Do you have an appraisal for this item?   Yes or No   Where is the appraisal located? _____
Additional Details:

| 13. | | | | | |

Do you have an appraisal for this item?   Yes or No   Where is the appraisal located? _____
Additional Details:

| 14. | | | | | |

Do you have an appraisal for this item?   Yes or No   Where is the appraisal located? _____
Additional Details:

Inventory List / Personal Possessions

Name: _____   Today's Date: _____

#	What's the Item? Personal belonging	What's the Value? Original cost, current value or is it sentimental	Description of the Item	Where is the Item Located?	Do you have a specific person you want to give this item to? *(Name of person or reference trust/will)*
15. Do you have an appraisal for this item? Yes or No Where is the appraisal located? _____ Additional Details:					
16. Do you have an appraisal for this item? Yes or No Where is the appraisal located? _____ Additional Details:					
17. Do you have an appraisal for this item? Yes or No Where is the appraisal located? _____ Additional Details:					
18. Do you have an appraisal for this item? Yes or No Where is the appraisal located? _____ Additional Details:					
19. Do you have an appraisal for this item? Yes or No Where is the appraisal located? _____ Additional Details:					
20. Do you have an appraisal for this item? Yes or No Where is the appraisal located? _____ Additional Details:					
21. Do you have an appraisal for this item? Yes or No Where is the appraisal located? _____ Additional Details:					

Inventory List / Personal Possessions (page 4 of 5)

Name: _____   **Today's Date:** _____

Inventory

#	What's the Item? Personal belonging	What's the Value? Original cost, current value or is it sentimental	Description of the Item	Where is the Item Located?	Do you have a specific person you want to give this item to? *(Name of person or reference trust/will)*
22. Do you have an appraisal for this item? Yes or No Where is the appraisal located? _____ Additional Details:					
23. Do you have an appraisal for this item? Yes or No Where is the appraisal located? _____ Additional Details:					
24. Do you have an appraisal for this item? Yes or No Where is the appraisal located? _____ Additional Details:					
25. Do you have an appraisal for this item? Yes or No Where is the appraisal located? _____ Additional Details:					
26. Do you have an appraisal for this item? Yes or No Where is the appraisal located? _____ Additional Details:					
27. Do you have an appraisal for this item? Yes or No Where is the appraisal located? _____ Additional Details:					
28. Do you have an appraisal for this item? Yes or No Where is the appraisal located? _____ Additional Details:					

Name: _____   Today's Date: _____

#	What's the Item? Personal belonging	What's the Value? Original cost, current value or is it sentimental	Description of the Item	Where is the Item Located?	Do you have a specific person you want to give this item to? *(Name of person or reference trust/will)*
29.					
Do you have an appraisal for this item? Yes or No Where is the appraisal located? _____ Additional Details:					
30.					
Do you have an appraisal for this item? Yes or No Where is the appraisal located? _____ Additional Details:					
31.					
Do you have an appraisal for this item? Yes or No Where is the appraisal located? _____ Additional Details:					
32.					
Do you have an appraisal for this item? Yes or No Where is the appraisal located? _____ Additional Details:					
33.					
Do you have an appraisal for this item? Yes or No Where is the appraisal located? _____ Additional Details:					
34.					
Do you have an appraisal for this item? Yes or No Where is the appraisal located? _____ Additional Details:					
35.					
Do you have an appraisal for this item? Yes or No Where is the appraisal located? _____ Additional Details:					

Prescription Drug Chart (page 1 of 2)

Name (Primary User): _____   Today's Date: _____

#	Medication (Drug Name)	Prescribing Doctor Name	Dosage (mg, drops)	Frequency				Notes (Monitoring, take with food, stop date, etc.)
				AM	Noon	PM	Bedtime	
1. Condition: Why do you take this medication? Do you have any side effects?								
				AM	Noon	PM	Bedtime	
2. Condition: Why do you take this medication? Do you have any side effects?								
				AM	Noon	PM	Bedtime	
3. Condition: Why do you take this medication? Do you have any side effects?								
				AM	Noon	PM	Bedtime	
4. Condition: Why do you take this medication? Do you have any side effects?								
				AM	Noon	PM	Bedtime	
5. Condition: Why do you take this medication? Do you have any side effects?								
				AM	Noon	PM	Bedtime	
6. Condition: Why do you take this medication? Do you have any side effects?								
				AM	Noon	PM	Bedtime	
7. Condition: Why do you take this medication? Do you have any side effects?								
				AM	Noon	PM	Bedtime	
8. Condition: Why do you take this medication? Do you have any side effects?								
				AM	Noon	PM	Bedtime	
9. Condition: Why do you take this medication? Do you have any side effects?								

Prescription Drug Chart (page 2 of 2)

Name (Primary User): _____ Today's Date: _____

#	Medication (Drug Name)	Prescribing Doctor Name	Dosage (mg, drops)	Frequency				Notes (Monitoring, take with food, stop date, etc.)
				AM	Noon	PM	Bedtime	
10. Condition: Why do you take this medication? Do you have any side effects?								
				AM	Noon	PM	Bedtime	
11. Condition: Why do you take this medication? Do you have any side effects?								
				AM	Noon	PM	Bedtime	
12. Condition: Why do you take this medication? Do you have any side effects?								
				AM	Noon	PM	Bedtime	
13. Condition: Why do you take this medication? Do you have any side effects?								
				AM	Noon	PM	Bedtime	
14. Condition: Why do you take this medication? Do you have any side effects?								
				AM	Noon	PM	Bedtime	
15. Condition: Why do you take this medication? Do you have any side effects?								
				AM	Noon	PM	Bedtime	
16. Condition: Why do you take this medication? Do you have any side effects?								

Additional Notes:

_____

_____

_____

_____

_____

Prescription Drug Chart (page 1 of 2)

Name (Secondary User): _____ Today's Date: _____

#	Medication (Drug Name)	Prescribing Doctor Name	Dosage (mg, drops)	Frequency				Notes (Monitoring, take with food, stop date, etc.)
				AM	Noon	PM	Bedtime	
1.								
Condition: Why do you take this medication?								
Do you have any side effects?								
				AM	Noon	PM	Bedtime	
2.								
Condition: Why do you take this medication?								
Do you have any side effects?								
				AM	Noon	PM	Bedtime	
3.								
Condition: Why do you take this medication?								
Do you have any side effects?								
				AM	Noon	PM	Bedtime	
4.								
Condition: Why do you take this medication?								
Do you have any side effects?								
				AM	Noon	PM	Bedtime	
5.								
Condition: Why do you take this medication?								
Do you have any side effects?								
				AM	Noon	PM	Bedtime	
6.								
Condition: Why do you take this medication?								
Do you have any side effects?								
				AM	Noon	PM	Bedtime	
7.								
Condition: Why do you take this medication?								
Do you have any side effects?								
				AM	Noon	PM	Bedtime	
8.								
Condition: Why do you take this medication?								
Do you have any side effects?								
				AM	Noon	PM	Bedtime	
9.								
Condition: Why do you take this medication?								
Do you have any side effects?								

Prescription Drug Chart

Name (Secondary User): _____   Today's Date: _____

#	Medication (Drug Name)	Prescribing Doctor Name	Dosage (mg, drops)	AM	Noon	PM	Bedtime	Notes (Monitoring, take with food, stop date, etc.)
10. Condition: Why do you take this medication? Do you have any side effects?								
11. Condition: Why do you take this medication? Do you have any side effects?								
12. Condition: Why do you take this medication? Do you have any side effects?								
13. Condition: Why do you take this medication? Do you have any side effects?								
14. Condition: Why do you take this medication? Do you have any side effects?								
15. Condition: Why do you take this medication? Do you have any side effects?								
16. Condition: Why do you take this medication? Do you have any side effects?								

Additional Notes:

_____

_____

_____

_____

_____

Over-the-Counter Medication / Supplements (page 1 of 2)

Name (Primary User): _____ Today's Date: _____

Supplements

# Name (Aspirin, vitamin, supplements)	Dosage	Frequency				Notes (Daily limit, take with food, etc.)
1.		AM	Noon	PM	Bedtime	
Why do you take this? Do you have any side effects?						
2.		AM	Noon	PM	Bedtime	
Why do you take this? Do you have any side effects?						
3.		AM	Noon	PM	Bedtime	
Why do you take this? Do you have any side effects?						
4.		AM	Noon	PM	Bedtime	
Why do you take this? Do you have any side effects?						
5.		AM	Noon	PM	Bedtime	
Why do you take this? Do you have any side effects?						
6.		AM	Noon	PM	Bedtime	
Why do you take this? Do you have any side effects?						
7.		AM	Noon	PM	Bedtime	
Why do you take this? Do you have any side effects?						
8.		AM	Noon	PM	Bedtime	
Why do you take this? Do you have any side effects?						
9.		AM	Noon	PM	Bedtime	
Why do you take this? Do you have any side effects?						

Over-the-Counter Medication / Supplements

Name (Primary User): _____   Today's Date: _____

# 	Name (Aspirin, vitamin, supplements)	Dosage	Frequency				Notes (Daily limit, take with food, etc.)
			AM	Noon	PM	Bedtime	
10. Why do you take this? Do you have any side effects?							
11. Why do you take this? Do you have any side effects?			AM	Noon	PM	Bedtime	
12. Why do you take this? Do you have any side effects?			AM	Noon	PM	Bedtime	
13. Why do you take this? Do you have any side effects?			AM	Noon	PM	Bedtime	
14. Why do you take this? Do you have any side effects?			AM	Noon	PM	Bedtime	
15. Why do you take this? Do you have any side effects?			AM	Noon	PM	Bedtime	
16. Why do you take this? Do you have any side effects?			AM	Noon	PM	Bedtime	

Additional Notes:

_____

_____

_____

_____

_____

Supplements

Over-the-Counter Medication / Supplements (page 1 of 2)

Name (Secondary User): _____ Today's Date: _____

Supplements

#	Name (Aspirin, vitamin, supplements)	Dosage	Frequency				Notes (Daily limit, take with food, etc.)
			AM	Noon	PM	Bedtime	
1. Why do you take this? Do you have any side effects?							
2. Why do you take this? Do you have any side effects?			AM	Noon	PM	Bedtime	
3. Why do you take this? Do you have any side effects?			AM	Noon	PM	Bedtime	
4. Why do you take this? Do you have any side effects?			AM	Noon	PM	Bedtime	
5. Why do you take this? Do you have any side effects?			AM	Noon	PM	Bedtime	
6. Why do you take this? Do you have any side effects?			AM	Noon	PM	Bedtime	
7. Why do you take this? Do you have any side effects?			AM	Noon	PM	Bedtime	
8. Why do you take this? Do you have any side effects?			AM	Noon	PM	Bedtime	
9. Why do you take this? Do you have any side effects?			AM	Noon	PM	Bedtime	

Over-the-Counter Medication / Supplements

Name (Secondary User): _____   Today's Date: _____

#	Name (Aspirin, vitamin, supplements)	Dosage	AM	Noon	PM	Bedtime	Notes (Daily limit, take with food, etc.)
10. Why do you take this? Do you have any side effects?							
11. Why do you take this? Do you have any side effects?							
12. Why do you take this? Do you have any side effects?							
13. Why do you take this? Do you have any side effects?							
14. Why do you take this? Do you have any side effects?							
15. Why do you take this? Do you have any side effects?							
16. Why do you take this? Do you have any side effects?							

Additional Notes:

_____

_____

_____

_____

_____

Supplements

Username and Password List with Security Questions

Name: _____   Today's Date: _____

#	Website	Username	Password	Email Used
1.				

Security Question/Answer:
Security Question/Answer:
Security Question/Answer:

Security PIN/Code: _____   Is 2-step verification turned on?   Yes or No   How is verification sent? Text Email Voice Message
Additional Details:

| 2. | | | | |

Security Question/Answer:
Security Question/Answer:
Security Question/Answer:

Security PIN/Code: _____   Is 2-step verification turned on?   Yes or No   How is verification sent? Text Email Voice Message
Additional Details:

| 3. | | | | |

Security Question/Answer:
Security Question/Answer:
Security Question/Answer:

Security PIN/Code: _____   Is 2-step verification turned on?   Yes or No   How is verification sent? Text Email Voice Message
Additional Details:

| 4. | | | | |

Security Question/Answer:
Security Question/Answer:
Security Question/Answer:

Security PIN/Code: _____   Is 2-step verification turned on?   Yes or No   How is verification sent? Text Email Voice Message
Additional Details:

| 5. | | | | |

Security Question/Answer:
Security Question/Answer:
Security Question/Answer:

Security PIN/Code: _____   Is 2-step verification turned on?   Yes or No   How is verification sent? Text Email Voice Message
Additional Details:

| 6. | | | | |

Security Question/Answer:
Security Question/Answer:
Security Question/Answer:

Security PIN/Code: _____   Is 2-step verification turned on?   Yes or No   How is verification sent? Text Email Voice Message
Additional Details:

Username and Password List with Security Questions

Name: _____   Today's Date: _____

#	Website	Username	Password	Email Used
7.				

Security Question/Answer:
Security Question/Answer:
Security Question/Answer:

Security PIN/Code: _____   Is 2-step verification turned on?   Yes or No   How is verification sent? Text   Email   Voice Message
Additional Details:

#	Website	Username	Password	Email Used
8.				

Security Question/Answer:
Security Question/Answer:
Security Question/Answer:

Security PIN/Code: _____   Is 2-step verification turned on?   Yes or No   How is verification sent? Text   Email   Voice Message
Additional Details:

#	Website	Username	Password	Email Used
9.				

Security Question/Answer:
Security Question/Answer:
Security Question/Answer:

Security PIN/Code: _____   Is 2-step verification turned on?   Yes or No   How is verification sent? Text   Email   Voice Message
Additional Details:

#	Website	Username	Password	Email Used
10.				

Security Question/Answer:
Security Question/Answer:
Security Question/Answer:

Security PIN/Code: _____   Is 2-step verification turned on?   Yes or No   How is verification sent? Text   Email   Voice Message
Additional Details:

#	Website	Username	Password	Email Used
11.				

Security Question/Answer:
Security Question/Answer:
Security Question/Answer:

Security PIN/Code: _____   Is 2-step verification turned on?   Yes or No   How is verification sent? Text   Email   Voice Message
Additional Details:

#	Website	Username	Password	Email Used
12.				

Security Question/Answer:
Security Question/Answer:
Security Question/Answer:

Security PIN/Code: _____   Is 2-step verification turned on?   Yes or No   How is verification sent? Text   Email   Voice Message
Additional Details:

Username and Password List with Security Questions

Name: _____ Today's Date: _____

#	Website	Username	Password	Email Used
13.				

Security Question/Answer:
Security Question/Answer:
Security Question/Answer:

Security PIN/Code: _____   Is 2-step verification turned on?   Yes or No   How is verification sent? Text   Email   Voice Message
Additional Details:

| 14. | | | | |

Security Question/Answer:
Security Question/Answer:
Security Question/Answer:

Security PIN/Code: _____   Is 2-step verification turned on?   Yes or No   How is verification sent? Text   Email   Voice Message
Additional Details:

| 15. | | | | |

Security Question/Answer:
Security Question/Answer:
Security Question/Answer:

Security PIN/Code: _____   Is 2-step verification turned on?   Yes or No   How is verification sent? Text   Email   Voice Message
Additional Details:

| 16. | | | | |

Security Question/Answer:
Security Question/Answer:
Security Question/Answer:

Security PIN/Code: _____   Is 2-step verification turned on?   Yes or No   How is verification sent? Text   Email   Voice Message
Additional Details:

| 17. | | | | |

Security Question/Answer:
Security Question/Answer:
Security Question/Answer:

Security PIN/Code: _____   Is 2-step verification turned on?   Yes or No   How is verification sent? Text   Email   Voice Message
Additional Details:

| 18. | | | | |

Security Question/Answer:
Security Question/Answer:
Security Question/Answer:

Security PIN/Code: _____   Is 2-step verification turned on?   Yes or No   How is verification sent? Text   Email   Voice Message
Additional Details:

Username and Password List with Security Questions

Name: _____   Today's Date: _____

#	Website	Username	Password	Email Used
19.				

Security Question/Answer:
Security Question/Answer:
Security Question/Answer:

Security PIN/Code: _____   Is 2-step verification turned on?   Yes or No   How is verification sent? Text   Email   Voice Message
Additional Details:

| 20. | | | | |

Security Question/Answer:
Security Question/Answer:
Security Question/Answer:

Security PIN/Code: _____   Is 2-step verification turned on?   Yes or No   How is verification sent? Text   Email   Voice Message
Additional Details:

| 21. | | | | |

Security Question/Answer:
Security Question/Answer:
Security Question/Answer:

Security PIN/Code: _____   Is 2-step verification turned on?   Yes or No   How is verification sent? Text   Email   Voice Message
Additional Details:

| 22. | | | | |

Security Question/Answer:
Security Question/Answer:
Security Question/Answer:

Security PIN/Code: _____   Is 2-step verification turned on?   Yes or No   How is verification sent? Text   Email   Voice Message
Additional Details:

| 23. | | | | |

Security Question/Answer:
Security Question/Answer:
Security Question/Answer:

Security PIN/Code: _____   Is 2-step verification turned on?   Yes or No   How is verification sent? Text   Email   Voice Message
Additional Details:

| 24. | | | | |

Security Question/Answer:
Security Question/Answer:
Security Question/Answer:

Security PIN/Code: _____   Is 2-step verification turned on?   Yes or No   How is verification sent? Text   Email   Voice Message
Additional Details:

Username and Password List with Security Questions

Name: _____ Today's Date: _____

#	Website	Username	Password	Email Used
25.				

Security Question/Answer:
Security Question/Answer:
Security Question/Answer:

Security PIN/Code: _____ Is 2-step verification turned on? Yes or No   How is verification sent? Text   Email   Voice Message
Additional Details:

| 26. | | | | |

Security Question/Answer:
Security Question/Answer:
Security Question/Answer:

Security PIN/Code: _____ Is 2-step verification turned on? Yes or No   How is verification sent? Text   Email   Voice Message
Additional Details:

| 27. | | | | |

Security Question/Answer:
Security Question/Answer:
Security Question/Answer:

Security PIN/Code: _____ Is 2-step verification turned on? Yes or No   How is verification sent? Text   Email   Voice Message
Additional Details:

| 28. | | | | |

Security Question/Answer:
Security Question/Answer:
Security Question/Answer:

Security PIN/Code: _____ Is 2-step verification turned on? Yes or No   How is verification sent? Text   Email   Voice Message
Additional Details:

| 29. | | | | |

Security Question/Answer:
Security Question/Answer:
Security Question/Answer:

Security PIN/Code: _____ Is 2-step verification turned on? Yes or No   How is verification sent? Text   Email   Voice Message
Additional Details:

| 30. | | | | |

Security Question/Answer:
Security Question/Answer:
Security Question/Answer:

Security PIN/Code: _____ Is 2-step verification turned on? Yes or No   How is verification sent? Text   Email   Voice Message
Additional Details:

Username and Password List with Security Questions

Name: _____   Today's Date: _____

#	Website	Username	Password	Email Used
31.				
Security Question/Answer: Security Question/Answer: Security Question/Answer: Security PIN/Code: _____ Is 2-step verification turned on? Yes or No How is verification sent? Text Email Voice Message Additional Details:				
32.				
Security Question/Answer: Security Question/Answer: Security Question/Answer: Security PIN/Code: _____ Is 2-step verification turned on? Yes or No How is verification sent? Text Email Voice Message Additional Details:				
33.				
Security Question/Answer: Security Question/Answer: Security Question/Answer: Security PIN/Code: _____ Is 2-step verification turned on? Yes or No How is verification sent? Text Email Voice Message Additional Details:				
34.				
Security Question/Answer: Security Question/Answer: Security Question/Answer: Security PIN/Code: _____ Is 2-step verification turned on? Yes or No How is verification sent? Text Email Voice Message Additional Details:				
35.				
Security Question/Answer: Security Question/Answer: Security Question/Answer: Security PIN/Code: _____ Is 2-step verification turned on? Yes or No How is verification sent? Text Email Voice Message Additional Details:				
36.				
Security Question/Answer: Security Question/Answer: Security Question/Answer: Security PIN/Code: _____ Is 2-step verification turned on? Yes or No How is verification sent? Text Email Voice Message Additional Details:				

Username and Password List with Security Questions

Name: _____   Today's Date: _____

#	Website	Username	Password	Email Used
37.				

Security Question/Answer:
Security Question/Answer:
Security Question/Answer:

Security PIN/Code: _____   Is 2-step verification turned on?   Yes or No   How is verification sent? Text   Email   Voice Message
Additional Details:

| 38. | | | | |

Security Question/Answer:
Security Question/Answer:
Security Question/Answer:

Security PIN/Code: _____   Is 2-step verification turned on?   Yes or No   How is verification sent? Text   Email   Voice Message
Additional Details:

| 39. | | | | |

Security Question/Answer:
Security Question/Answer:
Security Question/Answer:

Security PIN/Code: _____   Is 2-step verification turned on?   Yes or No   How is verification sent? Text   Email   Voice Message
Additional Details:

| 40. | | | | |

Security Question/Answer:
Security Question/Answer:
Security Question/Answer:

Security PIN/Code: _____   Is 2-step verification turned on?   Yes or No   How is verification sent? Text   Email   Voice Message
Additional Details:

| 41. | | | | |

Security Question/Answer:
Security Question/Answer:
Security Question/Answer:

Security PIN/Code: _____   Is 2-step verification turned on?   Yes or No   How is verification sent? Text   Email   Voice Message
Additional Details:

| 42. | | | | |

Security Question/Answer:
Security Question/Answer:
Security Question/Answer:

Security PIN/Code: _____   Is 2-step verification turned on?   Yes or No   How is verification sent? Text   Email   Voice Message
Additional Details:

Username and Password List with Security Questions

Name: _____   Today's Date: _____

#	Website	Username	Password	Email Used
43.				

Security Question/Answer:
Security Question/Answer:
Security Question/Answer:

Security PIN/Code: _____   Is 2-step verification turned on?   Yes or No   How is verification sent? Text   Email   Voice Message
Additional Details:

| 44. | | | | |

Security Question/Answer:
Security Question/Answer:
Security Question/Answer:

Security PIN/Code: _____   Is 2-step verification turned on?   Yes or No   How is verification sent? Text   Email   Voice Message
Additional Details:

| 45. | | | | |

Security Question/Answer:
Security Question/Answer:
Security Question/Answer:

Security PIN/Code: _____   Is 2-step verification turned on?   Yes or No   How is verification sent? Text   Email   Voice Message
Additional Details:

| 46. | | | | |

Security Question/Answer:
Security Question/Answer:
Security Question/Answer:

Security PIN/Code: _____   Is 2-step verification turned on?   Yes or No   How is verification sent? Text   Email   Voice Message
Additional Details:

| 47. | | | | |

Security Question/Answer:
Security Question/Answer:
Security Question/Answer:

Security PIN/Code: _____   Is 2-step verification turned on?   Yes or No   How is verification sent? Text   Email   Voice Message
Additional Details:

| 48. | | | | |

Security Question/Answer:
Security Question/Answer:
Security Question/Answer:

Security PIN/Code: _____   Is 2-step verification turned on?   Yes or No   How is verification sent? Text   Email   Voice Message
Additional Details:

www.ingramcontent.com/pod-product-compliance
Lightning Source LLC
Chambersburg PA
CBHW080954120626
46546CB00010B/2888